GOLF RULES ILLUSTRATED

The OFFICIAL ILLUSTRATED GUIDE to the RULES OF GOLF

hamlyn

C016371244

CONTENTS

Foreword 3

Principal Changes
Introduced in the
2016 Code 4

How to Use the Rule Book 5

A Quick Guide to
The Rules of Golf 6

SECTION 1
ETIQUETTE; BEHAVIOUR
ON THE COURSE 10

SECTION 2
DEFINITIONS 13

SECTION 3
THE RULES OF PLAY 24

THE GAME
1 The Game 24
2 Match Play 27
3 Stroke Play 31

CLUBS AND THE BALL
4 Clubs 33
5 The Ball 39

PLAYER'S RESPONSIBILITIES
6 The Player 43
7 Practice 52
8 Advice; Indicating
Line of Play 55
9 Information as
to Strokes Taken 57

ORDER OF PLAY
10 Order of Play 58

TEEING GROUND
11 Teeing Ground 61

PLAYING THE BALL
12 Searching For and
Identifying Ball 64
13 Ball Played as it Lies 68
14 Striking the Ball 74
15 Substituted Ball;
Wrong Ball 79

THE PUTTING GREEN
16 The Putting Green 82
17 The Flagstick 88

BALL MOVED, DEFLECTED
OR STOPPED
18 Ball at Rest Moved 92
19 Ball in Motion Deflected
or Stopped 98

RELIEF SITUATIONS AND
PROCEDURE
20 Lifting, Dropping and
Placing; Playing from
Wrong Place 102
21 Cleaning Ball 111
22 Ball Assisting or
Interfering with Play 111
23 Loose Impediments 114
24 Obstructions 118
25 Abnormal Ground
Conditions, Embedded
Ball and Wrong
Putting Green 127
26 Water Hazards (Including
Lateral Water Hazards) 136
27 Ball Lost or Out of
Bounds; Provisional Ball 141
28 Ball Unplayable 146

OTHER FORMS OF PLAY
29 Threesomes and
Foursomes 149
30 Three-Ball, Best-Ball and
Four-Ball Match Play 152
31 Four-Ball Stroke Play 155
32 Bogey, Par and
Stableford Competitions 158

ADMINISTRATION
33 The Committee 160
34 Disputes and Decisions 166

APPENDICES
Contents 169

APPENDIX I
LOCAL RULES; CONDITIONS
OF THE COMPETITION
Part A
Local Rules 170
Part B
Conditions of the
Competition 177

APPENDIX II
Design of Clubs 184

APPENDIX III
The Ball 190

APPENDIX IV
Devices and Other
Equipment 191

Acknowledgements 192

HOW TO USE THE RULE BOOK

It is understood that not everyone who has a copy of the Rules of Golf will read it from cover to cover. Most golfers only consult the Rule book when they have a Rules issue on the course that needs to be resolved. However, to ensure that you have a basic understanding of the Rules and that you play golf in a reasonable manner, it is recommended that you at least read the Quick Guide to the Rules of Golf and the Etiquette Section contained within this publication. The following points will assist you in using the Rule book efficiently and accurately:

UNDERSTAND THE WORDS

The Rule book is written in a very precise and deliberate fashion. You should be aware of and understand the following differences in word use:

o **may = optional**
o **should = recommendation**
o **must = instruction (and penalty if not carried out)**
o **a ball = you may substitute another ball (e.g. Rules 26, 27 and 28)**
o **the ball = you must not substitute another ball (e.g. Rules 24-2 and 25-1)**

KNOW THE DEFINITIONS

There are over fifty defined terms (e.g. abnormal ground condition, through the green, etc.) and these form the foundation around which the Rules of Play are written. A good knowledge of the defined terms (which are italicised throughout the book) is very important to the correct application of the Rules.

THE FACTS OF THE CASE

To answer any question on the Rules you must consider the facts of the case in some detail. You should identify:

o The form of play (e.g. match play or stroke play, single, foursome or four-ball)
o Who is involved (e.g. the player, his partner or caddie, an outside agency)
o Where the incident occurred (e.g. on the teeing ground, in a bunker or water hazard, on the putting green)
o What actually happened
o The player's intentions (e.g. what was he doing and what does he want to do)
o The timing of the incident (e.g. has the player now returned his score card, has the competition closed)

REFER TO THE BOOK

If in doubt on any of the Rules, play the course as you find it and play the ball as it lies. On returning to the Clubhouse, you can refer the matter to the Committee and it may be that reference to the *Decisions on the Rules of Golf* will assist in resolving any queries that are not entirely clear from the Rule book itself.

A Quick Guide to
THE RULES OF GOLF

This guide provides a simple explanation of common Rules situations. It is not a substitute for the Rules of Golf, which should be consulted whenever any doubt arises. For more information on the points covered, please refer to the relevant Rule.

GENERAL POINTS

The game of golf should be played in the correct spirit and in accordance with the Etiquette Section in the Rules of Golf. In particular:
- show consideration to other players,
- play at a good pace and be ready to invite faster moving groups to play through, and
- take care of the course by smoothing bunkers, replacing divots and repairing ball marks on the greens.

Before starting your round you are advised to:
- read the Local Rules on the score card and the notice board
- put an identification mark on your ball; many golfers play the same brand of ball and if you can't identify your ball, it is considered lost (Rules 12-2 and 27-1)
- count your clubs; you are allowed a maximum of 14 clubs (Rule 4-4).

During the round:
- don't ask for advice from anyone except your caddie, your partner (i.e. a player on your side) or your partner's caddie; don't give advice to any player except your partner; you may ask for or provide information on the Rules, distances and the position of hazards, the flagstick, etc. (Rule 8-1)
- don't play any practice shots during play of a hole (Rule 7-2).

At the end of your round:
- in match play, ensure the result of the match is posted
- in stroke play, ensure that your score card is completed properly and signed by you and your marker, and return it to the Committee as soon as possible (Rule 6-6).

THE RULES OF PLAY

Tee Shot (Rule 11)

You may change your ball before playing your tee shot, but it is good practice to advise a player in your group if you are changing your ball.

Play your tee shot from between, and not in front of, the tee-markers. You may play your tee shot from up to two club-lengths behind the front line of the tee-markers.

If you play your tee shot from outside this area:
- in match play there is no penalty, but your opponent may require you to replay your stroke provided he does so immediately;
- in stroke play you incur a two-stroke penalty, the stroke itself does not count and you must play a ball from within the correct area.

Playing the Ball (Rules 12, 13, 14 and 15)

If you think a ball is yours but cannot see your identification mark, after notifying your marker or opponent, you may mark the position of the ball and lift it to identify it. When lifted under this Rule, the ball may not be cleaned except to the extent necessary to identify it (Rule 12-2).

Play the ball as it lies. Don't improve your lie, the area of your intended stance or swing, or your line of play by:
- moving, bending or breaking anything fixed or growing, except in fairly taking your stance or making your swing, or
- pressing anything down (Rule 13-2).

If your ball is in a bunker or a water hazard, don't;
- touch the ground (or the water in a water hazard) with your hand or club before your downswing, or
- move loose impediments (Rule 13-4).

If you play a wrong ball (i.e. stray ball or ball being used by another player):
- in match play you lose the hole
- in stroke play you incur a two-stroke penalty, the strokes made with the wrong ball do not count and you must correct the mistake by playing the correct ball (Rule 15-3).

On the Putting Green (Rules 16 and 17)

On the putting green, you may:

- mark, lift and clean your ball (always replace it on the same spot), and
- repair ball marks and old hole plugs, but not any other damage, such as spike marks (Rule 16-1).

When making a stroke on the putting green, you should ensure that the flagstick is removed or attended. The flagstick may also be removed or attended when the ball lies off the putting green (Rule 17).

Ball at Rest Moved (Rule 18)

Generally, when your ball is in play, if you accidentally cause it to move, or you lift it when not permitted, add a penalty stroke and replace your ball.

If someone other than you, your caddie, your partner or your partner's caddie moves your ball at rest, or it is moved by another ball, replace your ball without penalty.

If a ball at rest is moved by wind or it moves of its own accord, play the ball as it lies without penalty.

Ball in Motion Deflected or Stopped (Rule 19)

If your ball in motion is deflected or stopped by you, your caddie, your partner, or your partner's caddie, or by equipment belonging to you or your partner, you incur a penalty of one stroke and play the ball as it lies (Rule 19-2).

If your ball in motion is deflected or stopped by another ball at rest, there is normally no penalty and the ball is played as it lies. However, in stroke play only, if both balls lay on the putting green before you made your stroke, you incur a two-stroke penalty (Rule 19-5a).

Lifting, Dropping and Placing the Ball (Rule 20)

Prior to lifting a ball that has to be replaced (e.g. when you lift your ball on the putting green to clean it), the position of the ball must be marked (Rule 20-1).

When your ball is being lifted in order to drop or place it in another position (e.g. dropping within two club-lengths under the unplayable ball Rule), it is not mandatory to mark its position although it is recommended that you do so.

When dropping, stand erect, hold the ball at shoulder height and arm's length and drop it.

Common situations where a dropped ball must be re-dropped include when it:
- rolls to a position where there is interference from the same condition from which free relief is being taken (e.g. an immovable obstruction)
- comes to rest more than two club-lengths from where it was dropped, or
- comes to rest nearer the hole than its original position, the nearest point of relief or where the ball last crossed the margin of a water hazard.

If a ball dropped for a second time rolls into any of these positions, you place it where it first struck the course when re-dropped (Rule 20-2c).

Ball Assisting or Interfering with Play (Rule 22)

You may:
- lift your ball or have any other ball lifted if you think the ball might assist another player, or
- have any ball lifted if it might interfere with your play.

You must not agree to leave a ball in position in order to assist another player.

A ball that is lifted because it is assisting or interfering with play must not be cleaned, except when it is lifted from the putting green.

Loose Impediments (Rule 23)

You may move a loose impediment (i.e. natural loose objects such as stones, detached leaves and twigs) unless the loose impediment and your ball are in the same hazard (i.e. bunker or water hazard). If you remove a loose impediment and this causes your ball to move, the ball must be replaced and (unless your ball was on the putting green) you incur a one-stroke penalty.

Movable Obstructions (Rule 24-1)

Movable obstructions (i.e. artificial movable objects such as rakes, bottles, etc.) located anywhere may be moved without penalty. If your ball moves as a result, it must be replaced without penalty.

If your ball is in or on a movable obstruction, the ball may be lifted, the obstruction removed and the ball dropped, without penalty, on the spot directly under where the ball lay on the obstruction, except that on the putting green, the ball is placed on that spot.

Immovable Obstructions and Abnormal Ground Conditions (Rules 24-2 and 25-1)

An immovable obstruction is an artificial object on the course that cannot be moved (e.g. a building) or cannot readily be moved (e.g. a firmly embedded direction post). Objects defining out of bounds are not treated as obstructions.

An abnormal ground condition is casual water, ground under repair or a hole or the cast from a hole made by a burrowing animal, a reptile or a bird.

Except when your ball is in a water hazard, relief without penalty is available from immovable obstructions and abnormal ground conditions when the condition physically interferes with the lie of the ball, your stance or your swing.

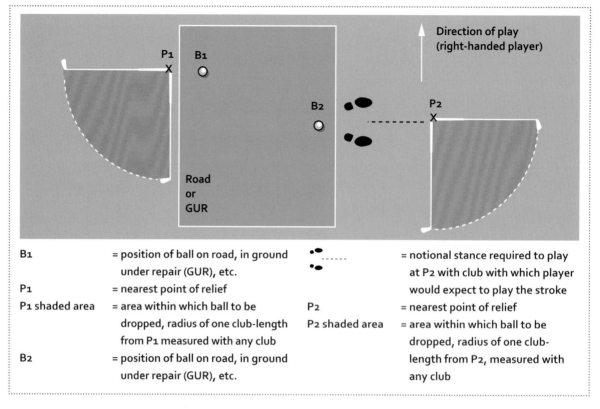

B1	= position of ball on road, in ground under repair (GUR), etc.		= notional stance required to play at P2 with club with which player would expect to play the stroke
P1	= nearest point of relief		
P1 shaded area	= area within which ball to be dropped, radius of one club-length from P1 measured with any club	P2	= nearest point of relief
		P2 shaded area	= area within which ball to be dropped, radius of one club-length from P2, measured with any club
B2	= position of ball on road, in ground under repair (GUR), etc.		

You may lift the ball and drop it within one club-length of the nearest point of relief (see Definition of "Nearest Point of Relief"), but not nearer the hole than the nearest point of relief (see diagram above). If the ball is on the putting green, you place it at the nearest point of relief, which may be off the putting green.

There is no relief for intervention on your line of play unless both your ball and the condition are on the putting green. As an additional option when your ball is in a bunker, you may take relief from the condition by dropping the ball outside and behind the bunker under penalty of one stroke.

The above diagram illustrates the term "nearest point of relief" in Rules 24-2 and 25-1 in the case of a right-handed player.

Water Hazards (Rule 26)

If your ball is in a water hazard (yellow stakes and/or lines) you may play it as it lies or, under penalty of one stroke:

o play a ball from where your last shot was played, or
o drop a ball any distance behind the water hazard keeping a straight line between the hole, the point where the ball last crossed the margin of the water hazard and the spot on which the ball is dropped.

If your ball is in a lateral water hazard (red stakes and/or lines), in addition to the options for a ball in a water hazard (see above), under penalty of one stroke, you may drop a ball

within two club-lengths of, and not nearer the hole than:

o the point where the ball last crossed the margin of the hazard, or
o a point on the opposite side of the hazard equidistant to the hole from the point where the ball last crossed the margin.

Ball Lost or Out of Bounds; Provisional Ball (Rule 27)

Check the Local Rules on the score card to identify the boundaries of the course. These are normally defined by fences, walls, white stakes or white lines.

If your ball is lost outside a water hazard or out of bounds you must play another ball from the spot where the last shot was played, under penalty of one stroke, i.e. stroke and distance.

You are allowed 5 minutes to search for a ball. If it is not found within 5 minutes, it is lost.

If, after playing a shot, you think your ball may be lost outside a water hazard or out of bounds you should play a provisional ball. You must announce that it is a provisional ball and play it before you go forward to search for the original ball.

If the original ball is lost (other than in a water hazard) or out of bounds, you must continue with the provisional ball, under penalty of one stroke. If the original ball is found in bounds within 5 minutes, you must continue play of the

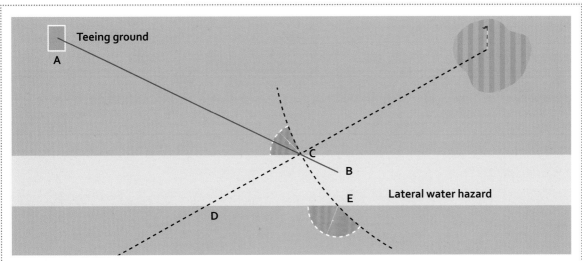

Ball played from teeing ground at Point A comes to rest in lateral water hazard at Point B having last crossed the margin of the hazard at Point C. Player's options are as follows:
- play ball as it lies without penalty at Point B, or under penalty of one stroke:
- play another ball from teeing ground

- drop a ball behind the hazard anywhere on the broken line from Point D backwards
- drop a ball in the shaded area at Point C (i.e. within two club-lengths of point C but not nearer the hole than Point C), or
- drop a ball in the shaded area at Point E (i.e. within two club-lengths of Point E but not nearer to the hole than Point E).

hole with it, and must stop playing the provisional ball.

Ball Unplayable (Rule 28)

If your ball is in a water hazard and you do not wish to play it as it lies, you must proceed under the water hazard Rule – the unplayable ball Rule does not apply. Elsewhere on the course, if you believe your ball is unplayable, you may, under penalty of one stroke:
- play a ball from where your last shot was played, or

- drop a ball any distance behind the point where the ball lay keeping a straight line between the hole, the point where the ball lay and the spot on which the ball is dropped, or
- drop a ball within two club-lengths of where the ball lay not nearer the hole.

If your ball is in a bunker you may proceed as above, except that if you are dropping back on a line or within two club-lengths, you must drop a ball in the bunker.

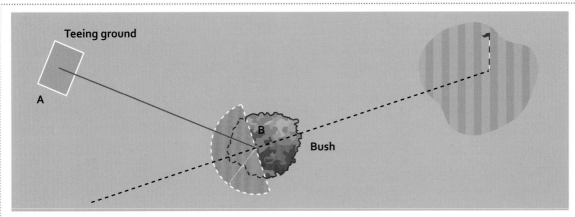

A ball played from teeing ground at Point A comes to rest in a bush at Point B. If the player deems the ball unplayable, the options, under penalty of one stroke, are as follows:
- play a ball from the teeing ground
- drop a ball behind Point B on the broken line, or
- drop a ball in the shaded area (i.e. within two club-lengths of Point B but not nearer the hole than Point B).

Section 1
ETIQUETTE; BEHAVIOUR ON THE COURSE

Introduction

This section provides guidelines on the manner in which the game of golf should be played. If they are followed, all players will gain maximum enjoyment from the game. The overriding principle is that consideration should be shown to others on the course at all times.

The Spirit of the Game

Golf is played, for the most part, without the supervision of a referee or umpire. The game relies on the integrity of the individual to show consideration for other players and to abide by the Rules. All players should conduct themselves in a disciplined manner, demonstrating courtesy and sportsmanship at all times, irrespective of how competitive they may be. This is the spirit of the game of golf.

Safety

Players should ensure that no one is standing close by or in a position to be hit by the club, the ball or any stones, pebbles, twigs or the like when they make a stroke or practice swing.

Players should not play until the players in front are out of range.

Players should always alert greenstaff nearby or ahead when they are about to make a stroke that might endanger them.

If a player plays a ball in a direction where there is a danger of hitting someone, he should immediately shout a warning. The traditional word of warning in such situations is "fore".

Consideration for Other Players

No Disturbance or Distraction Players should always show consideration for other players on the course and should not disturb their play by moving, talking or making unnecessary noise.

Players should ensure that any electronic device taken onto the course does not distract other players.

On the teeing ground, a player should not tee his ball until it is his turn to play.

Players should be ready to play as soon as it is their turn. This can be achieved by lining up putts while other players are playing, provided there is no disturbance or distraction for them. Here Phil Mickelson putts out while Tiger Woods prepares for his putt.

Players should not stand close to or directly behind the ball, or directly behind the hole, when a player is about to play.

On the Putting Green

On the putting green, players should not stand on another player's line of putt or, when he is making a stroke, cast a shadow over his line of putt.

Players should remain on or close to the putting green until all other players in the group have holed out.

Scoring In stroke play, a player who is acting as a marker should, if necessary, on the way to the next tee, check the score with the player concerned and record it.

Pace of Play

Play at Good Pace and Keep Up Players should play at a good pace. The Committee may establish pace of play guidelines that all players should follow.

It is a group's responsibility to keep up with the group in front. If it loses a clear hole and it is delaying the group behind, it should invite the group behind to play through, irrespective of the number of players in that group. Where a group has not lost a clear hole, but it is apparent that the group behind can play faster, it should invite the faster moving group to play through.

Be Ready to Play Players should be ready to play as soon as it is their turn to play. When playing on or near the putting green, they should leave their bags or carts in such a position as will enable quick movement off the green and towards the next tee. When the play of a hole has been completed, players should immediately leave the putting green.

Lost Ball

If a player believes his ball may be lost outside a water hazard or is out of bounds, to save time, he should play a provisional ball.

Players searching for a ball should signal the players in the group behind them to play through as soon as it becomes apparent that the ball will not easily be found. They should not search for five minutes before doing so. Having allowed the group behind to play through, they should not continue play until that group has passed and is out of range.

Priority on the Course

Unless otherwise determined by the Committee, priority on the course is determined by a group's pace of play. Any group playing a whole round is entitled to pass a

CARE OF THE COURSE

(1) Always repair divots, (2) carefully repair pitch-marks on the putting green and (3) smooth over footprints and other marks when leaving a bunker. (4) Do not lean on your putter when removing the ball from the hole.

group playing a shorter round. The term "group" includes a single player.

Care of the Course

Bunkers Before leaving a bunker, players should carefully fill up and smooth over all holes and footprints made by them and any nearby made by others. If a rake is within reasonable proximity of the bunker, the rake should be used for this purpose.

Repair of Divots, Ball-Marks and Damage by Shoes
Players should carefully repair any divot holes made by them and any damage to the putting green made by the impact of a ball (whether or not made by the player himself). On completion of the hole by all players in the group, damage to the putting green caused by golf shoes should be repaired.

Preventing Unnecessary Damage Players should avoid causing damage to the course by removing divots when taking practice swings or by hitting the head of a club into the ground, whether in anger or for any other reason.

Players should ensure that no damage is done to the putting green when putting down bags or the flagstick.

In order to avoid damaging the hole, players and

caddies should not stand too close to the hole and should take care during the handling of the flagstick and the removal of a ball from the hole. The head of a club should not be used to remove a ball from the hole.

Players should not lean on their clubs when on the putting green, particularly when removing the ball from the hole.

The flagstick should be properly replaced in the hole before the players leave the putting green.

Local notices regulating the movement of golf carts should be strictly observed.

Conclusion; Penalties for Breach

If players follow the guidelines in this section, it will make the game more enjoyable for everyone.

If a player consistently disregards these guidelines during a round or over a period of time to the detriment of others, it is recommended that the Committee considers taking appropriate disciplinary action against the offending player. Such action may, for example, include prohibiting play for a limited time on the course or in a certain number of competitions. This is considered to be justifiable in terms of protecting the interests of the majority of golfers who wish to play in accordance with these guidelines.

In the case of a serious breach of etiquette, the Committee may disqualify a player under Rule 33-7.

Q & A

Does a single player have any standing on the golf course?

Different players play at different speeds. Whilst players should not have to run round the course, they should be aware that there are other players on the course at the same time and should therefore act with common sense and courtesy towards those other players.

The Etiquette section suggests that, unless otherwise determined by the Committee, priority on the course is determined by a group's pace of play, and the term "group" includes a single player. The Pace of Play part of the Etiquette section also states that, "It is a group's responsibility to keep up with the group in front. If it loses a clear hole and it is delaying the group behind, it should invite the group behind to play through, irrespective of the number of players in that group. Where a group has not lost a clear hole, but it is apparent that the group behind can play faster, it should invite the faster moving group to play through." Therefore, a slow group should give way, where possible, to a faster group, and single golfers should have the same rights as all other players.

When should you let the group behind play through?

It is a group's responsibility to keep up with the group in front. Players need to be mindful of other players on the course and, while there are no hard and fast Rules as to when you should let the group behind through, there are some obvious situations where it would be appropriate to do so. For example:

o If your group loses a clear hole and is delaying the group behind
o Where it is apparent that the group behind can play faster
o Where you are searching for a ball and it is apparent that the ball may not be easily found.

Section 2
DEFINITIONS

The Definitions are listed alphabetically and, in the Rules themselves, defined terms are in *italics*.

Abnormal Ground Conditions An "*abnormal ground condition*" is any *casual water*, *ground under repair* or hole, cast or runway on the *course* made by a *burrowing animal*, a reptile or a bird.

Addressing the Ball A player has "*addressed the ball*" when he has grounded his club immediately in front of or immediately behind the ball, whether or not he has taken his *stance*.

Advice "*Advice*" is any counsel or suggestion that could influence a player in determining his play, the choice of a club or the method of making a *stroke*.

Information on the *Rules*, distance or matters of public information, such as the position of *hazards* or the *flagstick* on the *putting green*, is not *advice*.

Ball Deemed to Move See "*Move or Moved*".

Ball Holed See "*Holed*".

Ball Lost See "*Lost Ball*".

Ball in Play A ball is "*in play*" as soon as the player has made a *stroke* on the *teeing ground*. It remains *in play* until it is *holed*, except when it is *lost*, *out of bounds* or lifted, or another ball has been *substituted*, whether or not the substitution is permitted; a ball so *substituted* becomes the *ball in play*.

A *ball in play* that has been marked but not lifted remains *in play*. A ball that has been marked, lifted and replaced is back *in play* whether or not the ball-marker has been removed.

If a ball is played from outside the *teeing ground* when the player is starting play of a hole, or when attempting to correct this mistake, the ball is not *in play* and Rule 11-4 or 11-5 applies. Otherwise, *ball in play* includes a ball played from outside the *teeing ground* when the player elects or is required to play his next *stroke* from the *teeing ground*. **Exception in match play:** *Ball in play* includes a ball

ADDRESSING THE BALL

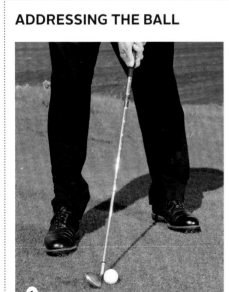

(1) A player has addressed the ball when he has grounded his club immediately in front of or immediately behind the ball, whether or not he has taken his stance.

(2) As the player has not grounded his putter immediately in front of or behind the ball, he has not "addressed" the ball.

played by the player from outside the *teeing ground* when starting play of a hole if the opponent does not require the *stroke* to be cancelled in accordance with Rule 11-4a.

Best-Ball See "*Forms of Match Play*".

Bunker A "*bunker*" is a *hazard* consisting of a prepared area of ground, often a hollow, from which turf or soil has been removed and replaced with sand or the like.

Grass-covered ground bordering or within a *bunker*, including a stacked turf face (whether grass-covered or earthen), is not part of the *bunker*. A wall or lip of the *bunker* not covered with grass is part of the *bunker*. The margin of a *bunker* extends vertically downwards, but not upwards.

A ball is in a *bunker* when it lies in or any part of it touches the *bunker*.

Burrowing Animal A "*burrowing animal*" is an animal (other than a worm, insect or the like) that makes a hole for habitation or shelter, such as a rabbit, mole, groundhog, gopher or salamander.

Note: A hole made by a non-burrowing animal, such as a dog, is not an *abnormal ground condition* unless marked or declared as *ground under repair*.

Caddie A "*caddie*" is one who assists the player in accordance with the Rules, which may include carrying or handling the player's clubs during play.

When one *caddie* is employed by more than one player,

CADDIE

A caddie will carry or handle the player's clubs and may offer advice on club selection, the direction of play and the line for putting.

he is always deemed to be the *caddie* of the player sharing the *caddie* whose ball (or whose *partner*'s ball) is involved, and *equipment* carried by him is deemed to be that player's *equipment*, except when the *caddie* acts upon specific directions of another player (or the *partner* of another player) sharing the *caddie*, in which case he is considered to be that other player's *caddie*.

BUNKER

Korean golfer Jeong Jin prepares to play from the road hole bunker on the 17th hole of the Old Course, St Andrews, Scotland. A bunker face consisting of stacked turf, whether grass-covered or earthen, is not part of the bunker.

CASUAL WATER

Casual water is an "abnormal ground condition" that is visible before or after the player takes his stance. A player may take relief from such a condition under Rule 25-1.

EQUIPMENT

Any small object, such as a coin or a tee, when used to mark the extent of an area in which a ball can be dropped is not equipment of the player.

Casual Water "*Casual water*" is any temporary accumulation of water on the *course* that is not in a *water hazard* and is visible before or after the player takes his *stance*. Snow and natural ice, other than frost, are either *casual water* or *loose impediments*, at the option of the player. Manufactured ice is an *obstruction*. Dew and frost are not *casual water*.

A ball is in *casual water* when it lies in or any part of it touches the *casual water*.

Committee The "*Committee*" is the committee in charge of the competition or, if the matter does not arise in a competition, the committee in charge of the *course*.

Competitor A "*competitor*" is a player in a stroke play competition. A "*fellow-competitor*" is any person with whom the *competitor* plays. Neither is *partner* of the other.

In stroke play *foursome* and *four-ball* competitions, where the context so admits, the word "*competito*r" or "*fellow-competitor*" includes his *partner*.

Course The "*course*" is the whole area within any boundaries established by the *Committee* (see Rule 33-2).

Equipment "*Equipment*" is anything used, worn, held or carried by the player or the player's *caddie*, except:
o any ball that the player has played at the hole being played, and
o any small object, such as a coin or a tee, when used to mark the position of the ball or the extent of an area in which a ball is to be dropped.

Note 1: A ball played at the hole being played is *equipment* when it has been lifted and not put back into play.

Note 2: *Equipment* includes objects placed on the course for the care of the *course*, such as rakes, while they are being held or carried.

Note 3: When *equipment* is shared by two or more players, the shared *equipment* is deemed to be the *equipment* of only one of the players sharing it.

If a shared golf cart is being moved by one of the players sharing it (or his *partner* or either of their *caddies*), the cart and everything in it are deemed to be that player's *equipment.* Otherwise, the cart and everything in it are deemed to be the *equipment* of the player sharing the cart whose ball (or whose *partner*'s ball) is involved.

Other shared *equipment* is deemed to be the *equipment* of the player who last used, wore, held or carried it. It remains that player's *equipment* until it is used, worn, held or carried by the other player (or his *partner* or either of their *caddies*).

Fellow-Competitor See "*Competitor*".

Flagstick The "*flagstick*" is a movable straight indicator, with or without bunting or other material attached, centred in the *hole* to show its position. It must be circular in cross-section. Padding or shock absorbent material that might unduly influence the movement of the ball is prohibited.

Forecaddie A "*forecaddie*" is one who is employed by the *Committee* to indicate to players the position of balls during play. He is an *outside agency*.

Forms of Match Play
Single: A match in which one player plays against another player.

Threesome: A match in which one player plays against two other players, and each *side* plays one ball.
Foursome: A match in which two players play against two other players, and each *side* plays one ball.
Three-Ball: Three players play a match against one another, each playing his own ball. Each player is playing two distinct matches.
Best-Ball: A match in which one player plays against the better ball of two other players or the *best-ball* of three other players.
Four-Ball: A match in which two players play their better ball against the better ball of two other players.

Forms of Stroke Play
Individual: A competition in which each *competitor* plays as an individual.
Foursome: A competition in which two *competitors* play as *partners* and play one ball.
Four-Ball: A competition in which two *competitors* play as *partners*, each playing his own ball. The lower score of the *partners* is the score for the hole. If one *partner* fails to complete the play of a hole, there is no penalty.
Note: For bogey, par and Stableford competitions, see Rule 32-1.

Four-Ball See "*Forms of Match Play*" and "*Forms of Stroke Play*".

Foursome See "*Forms of Match Play*" and "*Forms of Stroke Play*".

Ground Under Repair "*Ground under repair*" is any part of the *course* so marked by order of the *Committee* or so declared by its authorised representative. All ground and any grass, bush, tree or other growing thing within the *ground under repair* are part of the *ground under repair*. *Ground under repair* includes material piled for removal and a hole made by a greenkeeper, even if not so marked. Grass cuttings and other material left on the *course* that have been abandoned and are not intended to be removed are not *ground under repair* unless so marked.

When the margin of *ground under repair* is defined by stakes, the stakes are inside the *ground under repair*, and the margin of the *ground under repair* is defined by the nearest outside points of the stakes at ground level. When both stakes and lines are used to indicate *ground under repair*, the stakes identify the *ground under repair* and the lines define the margin of the *ground under repair*. When the margin of *ground under repair* is defined by a

GROUND UNDER REPAIR

Grass cuttings are ground under repair if they have been piled for removal or have been marked as ground under repair by the Committee. The player is not entitled to relief under Rule 25-1 if the grass cuttings have obviously been thrown away under a bush to rot. Grass cuttings are loose impediments, whether or not they are piled for removal, and may be removed by the player (see Rule 23-1).

line on the ground, the line itself is in the *ground under repair*. The margin of *ground under repair* extends vertically downwards but not upwards.

A ball is in *ground under repair* when it lies in or any part of it touches the *ground under repair*.

Stakes used to define the margin of or identify *ground under repair* are *obstructions*.

Note: The *Committee* may make a Local Rule prohibiting play from *ground under repair* or an environmentally-sensitive area defined as *ground under repair*.

Hazards A "*hazard*" is any *bunker* or *water hazard*.

Hole The "*hole*" must be 4¼ inches (108 mm) in diameter and at least 4 inches (101.6 mm) deep. If a lining is used, it must be sunk at least 1 inch (25.4 mm) below the *putting green* surface, unless the nature of the soil makes it impracticable to do so; its outer diameter must not exceed 4¼ inches (108 mm).

Holed A ball is "*holed*" when it is at rest within the circumference of the *hole* and all of it is below the level of the lip of the *hole*.

Honour The player who is to play first from the *teeing ground* is said to have the "*honour*".

Lateral Water Hazard A "*lateral water hazard*" is a *water hazard* or that part of a *water hazard* so situated that it is not possible, or is deemed by the *Committee* to be impracticable, to drop a ball behind the *water hazard* in accordance with Rule 26-1b. All ground and water within the margin of a *lateral water hazard* are part of the *lateral water hazard*.

When the margin of a *lateral water hazard* is defined by stakes, the stakes are inside the *lateral water hazard,* and the margin of the *hazard* is defined by the nearest outside points of the stakes at ground level. When both stakes and lines are used to indicate a *lateral water hazard*, the stakes identify the *hazard* and the lines define the *hazard* margin. When the margin of a *lateral water hazard* is defined by a line on the ground, the line itself is in the *lateral water hazard*. The margin of a *lateral water hazard* extends vertically upwards and downwards.

A ball is in a *lateral water hazard* when it lies in or any part of it touches the *lateral water hazard*.

Stakes used to define the margin of or identify a *lateral water hazard* are *obstructions*.

Note 1: That part of a *water hazard* to be played as a *lateral water hazard* must be distinctively marked. Stakes or lines used to define the margin of or identify a *lateral water hazard* must be red.

Note 2: The *Committee* may make a Local Rule prohibiting play from an environmentally-sensitive area defined as a *lateral water hazard*.

Note 3: The *Committee* may define a *lateral water hazard* as a *water hazard*.

Line of Play The "*line of play*" is the direction that the player wishes his ball to take after a *stroke*, plus a reasonable distance on either side of the intended direction. The *line of play* extends vertically upwards from the ground, but does not extend beyond the *hole*.

Line of Putt The "*line of putt*" is the line that the player wishes his ball to take after a *stroke* on the *putting green*. Except with respect to Rule 16-1e, the *line of putt* includes a reasonable distance on either side of the intended line. The *line of putt* does not extend beyond the *hole*.

Loose Impediments "*Loose impediments*" are natural objects, including:
o stones, leaves, twigs, branches and the like,
o dung, and
o worms, insects and the like, and the casts and heaps made by them,
provided they are not:
o fixed or growing,
o solidly embedded, or
o adhering to the ball.
Sand and loose soil are *loose impediments* on the *putting green*, but not elsewhere.

Snow and natural ice, other than frost, are either *casual water* or *loose impediments*, at the option of the player.

Dew and frost are not *loose impediments*.

Lost Ball A ball is deemed "*lost*" if:
a. It is not found or identified as his by the player within five minutes after the player's *side* or his or their *caddies* have begun to search for it; or
b. The player has made a *stroke* at a *provisional ball* from the place where the original ball is likely to be or from a point nearer the *hole* than that place (see Rule 27-2b); or
c. The player has put another *ball into play* under penalty of stroke and distance under Rule 26-1a, 27-1 or 28a; or
d. The player has put another *ball into play* because it is known or virtually certain that the ball, which has not been found, has been *moved* by an *outside agency* (see Rule 18-1), is in an *obstruction* (see Rule 24-3), is in an *abnormal ground condition* (see Rule 25-1c) or is in a

LOOSE IMPEDIMENTS

Natural objects such as:

dead rat

banana skin

pine cones

branches

stones

worm casts

insects

leaves

MOVABLE OBSTRUCTIONS

Artificial/manufactured objects such as:

litter

bottle

rake

booklet

tin can

tee

score card

water hazard (see Rule 26-1b or c); or

e. The player has made a *stroke* at a *substituted ball*. Time spent in playing a *wrong ball* is not counted in the five-minute period allowed for search.

Marker A "*marker*" is one who is appointed by the *Committee* to record a *competitor's* score in stroke play. He may be a *fellow-competitor*. He is not a *referee*.

Move or Moved A ball is deemed to have "*moved*" if it leaves its position and comes to rest in any other place.

Nearest Point of Relief The "*nearest point of relief*" is the reference point for taking relief without penalty from interference by an immovable *obstruction* (Rule 24-2), an *abnormal ground condition* (Rule 25-1) or a *wrong putting green* (Rule 25-3).

It is the point on the *course* nearest to where the ball lies:
(i) that is not nearer the *hole*, and
(ii) where, if the ball were so positioned, no interference by the condition from which relief is sought would exist for the *stroke* the player would have made from the original position if the condition were not there.

BALL DEEMED TO MOVE

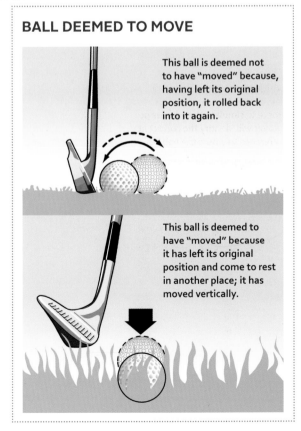

This ball is deemed not to have "moved" because, having left its original position, it rolled back into it again.

This ball is deemed to have "moved" because it has left its original position and come to rest in another place; it has moved vertically.

Note: In order to determine the *nearest point of relief* accurately, the player should use the club with which he would have made his next *stroke* if the condition were not there to simulate the *address* position, direction of play and swing for such a *stroke*.

Observer An "*observer*" is one who is appointed by the *Committee* to assist a *referee* to decide questions of fact and to report to him any breach of a *Rule*. An *observer* should not attend the *flagstick*, stand at or mark the position of the *hole*, or lift the ball or mark its position.

Obstructions An "*obstruction*" is anything artificial, including the artificial surfaces and sides of roads and paths and manufactured ice, except:

a. Objects defining o*ut of bounds*, such as walls, fences, stakes and railings;
b. Any part of an immovable artificial object that is *out of bounds*; and
c. Any construction declared by the *Committee* to be an integral part of the *course*.

An *obstruction* is a movable *obstruction* if it may be moved without unreasonable effort, without unduly delaying play and without causing damage. Otherwise, it is an immovable *obstruction*.

Note: The *Committee* may make a Local Rule declaring a movable *obstruction* to be an immovable *obstruction*.

Opponent An "*opponent*" is a member of a side against whom the player's *side* is competing in match play.

Out of Bounds "*Out of bounds*" is beyond the boundaries of the *course* or any part of the *course* so marked by the *Committee*.

When *out of bounds* is defined by reference to stakes or a fence or as being beyond stakes or a fence, the *out of bounds* line is determined by the nearest inside points at ground level of the stakes or fence posts (excluding angled supports). When both stakes and lines are used to indicate *out of bounds*, the stakes identify *out of bounds* and the lines define *out of bounds*. When *out of bounds* is defined by a line on the ground, the line itself is *out of bounds*. The *out of bounds* line extends vertically upwards and downwards.

A ball is *out of bounds* when all of it lies *out of bounds*. A player may stand *out of bounds* to play a ball lying within bounds.

Objects defining *out of bounds* such as walls, fences, stakes and railings are not *obstructions* and are deemed to be fixed. Stakes identifying *out of bounds* are not *obstructions* and are deemed to be fixed.

Note 1: Stakes or lines used to define *out of bounds* should be white.

NEAREST POINT OF RELIEF

The player should use the club with which she would have made her next stroke if the sprinkler head were not there to simulate the address position. By doing so the player will identify the correct nearest point of relief with reference to where the ball lies.

OUT OF BOUNDS

a. Defined by Stakes
   When out of bounds is defined by stakes, out of bounds is determined by the nearest inside points of the stakes at ground level. Ball 1 is considered in bounds as part of the ball still overhangs the course. Ball 2 is out of bounds because no part of it overhangs the course.
b. Defined by Line
   When out of bounds is defined by a line, the line itself is out of bounds. Ball 1 is in bounds because some of the ball overhangs the course. Ball 2 is out of bounds because no part of it overhangs the course.

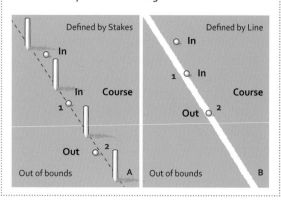

Note 2: A *Committee* may make a Local Rule declaring stakes identifying but not defining *out of bounds* to be *obstructions*.

Outside Agency In match play, an "*outside agency*" is any agency other than either the player's or *opponent's side*, any *caddie* of either *side*, any ball played by either *side* at the hole being played or any *equipment* of either *side*.

In stroke play, an *outside agency* is any agency other than the *competitor's side*, any *caddie* of the *side*, any ball played by the *side* at the hole being played or any *equipment* of the *side*.

An *outside agency* includes a *referee*, a *marker*, an *observer* and a *forecaddie*. Neither wind nor water is an *outside agency*.

Partner A "*partner*" is a player associated with another player on the same *side*.

In *threesome*, *foursome*, *best-ball* or *four-ball* play, where the context so admits, the word "player" includes his *partner* or *partners*.

Penalty Stroke A "*penalty stroke*" is one added to the score of a player or *side* under certain *Rules*. In a *threesome* or *foursome*, *penalty strokes* do not affect the order of play.

Provisional Ball A "*provisional ball*" is a ball played under Rule 27-2 for a ball that may be *lost* outside a *water hazard* or may be *out of bounds*.

Putting Green The "*putting green*" is all ground of the hole being played that is specially prepared for putting or otherwise defined as such by the *Committee*. A ball is on the *putting green* when any part of it touches the *putting green*.

R&A The "*R&A*" means R&A Rules Limited.

Referee A "*referee*" is one who is appointed by the *Committee* to decide questions of fact and apply the *Rules*. He must act on any breach of a *Rule* that he observes or is reported to him.

A *referee* should not attend the *flagstick*, stand at or mark the position of the *hole*, or lift the ball or mark its position.

Exception in match play: Unless a *referee* is assigned to accompany the players throughout a match, he has no authority to intervene in a match other than in relation to Rule 1-3, 6-7 or 33-7.

Rub of the Green A "*rub of the green*" occurs when a ball in

PARTNER

A partner is a player associated with another player on the same side.

motion is accidentally deflected or stopped by any *outside agency* (see Rule 19-1).

Rule or Rules The term "*Rule*" includes:
a. The Rules of Golf and their interpretations as contained in *Decisions on the Rules of Golf*;
b. Any Conditions of Competition established by the *Committee* under Rule 33-1 and Appendix I;
c. Any Local Rules established by the *Committee* under Rule 33-8a and Appendix I; and
d. The specifications on:
(i) clubs and the ball in Appendices II and III and their interpretations as contained in *A Guide to the Rules on Clubs and Balls*; and
(ii) devices and other equipment in Appendix IV.

Side A "*side*" is a player, or two or more players who are *partners*. In match play, each member of the opposing *side* is an *opponent*. In stroke play, members of all *sides* are *competitors* and members of different *sides* playing

TEEING GROUND

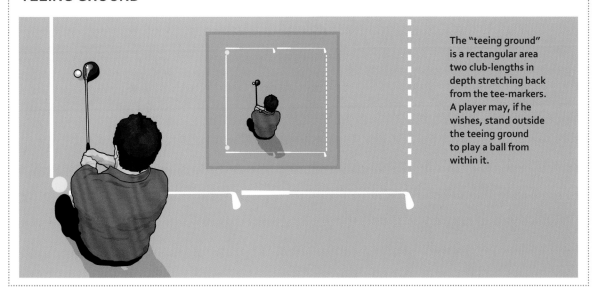

The "teeing ground" is a rectangular area two club-lengths in depth stretching back from the tee-markers. A player may, if he wishes, stand outside the teeing ground to play a ball from within it.

together are *fellow-competitors*.

Single See "*Forms of Match Play*" and "*Forms of Stroke Play*".

Stance Taking the "*stance*" consists in a player placing his feet in position for and preparatory to making a *stroke*.

Stipulated Round The "*stipulated round*" consists of playing the holes of the *course* in their correct sequence, unless otherwise authorised by the *Committee*. The number of holes in a *stipulated round* is 18 unless a smaller number is authorised by the *Committee*. As to extension of

stipulated round in match play, see Rule 2-3.

Stroke A "*stroke*" is the forward movement of the club made with the intention of striking at and moving the ball, but if a player checks his downswing voluntarily before the clubhead reaches the ball he has not made a *stroke*.

Substituted Ball A "*substituted ball*" is a ball put into play for the original ball that was either in *play*, *lost*, *out of bounds* or lifted, whether or not the substitution was permitted. A *substituted ball* becomes the *ball in play* when it has been dropped or placed (see Rule 20-4).

Teeing Ground The "*teeing ground*" is the starting place for the hole to be played. It is a rectangular area two club-lengths in depth, the front and the sides of which are defined by the outside limits of two tee-markers. A ball is outside the *teeing ground* when all of it lies outside the *teeing ground*.

Three-Ball See "*Forms of Match Play*".

Threesome See "*Forms of Match Play*".

Through the Green "*Through the green*" is the whole area of the *course* except:
a. The *teeing ground* and *putting green* of the hole being played; and
b. All *hazards* on the *course*.

Water Hazard A "*water hazard*" is any sea, lake, pond, river, ditch, surface drainage ditch or other open water

DEFINITION OF A STROKE

At this point, as the player has not started his downswing, he has not begun his stroke. Once the player begins his downswing he is considered to have made a stroke, unless he checks his downswing voluntarily.

course (whether or not containing water) and anything of a similar nature on the *course*. All ground and water within the margin of a *water hazard* are part of the *water hazard*.

When the margin of a *water hazard* is defined by stakes, the stakes are inside the *water hazard*, and the margin of the *hazard* is defined by the nearest outside points of the stakes at ground level. When both stakes and lines are used to indicate a *water hazard*, the stakes identify the *hazard* and the lines define the *hazard* margin. When the margin of a *water hazard* is defined by a line on the ground, the line itself is in the *water hazard*. The margin of a *water hazard* extends vertically upwards and downwards.

A ball is in a *water hazard* when it lies in or any part of it touches the *water hazard*.

Stakes used to define the margin of or identify a *water hazard* are *obstructions*.

Note 1: Stakes or lines used to define the margin of or identify a *water hazard* must be yellow.

Note 2: The *Committee* may make a Local Rule prohibiting play from an environmentally-sensitive area defined as a *water hazard*.

Wrong Ball A "*wrong ball*" is any ball other than the player's:
○ *ball in play*;
○ *provisional ball*; or
○ second ball played under Rule 3-3 or Rule 20-7c in stroke play.

Ball in play includes a ball *substituted* for the *ball in play*, whether or not the substitution is permitted. A *substituted ball* becomes the *ball in play* when it has been dropped or placed (see Rule 20-4).

Wrong Putting Green A "*wrong putting green*" is any *putting green* other than that of the hole being played. Unless otherwise prescribed by the *Committee*, this term includes a practice *putting green* or pitching green on the *course*.

INCIDENTS

Seung-Yul Noh was penalised for making a stroke from a wrong putting green during the second round of The Barclays Championship at Ridgewood Country Club in 2014. Noh's wayward tee shot on the 11th hole came to rest on the putting green of the adjacent 3rd hole from where he made a stroke.

As per the Definition of putting green, the putting green is all ground of the hole being played that is specially prepared for putting. All other putting greens, including practice putting greens or pitching greens on the course, are defined as wrong putting greens.

Rule 25-3 prohibits a player from making a stroke from a wrong putting green as it is desirable to protect the surface from any damage that may be caused by making a stroke. Consequently, the player must take relief from a wrong putting green, without penalty.

When Noh played his ball from the 3rd green, he played a stroke on a part of the course where the Rules do not permit a stroke to be made and was in breach of Rule 25-3. He was penalised two strokes.

Two-time Open Champion Padraig Harrington's short approach shot to the 11th hole during the final round of the 2014 Byron Nelson Championship bounced once on the putting green and into the hole, but the ball popped out again, coming to rest just inches away from the edge of the hole.

While some considered Harrington's ball to be holed, it was in fact still in play. Although the ball disappeared below the level of the lip of the hole and touched the bottom of the hole, it was not holed, as it did not come to rest within the hole. A ball is "holed" when it is at rest within the circumference of the hole and all of it is below the level of the lip of the hole. Therefore, Harrington had to tap the ball in to the hole to complete the play of the 11th hole.

At Merion Golf Club's East Course, distinctive baskets are used instead of the usual flags that are generally attached to the flagstick. The flagstick is a movable straight indicator, with or without a flag, to show the position of the hole. At Merion, large pear-shaped wicker tops are used; on the outward nine holes, the tops are red and on the inward nine holes, they are orange. William S. Flynn, the Merion greenkeeper patented the wicker baskets in 1915.

Q & A

How does a player establish the nearest point of relief?

If a player's ball lies on the fairway, the player would be entitled to relief without penalty if he has interference to the lie of the ball, or the area of intended stance or swing, from, for example, an abnormal ground condition (Rule 25-1). If the player opts to take relief, he is required to take relief from all three of these elements (that is, "complete relief"); he cannot choose to take relief from one but not the others. Thus, if his ball was in casual water (an abnormal ground condition), when determining his nearest point of relief, the player must ensure his ball is not in the casual water, and the casual water does not interfere with his stance or swing. He cannot take relief simply for the lie of the ball.

In order to determine the nearest point of relief accurately, the player should use the club with which he would have made his next stroke were the condition (the casual water) not there, and he should simulate the address position, direction of play and swing for such a stroke, making sure he is free of interference from the condition when doing so.

The nearest point of relief is the point on the course nearest to where the ball lies (i) that is not nearer the hole, and (ii) where, if the ball was positioned at that point, there would no longer be any interference from the condition, in this case, casual water.

What club must a player use to measure and to determine his nearest point of relief?

In determining the nearest point of relief the player should use the club with which he expects to play his next stroke. This is a recommendation, hence the use of the word "should" rather than "must", and the player cannot be penalised purely for failing to follow the recommendation. However, if a player uses a different club, for example a club with which it would not be at all reasonable to expect the player to play his next stroke, he is in danger of identifying a spot that is not, in fact, his nearest point of relief. If the player does this, he may, as a consequence, drop his ball in a wrong place and, if he plays from there, he will be penalised for playing from a wrong place.

Bill Haas measures a club-length from the nearest point of relief. Once the nearest point of relief has been established, the player may use any club to measure the area in which to drop the ball.

For example, say the player's ball lies 100 yards from the hole and he is standing in casual water. The player is entitled to relief without penalty from the casual water under Rule 25-1. The player should imagine that the casual water is not there and simply select which club he would normally hit with from that position – for example, a pitching wedge. The pitching wedge, therefore, would be the correct club to use in order to accurately determine the nearest point of relief. On the other hand, in measuring a one- or two club-length dropping area (depending on the Rule), the player may use any club.

Some Rules – for example immovable obstructions (Rule 24-2), abnormal ground conditions (Rule 25-1) – require a player to drop a ball within one club-length of the nearest point of relief. Other Rules, such as unplayable ball (Rule 28), simply require a player to drop a ball within a certain number of club-lengths: in the case of Rule 28c, within two club-lengths of where the ball lies.

Rule 1   THE GAME

DEFINITIONS
All defined terms are
in *italics* and are listed in
the Definitions section –
see pages 13–23.

1-1   General

The Game of Golf consists of playing a ball with a club from the *teeing ground* into the *hole* by a *stroke* or successive *strokes* in accordance with the *Rules*.

1-2   Exerting Influence on Movement of Ball or Altering Physical Conditions

A player must not (i) take an action with the intent to influence the movement of a *ball in play* or (ii) alter physical conditions with the intent of affecting the playing of a hole.

Exceptions

1   An action expressly permitted or expressly prohibited by another *Rule* is subject to that other *Rule*, not Rule 1-2.

2   An action taken for the sole purpose of caring for the *course* is not a breach of Rule 1-2.

---

* PENALTY
For breach of Rule 1-2:

EXERTING INFLUENCE ON MOVEMENT OF BALL OR ALTERING PHYSICAL CONDITIONS

Pressing down a raised piece of turf or repairing divot holes is not a breach of Rule 1-2 provided it is done for the sole purpose of caring for the course. However, if the action was taken with the intent of influencing the movement of the ball or to affect the playing of the hole, this would be a breach of Rule 1-2.

Match play – Loss of hole;

Stroke play – Two strokes.

* In the case of a serious breach of Rule 1-2, the *Committee* may impose a penalty of disqualification.

EQUITY: SOME EXAMPLES

Ball comes to rest near bees' nest. Player is entitled to relief – Decision 1-4/10.

Ball adheres to face of club after stroke. Player drops ball on spot where club was when ball stuck to it – Decision 1-4/2.

Bird's nest interferes with stroke. Player is entitled to relief – Decision 1-4/9.

Distractions are commonplace, but some problems less so. Wildlife needs to be protected and sometimes so does the golfer.

Ball comes to rest near snake. Player is entitled to relief – Decision 1-4/10.

A ball is either lost in casual water that is overflowing a water hazard or it is in the water hazard. Player must proceed under the water hazard Rule. Decision 1-4/7.

NOTE 1

A player is deemed to have committed a serious breach of Rule 1-2 if the *Committee* considers that the action taken in breach of this Rule has allowed him or another player to gain a significant advantage or has placed another player, other than his *partner*, at a significant disadvantage.

NOTE 2

In stroke play, except where a serious breach resulting in disqualification is involved, a player in breach of Rule 1-2 in relation to the movement of his own ball must play the ball from where it was stopped, or, if the ball was deflected, from where it came to rest. If the movement of a player's ball has been intentionally influenced by a *fellow-competitor* or other *outside agency*, Rule 1-4 applies to the player (see Note to Rule 19-1).

1-3   Agreement to Waive Rules

Players must not agree to exclude the operation of any *Rule* or to waive any penalty incurred.

PENALTY

For breach of Rule 1-3:

Match play – Disqualification of both *sides*;

Stroke play – Disqualification of *competitors* concerned.

(Agreeing to play out of turn in stroke play – see Rule 10-2c)

1-4   Points Not Covered by Rules

If any point in dispute is not covered by the *Rules*, the decision should be made in accordance with equity.

MATCH PLAY: AGREEMENT TO CONSIDER HOLE HALVED

An agreement to halve a hole being played is not an agreement to waive the Rules.

Rule 1 Incidents

As Pablo Larrazábal was preparing to play his second shot from the 5th fairway during the second round of the Malaysian Open in 2014, he was suddenly surrounded by hornets. After being stung more than 20 times, he jumped into a nearby lake to escape further harm.

"They were three times the size of bees," Larrazábal said. "Like 30 or 40 of them started to attack me. I didn't know what to do. My caddie told me to run so I started to run like crazy, but the hornets were still there. So I jumped in the lake. It was the scariest moment of my career."

It is unreasonable to expect a player to play when faced with a dangerous situation. It is also unreasonable to require the player to incur a penalty to avoid the danger. Decision 1-4/10 highlights the options for the player when faced with a dangerous situation. It is worth noting that a dangerous situation is one that is unrelated to conditions normally encountered on the course, such as a live rattlesnake or a bees' nest. Unpleasant lies in cacti or stinging nettles are common occurrences that are not considered dangerous and ones that players must accept.

As Larrazábal's ball was lying through the green, to avoid the danger of the hornets he was entitled to drop

Pablo Larrazábal jumps into a nearby lake to escape a swarm of hornets – in equity, a dangerous situation.

a ball, without penalty, within one club-length of and not nearer the hole than the nearest spot that was not dangerous.

By the time Larrazábal had dried off and composed himself, the hornets had disappeared and it was not necessary to apply the equity procedure. Despite the injuries he received from the stings, he went on to make a birdie on that hole.

Q & A

What constitutes an agreement to waive the Rules?
If the players are aware that they are excluding the operation of a Rule, then they are disqualified from the competition under this Rule. In order to be in breach of Rule 1–3 for agreeing to waive a Rule, the players must be aware that they are doing so.

Rule 2 MATCH PLAY

DEFINITIONS
All defined terms are in *italics* and are listed in the Definitions section – see pages 13–23.

2-1 General

A match consists of one *side* playing against another over a *stipulated round* unless otherwise decreed by the *Committee*.

In match play the game is played by holes.

Except as otherwise provided in the *Rules*, a hole is won by the *side* that *holes* its ball in the fewer *strokes*. In a handicap match, the lower net score wins the hole.

The state of the match is expressed by the terms: so many "holes up" or "all square", and so many "to play".

A *side* is "dormie" when it is as many holes up as there are holes remaining to be played.

WINNER OF THE MATCH: HOLE BY HOLE PLAY-OFF

The Committee has the authority to determine how a tie is decided. It is recommended that a match that ends all square should be played off hole by hole until one side wins. The play-off should start on the hole where the match began and any handicap strokes should be allowed as in the stipulated round.

2-2   Halved Hole

A hole is halved if each *side holes* out in the same number of *strokes*.

When a player has *holed* out and his opponent has been left with a *stroke* for the half, if the player subsequently incurs a penalty, the hole is halved.

2-3   Winner of Match

A match is won when one *side* leads by a number of holes greater than the number remaining to be played.

If there is a tie, the *Committee* may extend the *stipulated round* by as many holes as are required for a match to be won.

2-4   Concession of Match, Hole or Next Stroke

A player may concede a match at any time prior to the start or conclusion of that match.

A player may concede a hole at any time prior to the start or conclusion of that hole. A player may concede his *opponent*'s next *stroke* at any time, provided the *opponent*'s ball is at rest. The *opponent* is considered to have *holed* out with his next *stroke*, and the ball may be removed by either *side*.

A concession may not be declined or withdrawn.

(Ball overhanging hole – see Rule 16-2)

2-5   Doubt as to Procedure; Disputes and Claims

In match play, if a doubt or dispute arises between the players, a player may make a claim. If no duly authorised representative of the *Committee* is available within a reasonable time, the players must continue the match without delay. The *Committee* may consider a claim only if it has been made in a timely manner and if the player making the claim has notified his *opponent* at the time (i) that he is making a claim or wants a ruling and (ii) of the facts upon which the claim or ruling is to be based.

A claim is considered to have been made in a timely manner if, upon discovery of circumstances giving rise to a claim, the player makes his claim (i) before any player in the match plays from the next *teeing ground*, or (ii) in the case of the last hole of the match, before all players in the match leave the *putting green*, or (iii) when the circumstances giving rise to the claim are discovered after all the players in the match have left the *putting green* of the final hole, before the result of the match has been officially announced.

A claim relating to a prior hole in the match may only be considered by the *Committee* if it is based on facts previously unknown to the player making the claim and he had been given wrong information (Rules 6-2a or 9) by an *opponent*. Such a claim must be made in a timely manner.

Once the result of the match has been officially announced, a claim may not be considered by the *Committee*, unless it is satisfied that (i) the claim is based on facts which were previously unknown to the player making the claim at the time the result was officially announced, (ii) the player making the claim had been given wrong information by an *opponent* and (iii) the *opponent* knew he was giving wrong information. There is no time limit on considering such a claim.

NOTE 1

A player may disregard a breach of the *Rules* by his *opponent* provided there is no agreement by the *sides* to waive a Rule (Rule 1-3).

NOTE 2

In match play, if a player is doubtful of his rights or the correct procedure, he may not complete the play of the hole with two balls.

2-6 General Penalty

The penalty for a breach of a *Rule* in match play is loss of hole except when otherwise provided.

STATUS OF LATE CLAIM

Claims must be made in a timely manner, otherwise the Committee is unable to consider them. For example, a player realises that his opponent should have lost the 4th hole when he grounded his club in a bunker. For a claim to be made in a timely manner, the player would need to raise a claim before either player played a stroke from the 5th teeing ground.

RULE 2 INCIDENTS

In playing the 7th hole at the WGC Accenture Match Play Championship in 2014, Sergio Garcia offered to halve the hole with his opponent Ricky Fowler before they had both putted out. At the time, Fowler had a putt of 17ft for a par, while Garcia had much shorter putt of 6ft for his par.

Under the Rules, an agreement to halve a hole being played is permissible. However, if players agree to consider a hole halved without either player making a stroke on the hole, they are disqualified under Rule 1-3 for agreeing to exclude the operation of Rule 2-1 by failing to play the stipulated round.

Garcia's offer was therefore permitted and was obviously in favour of Fowler, who had the longer putt for par. The concession followed an incident on the previous hole, where Fowler had been forced to wait for a ruling that Garcia had requested. The ruling took some time to conclude and when it was eventually Fowler's turn to play, he missed his makeable birdie putt. When questioned about it later, Garcia explained, "I felt guilty that my drop on the 6th took so long. I felt like if I would have been in his position I would have been uncomfortable waiting so long to hit my birdie putt. So I just thought I have to do something. I have to do something to make sure that I feel OK with myself."

Garcia's sporting gesture was applauded, especially in light of the fact that he went on to lose the match by one hole to Fowler.

During the second day's four-ball match between Europe and the United States of America at the 2013 Solheim Cup, American golfer Lexi Thompson had a putt for a four to halve the hole with the European side. Her partner, Paula Creamer, had already played four so was unable to impact on the match.

However, Creamer's short putt for a five was on a similar line to Thompson's putt. Under Rule 30-3b, balls belonging to the same side may be played in the order the side considers best. As the European side had not conceded Creamer's putt, the American side decided that Creamer would putt first to show Thompson the line.

While Creamer was preparing to putt, the caddie of European player Jodie Ewart shouted out and conceded the putt, as he realised that it might assist Thompson and did not want the American side to benefit. Annoyed by this late call, Creamer called the referee over to ascertain if the caddie had acted alone or if her opponent, Ewart, had given him permission to concede the putt so late.

Although a concession cannot be declined or withdrawn, the player must make the concession. Rule 2-4 permits only the player to concede the opponent's next stroke. In this case, it was discovered that the caddie had acted without permission of his player, and as he did not have authority to concede the putt, the concession was invalid.

Despite the disruption, Thompson went on to make her putt to halve the hole with the European side.

Garcia and Fowler shake hands after their sporting match during the World Golf Championship Match Play Championship in 2014.

Q & A

Can a player putt out after a putt has been conceded?

While a concession cannot be declined, there is no penalty for holing out after a stroke has been conceded. However, if the act of holing out were to be of assistance to a partner in a four-ball or best-ball match, the partner is in equity (Rule 1-4) disqualified for the hole.

Rule 3

STROKE PLAY

DEFINITIONS

All defined terms are in *italics* and are listed in the Definitions section – see pages 13–23.

3-1   General; Winner

A stroke play competition consists of *competitors* completing each hole of a *stipulated round* or rounds and, for each round, returning a score card on which there is a gross score for each hole. Each *competitor* is playing against every other *competitor* in the competition.

The *competitor* who plays the *stipulated round* or rounds in the fewest *strokes* is the winner.

In a handicap competition, the *competitor* with the lowest net score for the *stipulated round* or rounds is the winner.

3-2   Failure to Hole Out

If a *competitor* fails to hole out at any hole and does not correct his mistake before he makes a *stroke* on the next *teeing ground* or, in the case of the last hole of the round, before he leaves the *putting green*, he is disqualified.

3-3   Doubt as to Procedure
3-3 a   Procedure for Competitor

In stroke play only, if a *competitor* is doubtful of his rights or the correct procedure during the play of a hole, he may, without penalty, complete the hole with two balls. To proceed under this Rule, he must decide to play two balls after the doubtful situation has arisen and before taking further action (e.g. making a stroke at the original ball).

The competitor should announce to his *marker* or a *fellow-competitor*:

o   that he intends to play two balls; and

o   which ball he wishes to count if the *Rules* permit the procedure used for that ball.

DOUBT AS TO PROCEDURE IN STROKE PLAY

A player who is doubtful of his rights or the correct procedure can play out the hole with two balls. He should announce to his fellow-competitor that he intends to play two balls and which ball he wishes to count if the Rules permit the procedure used for that ball.

Before returning his score card, the *competitor* must report the facts of the situation to the *Committee*. If he fails to do so, he is disqualified.

If the competitor has taken further action before deciding to play two balls, he has not proceeded under Rule 3-3 and the score with the original ball counts. The *competitor* incurs no penalty for playing the second ball.

3-3 b Committee Determination of Score for Hole

When the *competitor* has proceeded under this Rule, the *Committee* will determine his score as follows:

(i) If, before taking further action, the *competitor* has announced which ball he wishes to count and provided the *Rules* permit the procedure used for the selected ball, the score with that ball counts. If the *Rules* do not permit the procedure used for the selected ball, the score with the other ball counts provided the *Rules* permit the procedure used for that ball.

(ii) If, before taking further action, the *competitor* has failed to announce which ball he wishes to count, the score with the original ball counts provided the *Rules* permit the procedure used for that ball. Otherwise, the score with the other ball counts provided the *Rules* permit the procedure used for that ball.

(iii) If the *Rules* do not permit the procedures used for both balls, the score with the original ball counts unless the *competitor* has committed a serious breach with that ball by playing from a wrong place. If the *competitor* commits a serious breach in the play of one ball, the score with the other ball counts despite the fact that the *Rules* do not permit the procedure used for that ball. If the *competitor* commits a serious breach with both balls, he is disqualified.

NOTE 1

"*Rules* permit the procedure used for a ball" means that, after Rule 3-3 is invoked, either: (a) the original ball is played from where it had come to rest and play is permitted from that location, or (b) the *Rules* permit the procedure adopted for the ball and the ball is put into play in the proper manner and in the correct place as provided in the Rules.

NOTE 2

If the score with the original ball is to count, but the original ball is not one of the balls being played, the first ball put into play is deemed to be the original ball.

NOTE 3

After this Rule has been invoked, *strokes* made with the ball ruled not to count, and *penalty strokes* incurred solely by playing that ball, are disregarded. A second ball played under Rule 3-3 is not a *provisional ball* under Rule 27-2.

(Ball played from a wrong place – see Rule 20-7c)

3-4 Refusal to Comply with a Rule

If a *competitor* refuses to comply with a *Rule* affecting the rights of another *competitor*, he is disqualified.

3-5 General Penalty
The penalty for a breach of a *Rule* in stroke play is two strokes except when otherwise provided.

Q & A

Can I play a second ball in match play if I am unsure of what to do?

No. The Rules only permit a player to play a second ball in stroke play. In match play, a player may proceed as he thinks he is entitled to do. If a doubt or dispute arises between the players, the opponent may make a claim and raise it with the Committee in charge – see Rule 2-5.

Rule 4   CLUBS

DEFINITIONS
All defined terms are in *italics* and are listed in the Definitions section – see pages 13–23.

For detailed specifications and interpretations on the conformity of clubs under Rule 4 and the process for consultation and submission regarding clubs, see Appendix II.

4-1 Form and Make of Clubs
4-1 a General
The player's clubs must conform with this Rule and the provisions, specifications and interpretations set forth in Appendix II.

NOTE

The *Committee* may require, in the conditions of a competition (Rule 33-1), that any driver the player carries must have a clubhead, identified by model and loft, that is named on the current List of Conforming Driver Heads issued by the *R&A*.

4-1 b Wear and Alteration
A club that conforms with the *Rules* when new is deemed to conform after wear through normal use. Any part of a club that has been purposely altered is regarded as new and must, in its altered state, conform with the *Rules*.

4-2 Playing Characteristics Changed and Foreign Material
4-2 a Playing Characteristics Changed
During a *stipulated round*, the playing characteristics of a club must not be purposely changed by adjustment or by any other means.

NON-CONFORMING CLUB CARRIED BUT NOT USED

X

The penalty for carrying, but not making a stroke with, a non-conforming club is detailed in Rules 4-1 and 4-2. The player is only disqualified if he makes a stroke with a non-conforming club. This "chipper" is non-conforming as it has more than one striking face.

4-2 b Foreign Material

Foreign material must not be applied to the club face for the purpose of influencing the movement of the ball.

* PENALTY

For carrying, but not making *stroke* with, club or clubs in breach of Rule 4-1 or 4-2:

Match play – At the conclusion of the hole at which the breach is discovered, the state of the match is adjusted by deducting one hole for each hole at which a breach occurred; maximum deduction per round – Two holes.

Stroke play – Two strokes for each hole at which any breach occurred; maximum penalty per round – Four strokes (two strokes at each of the first two holes at which any breach occurred).

Match play or stroke play – If a breach is discovered between the play of two holes, it is deemed to have been discovered during play of the next hole, and the penalty must be applied accordingly.

Bogey and par competitions – See Note 1 to Rule 32-1a

Stableford competitions – See Note 1 to Rule 32-1b.

*Any club or clubs carried in breach of Rule 4-1 or 4–2 must be declared out of play by the player to his *opponent* in match play or his *marker* or a *fellow-competitor* in stroke play immediately upon discovery that a breach has occurred. If the player fails to do so, he is disqualified.

PENALTY

For making stroke with club in breach of Rule 4-1 or 4-2:

Disqualification.

BREACH OF FOURTEEN-CLUB RULE IN MATCH PLAY

4-3 Damaged Clubs: Repair and Replacement
4-3 a Damage in Normal Course of Play

If, during a *stipulated round*, a player's club is damaged in the normal course of play, he may:

(i) use the club in its damaged state for the remainder of the *stipulated round*; or

(ii) without unduly delaying play, repair it or have it repaired; or

(iii) as an additional option available only if the club is unfit for play, replace the damaged club with any club. The replacement of a club must not unduly delay play (Rule 6-7) and must not be made by borrowing any club selected for play by any other person playing on the *course* or by assembling components carried by or for the player during the *stipulated round*.

PENALTY

For breach of Rule 4-3a:

See Penalty Statements for Rule 4-4a or b, and Rule 4-4c.

NOTE

A club is unfit for play if it is substantially damaged, e.g. the shaft is dented, significantly bent or breaks into pieces; the clubhead becomes loose, detached or significantly deformed; or the grip becomes loose. A club is not unfit for play solely because the club's lie or loft has been altered, or the clubhead is scratched.

4-3 b Damage Other Than in Normal Course of Play

If, during a *stipulated round*, a player's club is damaged other than in the normal course of play rendering it non-conforming or changing its playing characteristics, the club must not subsequently be used or replaced during the round.

4-3 c Damage Prior to Round

A player may use a club damaged prior to a round, provided the club, in its damaged state, conforms with the *Rules*.

Damage to a club that occurred prior to a round may be repaired during the round, provided the playing characteristics are not changed and play is not unduly delayed

4-4 Maximum of Fourteen Clubs
4-4 a Selection and Addition of Clubs

The player must not start a *stipulated round* with more than fourteen clubs. He is limited to the clubs thus selected for that round, except that if he started with fewer than fourteen clubs, he may add any number, provided his total number does not exceed fourteen.

The addition of a club or clubs must not unduly delay play (Rule 6-7) and the player must not add or borrow any club selected for play by any other person playing on the *course* or by assembling components carried by or for the player during the *stipulated round*.

MAXIMUM OF FOURTEEN CLUBS

Felipe Aguilar incurred the maximum penalty of four strokes for a breach of Rule 4-4a.

4-4 b Partners May Share Clubs

Partners may share clubs, provided that the total number of clubs carried by the *partners* so sharing does not exceed fourteen.

Rule 4 Incidents

At the 2014 Memorial Tournament held at Muirfield Village, Ohio, Hideki Matsuyama birdied the final hole to force a hole-by-hole play-off against Kevin Na. After pushing his tee shot on the 18th hole, Matsuyama took out some of his frustration on his driver by slamming it into the ground, rendering it visibly damaged. Fortunately, his ball took a favourable bounce and landed back on the fairway, allowing him to hit the green in regulation and sink the birdie putt to secure a place in the play-off.

If, during a stipulated round, a player's club is damaged other than in the normal course of play, rendering it non-conforming or changing its playing characteristics, the club must not be used or replaced (Rule 4-3b). As Matsuyama's driver was not damaged in the normal course of play (e.g. in playing a stroke or by accidentally dropping it), he was not permitted to use the club for the remainder of the stipulated round.

However, Matsuyama's stipulated round finished when he birdied the 18th hole. Decision 4-3/12 clarifies that the hole-by-hole play-off constitutes a new round, so fortunately for Matsuyama, he was entitled to replace his broken club for the play-off.

Unable to find a replacement in time, Matsuyama teed off on the first extra hole with his 3-wood, finding a fairway bunker. Nevertheless, he played from the bunker and found the putting green, sinking his 10 foot putt for a par to win the tournament.

Felipe Aguilar started his second round of the Turkish Airlines Open in 2014 with 14 clubs in his bag but was penalised when he changed one of the clubs in his bag during an overnight suspension of play for bad weather.

After play had resumed the next day, Aguilar realised he had a different selection of clubs than the day before, so before signing his score card, he asked a referee for a ruling.

Rule 4-4a stipulates that a player must not start a round with more than fourteen clubs and that he is limited to the clubs thus selected for that round, except that if he has fewer than 14 clubs in the bag, he may add to the selection, provided the total number of clubs does not exceed 14.

Aguilar had 14 clubs in his bag at the start of his round, so he was restricted to those clubs and was not permitted to change any. Switching one club for another club overnight resulted in him carrying 15 different clubs over the course of his stipulated second round.

The penalty for a breach of Rule 4-4a is two strokes for each hole at which any breach occurred, with a maximum penalty per round of four strokes. As Aguilar had the switched club for all the 6 holes he played after play was resumed, he incurred the maximum penalty of four strokes (two strokes at the 13th hole and two strokes at the 14th hole).

Probably the most memorable case involving Rule 4-4a was during the 2001 Open Championship at Royal Lytham & St Annes. Ian Woosnam started the final round as joint leader and tapped in for a birdie two at the first hole, a fantastic start to his final round.

Standing on the second tee, Miles Byrne, Woosnam's caddie, turned to him and said, "You're going to go ballistic. We have 15 clubs in the bag." On the practice ground, Woosnam had been testing two drivers and, rushing from the practice ground to the first tee, he had not counted his clubs to ensure that he had no more than the stipulated 14. Under Rule 4-4a, Woosnam incurred a two-stroke penalty at the first hole and his birdie two became a bogey four, effectively spoiling his chances of a second Major title.

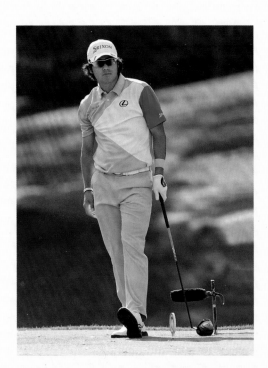

Hideki Matsuyama holds his broken club on the 18th hole during the final round of the 2014 Memorial Tournament.

PENALTY

For breach of Rule 4-4a or b, regardless of number of excess clubs carried:

Match play – At the conclusion of the hole at which the breach is discovered, the state of the match is adjusted by deducting one hole for each hole at which a breach occurred; maximum deduction per round – Two holes.

Stroke play – Two strokes for each hole at which any breach occurred; maximum penalty per round – Four strokes (two strokes at each of the first two holes at which any breach occurred).

Match play or stroke play – If a breach is discovered between the play of two holes, it is deemed to have been discovered during play of the hole just completed, and the penalty for a breach of Rule 4-4a or b does not apply to the next hole.

Bogey and par competitions – See Note 1 to Rule 32-1a.

Stableford competitions – See Note 1 to Rule 32-1b.

4-4 c Excess Club Declared Out of Play

Any club or clubs carried or used in breach of Rule 4-3a(iii) or Rule 4-4 must be declared out of play by the player to his *opponent* in match play or his *marker* or a *fellow-competitor* in stroke play immediately upon discovery that a breach has occurred. The player must not use the club or clubs for the remainder of the *stipulated round*.

PENALTY

For breach of Rule 4-4c:

Disqualification.

Q & A

Can a player play with both right-handed and left-handed clubs?

The Rules of Golf do not restrict a player in his choice of clubs in terms of whether they are left-handed or right-handed. The player may select up to 14 clubs (the maximum permitted under Rule 4-4) and they can consist of right- and left-handed clubs. For example, some players prefer to play right-handed, but will putt left-handed, and so carry a left-handed putter. This is permitted by the Rules provided the total number of clubs selected does not exceed 14 and all clubs conform to the Rules.

Can I use a "chipper" in a stipulated round?

A "chipper" is an iron club designed primarily for use off the putting green. It is permitted to use a chipper in a stipulated round provided the:

o   shaft is attached to the chipper head at the heel;

o   chipper has only one grip and the grip is circular in cross-section;

o   chipper has only one striking face;

o   face of the chipper conforms to the specifications with regard to hardness, surface roughness, material and markings in the impact area (see Appendix II and Decision 4-1/3).

Rule 5

THE BALL

DEFINITIONS
All defined terms are in *italics* and are listed in the Definitions section – see pages 13–23.

For detailed specifications and interpretations on the conformity of balls under Rule 5 and the process for consultation and submission regarding balls, see Appendix III.

5-1 General

The ball the player plays must conform to the requirements specified in Appendix III.

> **NOTE**
> The *Committee* may require, in the conditions of a competition (Rule 33-1), that the ball the player plays must be named on the current List of Conforming Golf Balls issued by the *R&A*.

5-2 Foreign Material

The ball the player plays must not have foreign material applied to it for the purpose of changing its playing characteristics.

> **PENALTY**
> For breach of Rule 5-1 or 5-2:
> Disqualification.

THE BALL

An "x-out" is a common name used for a golf ball that a manufacturer considers to be imperfect due to aesthetic reasons. In the absence of strong evidence to suggest that it does not conform to the Rules, it is permissible to use such a ball.

5-3 Ball Unfit for Play

A ball is unfit for play if it is visibly cut, cracked or out of shape. A ball is not unfit for play solely because mud or other materials adhere to it, its surface is scratched or scraped or its paint is damaged or discoloured.

If a player has reason to believe his ball has become unfit for play during play of the hole being played, he may lift the ball, without penalty, to determine whether it is unfit. Before lifting the ball, the player must announce his intention to his *opponent* in match play or his *marker* or a *fellow-competitor* in stroke play and mark the position of the ball. He may then lift and examine it, provided that he gives his *opponent*, *marker* or *fellow-competitor* an opportunity to examine the ball and observe the lifting and replacement. The ball must not be cleaned when lifted under Rule 5-3.

If the player fails to comply with all or any part of this procedure, or if he lifts the ball without having reason to believe that it has become unfit for play during play of the hole being played, he incurs a penalty of one stroke.

If it is determined that the ball has become unfit for play during play of the hole being played, the player may *substitute* another ball, placing it on the spot where the original ball lay. Otherwise, the original ball must be replaced. If a player *substitutes* a ball when not permitted and makes a *stroke* at the incorrectly *substituted ball*, he incurs the general penalty for a breach of Rule 5-3, but there is no additional penalty under this Rule or Rule 15-2.

If a ball breaks into pieces as a result of a *stroke*, the *stroke* is cancelled and the player must play a ball, without penalty, as nearly as possible at the spot from which the original ball was played (see Rule 20-5).

RULE 5 INCIDENTS

Despite the advances in the design and technology of the golf ball, it is still occasionally possible to experience a cut or cracked golf ball.

A ball is not unfit for play solely because mud or other materials adhere to it. Equally, a ball is not unfit for play if its surface is scratched or scraped, or if its paint is damaged or discoloured. It must be visibly cut, cracked or out of shape to be considered unfit for play. After playing out of a bunker at the 16th hole on day three of The Open Championship at Royal Lytham & St Annes in 2012, Jeev Milkha Singh queried whether his ball was unfit for play with a referee. When a player has reason to believe that his ball has become unfit for play during the play of a hole, he may lift the ball, without penalty, to determine if it is unfit.

Under Rule 5-3, the player must first announce his intention to lift and examine the ball to his opponent, marker or fellow-competitor. However, the referee may also fulfil the responsibility of the opponent, marker or fellow-competitor to observe and determine if a ball is unfit for play. The player must also mark the position of the ball under this Rule.

If a player fails to comply with all or any part of the procedure in Rule 5-3, he incurs a penalty of one stroke. Thereafter, if it is determined that the ball has become unfit for play, the player may substitute another ball, placing it on the spot where the original ball lay, without penalty. Otherwise, the player must replace the original ball.

The referee agreed with Singh that his ball was damaged to such a degree that it was unfit for play. Singh substituted another ball on the same spot, without penalty, and continued play of the hole.

BALL UNFIT FOR PLAY

A player who has reason to believe that their ball has become unfit for play must give the opponent, marker or fellow-competitor an opportunity to examine the ball and observe the lifting and replacement.

* PENALTY

For breach of Rule 5-3:

Match play – Loss of hole;

Stroke play – Two strokes.

*If a player incurs the general penalty for a breach of Rule 5-3, there is no additional penalty under this Rule.

NOTE 1

If the *opponent, marker or fellow-competitor* wishes to dispute a claim of unfitness, he must do so before the player plays another ball.

NOTE 2

If the original lie of a ball to be placed or replaced has been altered, see Rule 20-3b.

(Cleaning ball lifted from putting green or under any other Rule – see Rule 21)

5

A referee may fulfil the responsibilities of the opponent, marker or fellow-competitor in determining if a ball is unfit for play. Here, Ernie Els gives his fellow-competitor Soren Kjeldsen and the referee an opportunity to inspect a ball that he believes is damaged during the play of a hole.

Q & A

Can I use an "x-out", "refurbished" or "practice" ball to play a round of golf?

"X-out' is the common name used for a golf ball that a manufacturer considers to be imperfect (usually for aesthetic reasons only: for example, paint or printing errors) and, therefore, has crossed out the brand name. A "refurbished" golf ball is a second-hand ball that has been cleaned and stamped as "refurbished".

In the absence of strong evidence to suggest that an "x-out" or "refurbished" ball does not conform to the Rules, it is permissible for such a ball to be used. However, in a competition where the Committee has adopted the condition that the ball the player uses must be named on the List of Conforming Golf Balls (see Note to Rule 5-1), such a ball may not be used, even if the ball in question (without the "x"s or without the "refurbished" stamp) does appear on the List.

In most cases, "practice" balls are simply listed conforming golf balls that have been stamped "PRACTICE" (for example, just like a ball with a golf club's logo). Such balls may be used even where the Committee has adopted the condition that the ball the player uses must be named on the List of Conforming Golf Balls.

May a player borrow golf balls from an opponent or fellow-competitor if he runs out of golf balls during the round?

The Rules of Golf do not prevent a player from borrowing a golf ball from another player on the course. The Rules only limit the borrowing of clubs and not golf balls.

What does the "One Ball Condition" mean?

The Rules do not require the player to use the same brand and type of golf ball throughout the stipulated round. A player may use a different golf ball to start each hole and must continue with this ball, unless it is lost or the Rules permit a substitution.

However, the Committee may adopt the "one ball condition" as a Condition of Competition. When this condition is adopted, players are required to use the same brand and type of golf ball throughout the stipulated round at all times.

Rule 6

THE PLAYER

DEFINITIONS
All defined terms are
in *italics* and are listed in
the Definitions section –
see pages 13–23.

6-1 Rules

The player and his *caddie* are responsible for knowing the *Rules*. During a *stipulated round*, for any breach of a *Rule* by his *caddie*, the player incurs the applicable penalty.

6-2 Handicap
6-2 a Match Play

Before starting a match in a handicap competition, the players should determine from one another their respective handicaps. If a player begins a match having declared a handicap higher than that to which he is entitled and this affects the number of strokes given or received, he is disqualified; otherwise, the player must play off the declared handicap.

6-2 b Stroke Play

In any round of a handicap competition, the *competitor* must ensure that his handicap is recorded on his score card before it is returned to the *Committee*. If no handicap is recorded on his score card before it is returned (Rule 6-6b), or if the recorded handicap is higher than that to which he is entitled and this affects the number of strokes received, he is disqualified from the handicap competition; otherwise, the score stands.

NOTE

It is the player's responsibility to know the holes at which handicap strokes are to be given or received.

6-3 Time of Starting and Groups
6-3 a Time of Starting

The player must start at the time established by the *Committee*.

PENALTY

For breach of Rule 6-3a:

If the player arrives at his starting point, ready to play, within five minutes after his starting time, the penalty for failure to start on time is loss of the first hole in match play or two strokes at the first hole in stroke play. Otherwise, the penalty for breach of this Rule is disqualification.

Bogey and par competitions – See Note 2 to Rule 32-1a.

Stableford competitions – See Note 2 to Rule 32-1b.

Exception

Where the *Committee* determines that exceptional circumstances have prevented a player from starting on time, there is no penalty.

6-3 b Groups

In stroke play, the *competitor* must remain throughout the round in the group arranged by the *Committee*, unless the *Committee* authorises or ratifies a change.

PENALTY

For breach of Rule 6-3b:

Disqualification.

(*Best-ball* and *four-ball play* – see Rules 30-3a and 31-2)

6-4 Caddie

The player may be assisted by a *caddie*, but he is limited to only one *caddie* at any one time.

* PENALTY

For breach of Rule 6-4:

Match play – At the conclusion of the hole at which the breach is discovered, the state of the match is adjusted by deducting one hole for each hole at which a breach occurred; maximum deduction per round – Two holes.

Stroke play – Two strokes for each hole at which any breach occurred; maximum penalty per round – Four strokes (two strokes at each of the first two holes at which any breach occurred).

Match play or stroke play – If a breach is discovered between the play of two holes, it is deemed to have been discovered during play of the next hole, and the penalty must be applied accordingly.

Bogey and par competitions – See Note 1 to Rule 32-1a.

Stableford competitions – See Note 1 to Rule 32-1b.

*A player having more than one caddie in breach of this Rule must immediately upon discovery that a breach has occurred ensure that he has no more than one caddie at any one time during the remainder of the stipulated round. Otherwise, the player is disqualified.

NOTE

The *Committee* may, in the conditions of a competition (Rule 33-1), prohibit the use of *caddies* or restrict a player in his choice of *caddie*.

6-5 Ball

The responsibility for playing the proper ball rests with the player. Each player should put an identification mark on his ball.

6-6 Scoring in Stroke Play
6-6 a Recording Scores

After each hole the *marker* should check the score with the *competitor* and record it. On completion of the round the *marker* must sign the score card and hand it to the *competitor*. If more than one *marker* records the scores, each must sign for the part for which he is responsible.

6-6 b Signing and Returning Score Card

After completion of the round, the *competitor* should check his score for each hole and settle any doubtful points with the *Committee*. He must ensure that the *marker* or *markers* have signed the score card, sign the score card himself and return it to the *Committee* as soon as possible.

PENALTY

For breach of Rule 6-6b:

Disqualification.

6-6 c Alteration of Score Card

No alteration may be made on a score card after the *competitor* has returned it to the *Committee*.

6-6 d Wrong Score for Hole

The *competitor* is responsible for the correctness of the score recorded for each hole on his score card. If he returns a score for any hole lower than actually taken, he is disqualified. If he returns a score for any hole higher than actually taken, the score as returned stands.

Exception

If a competitor returns a score for any hole lower than actually taken due to failure to include one or more *penalty strokes* that, before returning his score card, he did not know he had incurred, he is not disqualified. In such circumstances, the competitor incurs the penalty prescribed by the applicable *Rule* and an additional penalty of two strokes for each hole at which the *competitor* has committed a breach of Rule 6-6d. This Exception does not apply when the applicable penalty is disqualification from the competition.

NOTE 1

The *Committee* is responsible for the addition of scores and application of the handicap recorded on the score card – see Rule 33-5.

NOTE 2

In *four-ball* stroke play, see also Rule 31-3 and 31-7a.

Japan's Ryo Ishikawa has a cartoon image of himself as an identification mark.

So Yeon Ryu of South Korea marks up golf balls in advance of her starting time.

6-7 Undue Delay; Slow Play

The player must play without undue delay and in accordance with any pace of play guidelines that the *Committee* may establish. Between completion of a hole and playing from the next *teeing ground*, the player must not unduly delay play.

PENALTY

For breach of Rule 6-7:

Match play – Loss of hole;

Stroke play – Two strokes.

Bogey and par competitions – See Note 2 to Rule 32-1a.

Stableford competitions – See Note 2 to Rule 32-1b.

For subsequent offence – Disqualification.

NOTE 1

If the player unduly delays play between holes, he is delaying the play of the next hole and, except for bogey, par and Stableford competitions (see Rule 32), the penalty applies to that hole.

NOTE 2

For the purpose of preventing slow play, the *Committee* may, in the conditions of a competition (Rule 33-1), establish pace of play guidelines including maximum periods of time allowed to complete a *stipulated round*, a hole or a *stroke*.

In match play, the *Committee* may, in such a condition, modify the penalty for a breach of this Rule as follows:

First offence – Loss of hole;

Second offence – Loss of hole;

For subsequent offence – Disqualification.

UNDUE DELAY: ENTERING CLUBHOUSE

A player may enter the clubhouse or a "half-way" house without penalty provided the player does not unduly delay either his own play or that of his opponent or any other competitor (Rule 6-7).

SCORING IN STROKE PLAY

COMPETITION **SPRING STROKE PLAY**   DATE **14 . 6 . 15**

PLAYER **D. BROWN**   HANDICAP **10**   Game No **21**

Hole	Yards	Par	Stroke Index	Score	W = + L = - H = 0 POINTS	Mar Score	Hole	Yards	Par	Stroke Index	Score	W = + L = - H = 0 POINTS	Mar Score
1	312	4	17	5		6	10	369	4	12	6̸5	c	
2	446	4	1	4		4	11	433	4	2	3		
3	310	4	13	4		3	12	361	4	14	4		
4	370	4	9	5	b	5	13	415	4	6	5		
5	478	5	3	6			14	155	3	16	6		
8̸7	429	4	11	4			15	338	4	8	5		
7̸6	385	4	5	3			16	316	4	10	4		
8	178	3	7	4			17	191	3	4	5		
9	354	4	15	6			18	508	5	18	7		
OUT	3262			41			IN	3086	35		44		
							OUT	3262	36		41		
							TOTAL	6348	71		85		

a

e & f

Markers Signature **D.B.**

Players Signature **Bill White**

HANDICAP **10**
NETT **75**   d

Competitor's Responsibilities:

1 To record the correct handicap somewhere on the score card before it is returned to the *Committee*.

2 To check the gross score recorded for each hole is correct.

3 To ensure that the *marker* has signed the card and to countersign the card himself before it is returned to the *Committee*.

Committee Responsibilities:

1 Issue to each *competitor* a score card containing the date and the *competitor's* name.

2 To add the scores for each hole and apply the handicap recorded on the card.

Points to Note:

(a) Hole numbers may be altered if hole scores have been recorded in the wrong boxes.

(b) A *marker* need not keep a record of his own score, however it is recommended.

(c) There is nothing in the Rules that requires an alteration to be initialled.

(d) The *competitor* is responsible only for the correctness of the score recorded for each hole. If the *competitor* records a wrong total score or net score, the *Committee* must correct the error, without penalty to the *competitor*. In this instance, the *Committee* have added the scores for each hole and applied the handicap.

(e) There is no penalty if a *marker* signs the *competitor's* score card in the space provided for the *competitor's* signature, and the *competitor* then signs in the space provided for the *marker's* signature.

(f) The initialling of the score card by the *competitor* is sufficient for the purpose of countersignature.

In stroke play, the *Committee* may, in such a condition, modify the penalty for a breach of this Rule as follows:

First offence – One stroke;

Second offence – Two strokes;

For subsequent offence – Disqualification.

6-8 Discontinuance of Play; Resumption of Play
6-8 a When Permitted

The player must not discontinue play unless:

(i) the *Committee* has suspended play;

(ii) he believes there is danger from lightning;

(iii) he is seeking a decision from the *Committee* on a doubtful or disputed point (see Rules 2-5 and 34-3); or

(iv) there is some other good reason such as sudden illness.

Bad weather is not of itself a good reason for discontinuing play.

If the player discontinues play without specific permission from the *Committee*, he must report to the *Committee* as soon as practicable. If he does so and the *Committee* considers his reason satisfactory, there is no penalty. Otherwise, the player is disqualified.

Exception in match play: Players discontinuing match play by agreement are not subject to disqualification, unless by so doing the competition is delayed.

NOTE

Leaving the course does not of itself constitute discontinuance of play.

DISCONTINUANCE OF PLAY

In stroke play, players may not discontinue play simply because of bad weather. However, in match play, players may agree to discontinue play for whatever reason, for example darkness, as long as the competition is not delayed as a result.

Stroke play

Match play

6-8 b Procedure When Play Suspended by Committee

When play is suspended by the *Committee*, if the players in a match or group are between the play of two holes, they must not resume play until the *Committee* has ordered a resumption of play. If they have started play of a hole, they may discontinue play immediately or continue play of the hole, provided they do so without delay. If the players choose to continue play of the hole, they are permitted to discontinue play before completing it. In any case, play must be discontinued after the hole is completed.

The players must resume play when the *Committee* has ordered a resumption of play.

PENALTY

For breach of Rule 6-8b:

Disqualification.

NOTE

The *Committee* may provide, in the conditions of a competition (Rule 33-1), that in potentially dangerous situations play must be discontinued immediately following a suspension of play by the *Committee*. If a player fails to discontinue play immediately, he is disqualified, **unless circumstances warrant waiving the penalty as provided in Rule 33-7.**

6-8 c Lifting Ball When Play Discontinued

When a player discontinues play of a hole under Rule 6-8a, he may lift his ball, without penalty, only if the *Committee* has suspended play or there is a good reason to lift it. Before lifting the ball the player must mark its position. If the player discontinues play and lifts his ball without specific permission from the *Committee*, he must, when reporting to the *Committee* (Rule 6-8a), report the lifting of the ball.

If the player lifts the ball without a good reason to do so, fails to mark the position of the ball before lifting it or fails to report the lifting of the ball, he incurs a penalty of one stroke.

6-8 d Procedure When Play Resumed

Play must be resumed from where it was discontinued, even if resumption occurs on a subsequent day. The player must, either before or when play is resumed, proceed as follows:

(i)   if the player has lifted the ball, he must, provided he was entitled to lift it under Rule 6-8c, place the original ball or a *substituted ball* on the spot from which the original ball was lifted. Otherwise, the original ball must be replaced;

(ii) if the player has not lifted his ball, he may, provided he was entitled to lift it under Rule 6-8c, lift, clean and replace the ball, or substitute a ball, on the spot from which the original ball was lifted. Before lifting the ball he must mark its position; or

(iii) if the player's ball or ball-marker is moved (including by wind or water) while play is discontinued, a ball or ball-marker must be placed on the spot from which the original ball or ball-marker was moved.

NOTE

If the spot where the ball is to be placed is impossible to determine, it must be estimated and the ball placed on the estimated spot. The provisions of Rule 20-3c do not apply.

---

* PENALTY

For breach of Rule 6-8d:

Match play – Loss of hole;

Stroke play – Two strokes.

*If a player incurs the general penalty for a breach of Rule 6-8d, there is no additional penalty under Rule 6-8c.

RULE 6 INCIDENTS

Rory McIlroy needed a police car to take him to Medinah Country Club after he confused his time zones and nearly missed his tee time for his singles match in the 2012 Ryder Cup.

McIlroy was due to play Keegan Bradley at 11.25 a.m. local time, but only managed to arrive at the course at 11.15 a.m. McIlroy had confused Eastern Standard Time with Central Standard Time and thought he had 1 hour and 25 minutes to go. After a mad dash to the course courtesy of a helpful police officer, he said, "I was just casually walking out of my hotel room and got a phone call saying you've got 25 minutes until you tee off. I've never been so worried driving to the golf course."

Rule 6-3a stipulates that the player must start at the time established by the Committee. In McIlroy's case, his match tee off time was established at 11.25 a.m. Being match play, the consequences of missing his tee time could have been significant: had McIlroy arrived at his starting point, ready to play, within five minutes after his starting time, the penalty for failure to start on time would have been loss of hole. Had he arrived more than five minutes late, he would have been disqualified, handing a valuable point to the United States of America.

Fortunately, thanks to the lift from the police officer, McIlroy made it to the course with minutes to spare. With no time to warm up, he had to head straight to the first tee to ensure he made his tee time. Composing himself quickly, he went on to win the match 2&1.

A player may be assisted by a caddie, but is limited to only one caddie at any one time (Rule 6-4). At the 2011 Walker Cup, Jack Senior was assisted by his brother Joe in his foursomes match against the US. It was a condition of competition that players were prohibited from having a professional golfer as a caddie. The player and his caddie are responsible for knowing the Rules, which includes any local rules or conditions of competition (Rule 6-1).

Jack's brother was a professional golfer and his professional status was not discovered until after the GB&I side won the match 2&1 and the result of the match was announced. Rule 2-5 prohibits a Committee from considering a claim after the result of a match has been officially announced.

"We were alerted to the fact that Jack Senior's caddie may be a professional golfer after the match had finished," explained R&A chief executive Peter Dawson.

"We verified with Jack that was in fact the case. There is a condition of competition of this Walker Cup that professional golfers should not caddie for a player."

Dawson went on to clarify, "The breach of that condition was discovered after the match had finished. Had it been discovered during the match, an adjustment to the state of the match would have had to have been made and the caddie would have had to have been changed mid-round. But because it wasn't discovered until after the result had been officially declared, the Rules of Golf stipulate that the result should stand."

The incident highlighted to the players the importance of knowing the Rules and conditions of competition. Following the 2011 Walker Cup, this condition of competition was amended so that players are no longer able to appoint their own caddies. Caddies that meet the conditions of competition for both teams are now found from the host club, local clubs or other nearby sources.

Stephen Gallacher was satisfied with his second place behind Louis Oosthuizen at the Malaysian Open in 2012 after signing for a wrong score.

Gallacher signed for a wrong score after the third round by marking a 4 instead of a birdie 3 for one of the holes. After submitting his card he reflected on his score and realised that he had signed for a 69 when he had actually shot a 68.

The competitor is responsible for the correctness of the score recorded for each hole on his score card. Although the marker may have physically written the score on the score card, it is still the player's responsibility to ensure that the gross score recorded for each hole is correct. If the player returns a score for any hole lower than actually taken, he is disqualified. If he returns a score for any hole higher than actually taken, the score as returned stands (Rule 6-6d).

In Gallacher's case the score for the hole was recorded as a 4 although he had actually scored a 3 on that particular hole. Consequently, he had to accept the 4.

"Luckily, it didn't really affect me that much," he said of his mistake. "I thought I was tied for the lead and then was suddenly one behind. It's one of those things that you learn from."

Rory McIlroy arrives just in time for his 11.25 a.m. tee time. The player must start at the time established by the Committee – Rule 6-3a.

Q & A

Must a player enter his handicap in the box provided on the score card?

Although under Rule 6-2b a competitor must ensure that his handicap is recorded on his score card before it is returned to the Committee, it does not stipulate where the handicap must be recorded; as long as it appears somewhere on the card, the competitor has fulfilled his duty. Consequently, a competitor cannot be disqualified for failure to record his handicap in the "official" box provided on the score card.

Can a player be disqualified for an omission or error in entering his score into a computer?

The Rules of Golf do not require a competitor to enter scores into a computer. Therefore, a competitor may not be penalised or disqualified under the Rules of Golf if the scores entered into the computer are incorrect, or indeed if he fails to enter these scores. The Committee could, however, impose a disciplinary penalty (for example, ineligibility to enter the next Club competition) under its Club regulations for failure to enter scores into a computer.

Can a player be disqualified for not initialling any alterations made on his score card?

A Committee cannot require that alterations made on score cards be initialled. Consequently, a player cannot be disqualified for failure to do so.

Do I have to record my score on the card that I am marking?

No. The Rules of Golf do not require the marker to record his score on the card that he is marking. If the marker does record his score on the card he is marking, it is simply for reference purposes when checking his own score. The noting of a marker's score on a card has no standing in terms of Rule 6-6d but may alert the player to a discrepancy on his own score card.

Rule 7 PRACTICE

DEFINITIONS
All defined terms are in *italics* and are listed in the Definitions section – see pages 13–23.

7-1 Before or Between Rounds
7-1 a Match Play
On any day of a match play competition, a player may practise on the competition *course* before a round.

7-1 b Stroke Play
Before a round or play-off on any day of a stroke play competition, a *competitor* must not practise on the competition *course* or test the surface of any *putting green* on the *course* by rolling a ball or roughening or scraping the surface.

When two or more rounds of a stroke play competition are to be played over consecutive days, a *competitor* must not practise between those rounds on any competition *course* remaining to be played, or test the surface of any *putting green* on such *course* by rolling a ball or roughening or scraping the surface.

Exception

Practice putting or chipping on or near the first *teeing ground* or any practice area before starting a round or play-off is permitted.

PENALTY
For breach of Rule 7-1b:
Disqualification.

NOTE

The *Committee* may, in the conditions of a competition (Rule 33-1), prohibit practice on the competition *course* on any day of a match play competition or permit practice on the competition *course* or part of the *course* (Rule 33-2c) on any day of or between rounds of a stroke play competition.

7-2   During Round

A player must not make a practice *stroke* during play of a hole.

Between the play of two holes a player must not make a practice *stroke*, except that he may practise putting or chipping on or near:

a. the *putting green* of the hole last played,

b. any practice *putting green*, or

c. the *teeing ground* of the next hole to be played in the round, provided a practice *stroke* is not made from a *hazard* and does not unduly delay play (Rule 6-7).

Strokes made in continuing the play of a hole, the result of which has been decided, are not practice *strokes*.

Exception

When play has been suspended by the *Committee*, a player may, prior to resumption of play, practise (a) as provided in this Rule, (b) anywhere other than on the competition *course* and (c) as otherwise permitted by the *Committee*.

PRACTICE DURING A ROUND

Practice putting and chipping on or near the teeing ground of the next hole to be played is permitted as long as play is not delayed.

PENALTY

For breach of Rule 7-2:

Match play – Loss of hole;

Stroke play – Two strokes.

In the event of a breach between the play of two holes, the penalty applies to the next hole.

NOTE 1

A practice swing is not a practice *stroke* and may be taken at any place, provided the player does not breach the *Rules*.

NOTE 2

The *Committee* may, in the conditions of a competition (Rule 33-1), prohibit:

(a)   practice on or near the *putting green* of the hole last played, and

(b)   rolling a ball on the *putting green* of the hole last played.

RULE 7 INCIDENTS

Corey Pavin and Colin Montgomerie took the decision to prohibit practice during the round at Celtic Manor for the 2010 Ryder Cup matches. Due to the diminishing autumn daylight, the captains agreed to introduce a condition of competition to prohibit practice on or near the putting green of the hole last played (see Note 2 to Rule 7-2) in an effort to ensure that there was no delay in play.

Montgomerie was adamant that play would proceed according to schedule. "I see no reason why a four-ball should not be round in four and a half hours, even with the pressures of a Ryder Cup situation," he stated in advance of the event. "We do not want to be coming back on Saturday morning and Sunday morning to finish off games from the day before."

However, Montgomerie did not get his wish to proceed according to schedule. Despite the captains' best efforts to ensure there was no time wasted in practising after the result of a hole was decided, it was the weather that delayed play and resulted in the matches being concluded a day late.

Q & A

May a player practise on the competition course?

Before a match, a player may practise on the competition course, unless prohibited by the Committee in the conditions of competition.

In stroke play, a competitor is not permitted to practise on the competition course before the competition, or test the surface of any putting green, unless permitted to do so by the Committee in the conditions of competition – see Note to Rule 7-1.

In match or stroke play, during the round, a player is not permitted to play a practice stroke either during the play of a hole or between play of two holes, except that, between the play of two holes, the player may practise putting or chipping on or near:

o the putting green of the hole last played,

o any practice putting green, or

o the teeing ground of the next hole to be played.

A player should check the conditions of competition to see if the Committee has laid down any restrictions on practising during a round.

Rule 8

ADVICE; INDICATING LINE OF PLAY

DEFINITIONS
All defined terms are in *italics* and are listed in the Definitions section – see pages 13–23.

8-1   Advice

During a *stipulated round*, a player must not:

a. give *advice* to anyone in the competition playing on the *course* other than his *partner*, or

b. ask for *advice* from anyone other than his *partner* or either of their *caddies*.

8-2   Indicating Line of Play
8-2 a   Other Than on Putting Green

Except on the *putting green*, a player may have the *line of play* indicated to him by anyone, but no one may be positioned by the player for that purpose on or close to the line or an extension of the line beyond the *hole* while the *stroke* is being made. Any mark placed by the player or with his knowledge, for the purpose of indicating the *line of play*, must be removed before the *stroke* is made.

Exception

Flagstick attended or held up – see Rule 17-1.

8-2 b   On the Putting Green

When the player's ball is on the *putting green*, the *line of putt* may be indicated before, but not during, the *stroke* by the player, his *partner* or either of their *caddies*; in doing so the *putting green* must not be touched. A mark must not be placed anywhere for the purpose of indicating a *line of putt*.

(Touching line of putt – see Rule 16-1a)

ADVICE: INFORMATION ON DISTANCE

Information regarding distance is public information and not advice and therefore may be exchanged between players.

INDICATING LINE OF PLAY

A player must not place a mark to indicate the line of play while the stroke is being made. Any mark placed by the player, for the purpose of indicating the line of play, must be removed before the stroke is made.

PENALTY

For breach of Rule:

Match play – Loss of hole;

Stroke play – Two strokes.

NOTE

The *Committee* may, in the conditions of a team competition (Rule 33-1), permit each team to appoint one person who may give *advice* (including pointing out a *line of putt*) to members of that team. The *Committee* may establish conditions relating to the appointment and permitted conduct of that person, who must be identified to the *Committee* before giving *advice*.

RULE 8 INCIDENTS

John Paramor, Chief Referee on the European Tour, was appointed with the task of briefing the respective European and US Ryder Cup teams prior to the start of the 2010 Ryder Cup matches that were played at Celtic Manor. It was essential that both teams were familiar with the details of the Captains' Agreement, which forms the conditions of play and the Local Rules for the event.

One of the key points that Paramor had to address was the fact that the Captains' Agreement included a condition of competition permitting each team to appoint one person who may give advice to members of that team. The Note to Rule 8 facilitates such a condition and highlights that the person appointed to give advice must be identified to the Committee.

In the case of the Ryder Cup, the person appointed to give advice in accordance to the Note to Rule 8 was the respective team captains – Colin Montgomerie for Europe and Corey Pavin for the USA.

During the briefing of the US team, one of Pavin's co-captains asked what constituted advice. Paramor explained using the example of Bubba Watson selecting an 8-iron for a stroke and later Tiger Woods, when faced with the same shot, swithering between an 8-iron or a 7-iron. The co-captain could inform the team captain of the fact that Watson had used an 8-iron, but it was only the team captain that could pass this information on to Woods. Amused, Woods commented with a smile, "There would have been no doubt – I would have hit an 8-iron!".

Q & A

May players share information obtained from a distance-measuring device?

Information regarding the distance between two objects is public information and not advice. It is therefore permissible for players to exchange information relating to the distance between two objects.

It is only permissible to use a distance measuring device in competitions if the Committee have introduced a Local Rule permitting the use of such devices. If the Local Rule is in place, information on distance obtained from such a device can be shared between the player, partner, fellow-competitor or opponent.

Moreover, asking for information which has been obtained by a distance measuring device is not a breach of Rule 8-1 but there is no obligation under the Rules on the person who has the device to share the information with another player.

Rule 9   INFORMATION AS TO STROKES TAKEN

DEFINITIONS
All defined terms are in *italics* and are listed in the Definitions section – see pages 13–23.

9-1   General

The number of *strokes* a player has taken includes any *penalty strokes* incurred.

9-2   Match Play

9-2 a   Information as to Strokes Taken

An opponent is entitled to ascertain from the player, during the play of a hole, the number of *strokes* he has taken and, after play of a hole, the number of *strokes* taken on the hole just completed.

9-2 b   Wrong Information

A player must not give wrong information to his *opponent*. If a player gives wrong information, he loses the hole.

A player is deemed to have given wrong information if he:

(i) fails to inform his *opponent* as soon as practicable that he has incurred a penalty, unless (a) he was obviously proceeding under a *Rule* involving a penalty and this was observed by his *opponent*, or (b) he corrects the mistake before his *opponent* makes his next *stroke*; or

(ii) gives incorrect information during play of a hole regarding the number of *strokes* taken and does not correct the mistake before his *opponent* makes his next *stroke*; or

(iii) gives incorrect information regarding the number of *strokes* taken to complete a hole and this affects the *opponent's* understanding of the result of the hole, unless he corrects the mistake before any player makes a *stroke* from the next *teeing ground* or, in the case of the last hole of the match, before all players leave the *putting green*.

A player has given wrong information even if it is due to the failure to include a penalty that he did not know he had incurred. It is the player's responsibility to know the *Rules*.

9-3   Stroke Play

A *competitor* who has incurred a penalty should inform his *marker* as soon as practicable.

Rule 10   ORDER OF PLAY

DEFINITIONS
All defined terms are in *italics* and are listed in the Definitions section – see pages 13–23.

10-1   Match Play

10-1 a   When Starting Play of Hole

The *side* that has the *honour* at the first *teeing ground* is determined by the order of the draw. In the absence of a draw, the *honour* should be decided by lot.

The *side* that wins a hole takes the *honour* at the next *teeing ground*. If a hole has been halved, the *side* that had the *honour* at the previous *teeing ground* retains it.

10-1 b During Play of Hole

After both players have started play of the hole, the ball farther from the *hole* is played first. If the balls are equidistant from the *hole* or their positions relative to the *hole* are not determinable, the ball to be played first should be decided by lot.

Exception

Rule 30-3b (*best-ball* and *four-ball* match play).

> **NOTE**
>
> When it becomes known that the original ball is not to be played as it lies and the player is required to play a ball as nearly as possible at the spot from which the original ball was last played (see Rule 20-5), the order of play is determined by the spot from which the previous *stroke* was made. When a ball may be played from a spot other than where the previous *stroke* was made, the order of play is determined by the position where the original ball came to rest.

10-1 c Playing Out of Turn

If a player plays when his opponent should have played, there is no penalty, but the opponent may immediately require the player to cancel the *stroke* so made and, in correct order, play a ball as nearly as possible at the spot from which the original ball was last played (see Rule 20-5).

10-2 Stroke Play
10-2 a When Starting Play of Hole

The *competitor* who has the *honour* at the first *teeing ground* is determined by the order of the draw. In the absence of a draw, the *honour* should be decided by lot.

ORDER OF PLAY

The player who is furthest from the hole is entitled to play first, even though the other player is not on the putting green.

The *competitor* with the lowest score at a hole takes the *honour* at the next *teeing ground*. The *competitor* with the second lowest score plays next and so on. If two or more *competitors* have the same score at a hole, they play from the next *teeing ground* in the same order as at the previous *teeing ground*.

Exception

Rule 32-1 (handicap bogey, par and Stableford competitions).

10-2 b During Play of Hole

After the *competitors* have started play of the hole, the ball farthest from the *hole* is played first. If two or more balls are equidistant from the *hole* or their positions relative to the *hole* are not determinable, the ball to be played first should be decided by lot.

Exceptions

Rules 22 (ball assisting or interfering with play) and 31-4 (*four-ball* stroke play).

NOTE

When it becomes known that the original ball is not to be played as it lies and the *competitor* is required to play a ball as nearly as possible at the spot from which the original ball was last played (see Rule 20-5), the order of play is determined by the spot from which the previous *stroke* was made. When a ball may be played from a spot other than where the previous *stroke* was made, the order of play is determined by the position where the original ball came to rest.

10-2 c Playing Out of Turn

If a *competitor* plays out of turn, there is no penalty and the ball is played as it lies. If, however, the *Committee* determines that *competitors* have agreed to play out of turn to give one of them an advantage, they are disqualified.

(Making stroke while another ball in motion after stroke from putting green – see Rule 16-1f)

(Incorrect order of play in foursome stroke play – see Rule 29-3)

10-3 Provisional Ball or Another Ball from Teeing Ground

If a player plays a *provisional ball* or another ball from the *teeing ground*, he must do so after his *opponent* or *fellow-competitor* has made his first *stroke*. If more than one player elects to play a *provisional ball* or is required to play another ball from the *teeing ground*, the original order of play must be retained. If a player plays a *provisional ball* or another ball out of turn, Rule 10-1c or 10-2c applies.

Q & A

What is the penalty and procedure if you play out of turn in match play?

There is no penalty but your opponent has the option to immediately require you to cancel the stroke and play again, in the correct order.

RULE 10 INCIDENTS

On the second day of the 2003 Walker Cup at Ganton, the Great Britain & Ireland pairing of Gary Wolstenholme and Oliver Wilson were up against Trip Kuehne and Bill Haas of the USA in the morning foursomes.

Kuehne played first from the 2nd tee, hitting a long but wayward drive into some gorse bushes, then Wolstenholme followed with a shorter drive into a fairway bunker. When the players arrived at their balls, a search for the USA ball was ongoing. Before the end of the five-minute search period, Wilson played out of the bunker for Great Britain & Ireland and then Wolstenholme played the ball on to the green.

At this point, the USA side queried whether the home team had played out of turn as Wolstenholme may have played from closer to the hole than the point where the USA's lost ball could have been. It was ruled that, as the USA ball could not be found, its position for establishing the correct order of play had to be estimated and the match referee decided that, on the basis of this estimation, the Great Britain & Ireland ball had been farther from the hole and therefore had not played out of turn.

It was recognised at the time that the Rules would benefit from greater clarification in this type of situation and the Note to Rule 10-1b now provides that, when it becomes known that the original ball is not to be played as it lies (for example, if it is not found within five minutes) and the player is required to play a ball as near as possible to the spot where the original ball was last played, the order of play is determined by the spot from where the original ball was last played. Therefore, in the Walker Cup case, at the point where the USA ball became lost it would have been their turn to play as they were required to play again from the teeing ground.

Bob Lewis, the USA 2003 Walker Cup captain, queries with the referee walking with the match whether the Great Britain & Ireland team had played out of turn and in breach of Rule 10-1b.

Rule 11 TEEING GROUND

DEFINITIONS
All defined terms are in *italics* and are listed in the Definitions section – see pages 13–23.

11-1 Teeing

When a player is putting a ball into play from the *teeing ground*, it must be played from within the *teeing ground* and from the surface of the ground or from a conforming *tee* (see Appendix IV) in or on the surface of the ground.

For the purposes of this Rule, the surface of the ground includes an irregularity of surface (whether or not created by the player) and sand or other natural substance (whether or not placed by the player).

If a player makes a *stroke* at a ball on a non-conforming tee, or at a ball teed in a manner not permitted by this Rule, he is disqualified.

A player may stand outside the *teeing ground* to play a ball within it.

11-2 Tee-Markers

Before a player makes his first *stroke* with any ball on the *teeing ground* of the hole being played, the tee-markers are deemed to be fixed. In these circumstances, if the player moves or allows to be moved a tee-marker for the purpose of avoiding interference with his *stance*, the area of his intended swing or his *line of play*, he incurs the penalty for a breach of Rule 13-2.

11-3 Ball Falling off Tee

If a ball, when not *in play*, falls off a *tee* or is knocked off a *tee* by the player in *addressing* it, it may be re-teed, without penalty. However, if a *stroke* is made at the ball in these circumstances, whether the ball is moving or not, the *stroke* counts, but there is no penalty.

11-4 Playing from Outside Teeing Ground
11-4 a Match Play

If a player, when starting a hole, plays a ball from outside the *teeing ground*, there is no penalty, but the *opponent* may immediately require the player to cancel the *stroke* and play a ball from within the *teeing ground*.

PLAYING FROM THE WRONG TEE IN STROKE PLAY

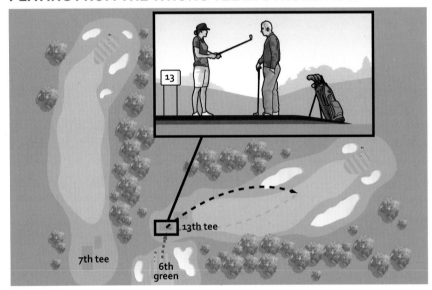

A competitor is penalised two strokes for playing from a wrong teeing ground and must rectify the error by playing from the correct teeing ground. The strokes made from the wrong teeing ground and any subsequent strokes prior to the correction of the error do not count in the competitor's score.

TEEING

(1) The ball may be played from the surface of the ground... (2) or from a conforming tee in the surface of the ground... (3) or from an irregularity of surface.

11-4 b Stroke Play

If a *competitor*, when starting a hole, plays a ball from outside the *teeing ground*, he incurs a penalty of two strokes and must then play a ball from within the *teeing ground*.

If the *competitor* makes a *stroke* from the next *teeing ground* without first correcting his mistake or, in the case of the last hole of the round, leaves the *putting green* without first declaring his intention to correct his mistake, he is disqualified.

The *stroke* from outside the *teeing ground* and any subsequent *strokes* by the *competitor* on the hole prior to his correction of the mistake do not count in his score.

11-5 Playing from Wrong Teeing Ground

The provisions of Rule 11-4 apply.

RULE 11 INCIDENTS

During the 2011 Wales Open at The Celtic Manor Resort, Phillip Price incurred a penalty as a result of breaching Rule 11-4 and narrowly escaped disqualification thanks to the situation being brought to the referee's attention before Price teed off on the next hole.

In his attempt to birdie the 373 yard, 15th hole on the Twenty Ten course, Price decided to cut the corner of the dog-leg, so teed up with the aim of playing over the trees to the front of the green, some 260 yards away. To do this he had to tee the ball at an angle to the tee-markers and, unbeknown to him, played his tee shot approximately nine inches in front of the tee-markers.

The error was identified to the Chief Referee, who was able to review TV footage that confirmed Price had in fact teed up outside of the teeing ground. Meanwhile, Price had completed play of the 15th hole and was preparing to tee up on the 16th hole when he was informed of the breach. Thankfully, he had not yet played from the 16th tee so was able to correct the error as per Rule 11-4.

Phillip Price of Wales in action during the 2011 Wales Open on the Twenty Ten course at The Celtic Manor Resort. Price incurred a two-stroke penalty when he played from outside the teeing ground on the 15th hole.

Q & A

If you knock your ball off the tee when addressing it, is there a penalty?
As the ball was not yet in play (see Definition of Ball in Play), there is no penalty. The ball may be re-teed and played.

What do you do if you play from the wrong teeing ground?
In stroke play, you must correct the mistake and play a ball from the correct teeing ground, incurring a penalty of two strokes. The stroke made from the wrong teeing ground, and any subsequent strokes made on the wrong hole, do not count in your score.

In match play, there is no penalty and you continue with the ball played from the wrong teeing ground, unless your opponent immediately requires you to cancel the stroke and play a ball from within the correct teeing ground.

Rule 12 SEARCHING FOR AND IDENTIFYING BALL

DEFINITIONS
All defined terms are in *italics* and are listed in the Definitions section – see pages 13–23.

12-1 Seeing Ball; Searching for Ball

A player is not necessarily entitled to see his ball when making a *stroke*.

In searching for his ball anywhere on the *course*, the player may touch or bend long grass, rushes, bushes, whins, heather or the like, but only to the extent necessary to find or identify the ball, provided that this does not improve the lie of the ball, the area of his intended stance or swing or his *line of play*; if the ball is moved, Rule 18-2 applies except as provided in clauses a - d of this Rule.

In addition to the methods of searching for and identifying a ball that are otherwise permitted by the Rules, the player may also search for and identify a ball under Rule 12-1 as follows:

a. Searching for or Identifying Ball Covered by Sand

If the player's ball lying anywhere on the course is believed to be covered by sand, to the extent that he cannot find or identify it, he may, without penalty, touch or move the sand in order to find or identify the ball. If the ball is found, and identified as his, the player must re-create the lie as nearly as possible by replacing the sand. If the ball is moved during the touching or moving of sand while searching for or identifying the ball or during the re-creation of the lie, there is no penalty; the ball must be replaced and the lie re-created.

In re-creating a lie under this Rule, the player is permitted to leave a small part of the ball visible.

b. Searching for or Identifying Ball Covered by Loose Impediments in Hazard

In a *hazard*, if the player's ball is believed to be covered by *loose impediments* to the extent that he cannot find or identify it, he may, without penalty, touch or move *loose impediments* in order to find or identify the ball. If the ball is found or identified as his, the player must replace the *loose impediments*. If the ball is moved during the touching or moving of *loose impediments* while searching for or identifying the ball, Rule 18-2 applies; if the ball is moved during the replacement of the *loose impediments*, there is no penalty and the ball must be replaced.

If the ball was entirely covered by *loose impediments*, the player must re-cover the ball but is permitted to leave a small part of the ball visible.

c. Searching for Ball in Water in Water Hazard

If a ball is believed to be lying in water in a *water hazard*, the player may, without penalty, probe for it with a club or otherwise. If the ball in water is accidentally *moved* while probing, there is no penalty; the ball must be replaced, unless the player elects to proceed under Rule 26-1. If the *moved* ball was not lying in water or the ball was accidentally *moved* by the player other than while probing, Rule 18-2 applies.

d. Searching for Ball Within Obstruction or Abnormal Ground Condition

If a ball lying in or on an obstruction or in an abnormal ground condition is accidentally moved during search, there is no penalty; the ball must be replaced unless the player elects to proceed under Rule 24-1b, 24-2b or 25-1b as applicable. If the player replaces the ball, he may still proceed under one of those Rules, if applicable.

PENALTY
For breach of Rule 12-1:
Match play – Loss of hole;

SEARCHING FOR A BALL IN A BUNKER

(1) If a player's ball is believed to be buried in sand, he may touch or move the sand with a club, hand or otherwise. (2) If the ball is moved during the search, there is no penalty, but the ball must be replaced. (3) The player must re-create the lie by replacing the sand, recovering the ball. It is permitted to leave a small part of the ball visible.

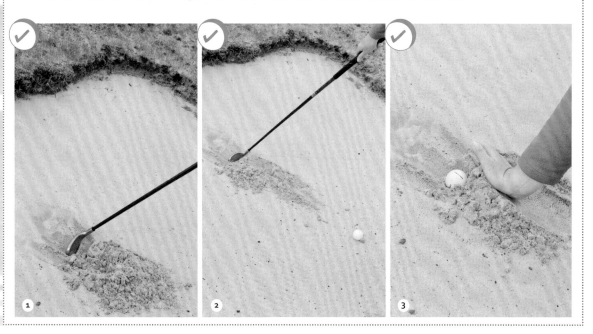

Stroke play – Two strokes.

(Improving lie, area of intended *stance* or swing, or *line of play* – see Rule 13-2)

12-2 Lifting Ball for Identification

The responsibility for playing the proper ball rests with the player. Each player should put an identification mark on his ball.

If a player believes that a ball at rest might be his, but he cannot identify it, the player may lift the ball for identification, without penalty. The right to lift a ball for identification is in addition to the actions permitted under Rule 12-1.

Before lifting the ball, the player must announce his intention to his *opponent* in match play or his *marker* or a *fellow-competitor* in *stroke play* and mark the position of the ball. He may then lift the ball and identify it, provided that he gives his *opponent*, *marker* or *fellow-competitor* an opportunity to observe the lifting and replacement. The ball must not be cleaned beyond the extent necessary for identification when lifted under Rule 12-2.

If the ball is the player's ball and he fails to comply with all or any part of this procedure, or he lifts his ball in order to identify it without having good reason to do so, he incurs a penalty of one stroke. If the lifted ball is the player's ball, he must replace it. If he fails to do so, he incurs the general penalty for a breach of Rule 12-2, but there is no additional penalty under this Rule.

NOTE

If the original lie of a ball to be replaced has been altered, see Rule 20-3b.

IDENTIFYING A BALL IN A HAZARD

A player may lift a ball in order to identify it, even if the ball lies in a bunker or water hazard. The position of the ball must be marked before it is lifted and the player must tell his opponent, fellow-competitor or marker what he intends doing before he lifts the ball. The ball must not be cleaned beyond the extent necessary to identify it.

* PENALTY
For breach of Rule 12-2:
Match play – Loss of hole;
Stroke play – Two strokes.
*If a player incurs the general penalty for a breach of Rule 12-2, there is no additional penalty under this Rule.

Q & A

Is it permissible to put an identification mark on a ball, in the form of a line that completely encircles the ball?
Yes. It is recommended that each player puts a personal identification mark on his ball. This can take any form, including a line encircling the ball, which the player may then use to help with alignment.

A player may draw a line on the ball and may position the ball so that the line indicates the line of play.

RULE 12 INCIDENTS

South African Branden Grace's progress in the first round of the 2012 Hassan Trophy in Morocco was hampered when he lost his ball in a bunker. Grace found the greenside bunker with his tee shot on the par-3 16th hole.

As the ball was not immediately visible, Grace started to search for it in the sand. Although a player is prohibited from touching the sand when his ball is in a bunker, if the ball is believed to be covered by sand, the player may, without penalty, touch or move the sand in order to find or identify the ball (Rule 12-1a). The player can use his hand, club or otherwise to search for the ball in the sand. If the ball is moved during the touching or moving of the sand while searching for or identifying the ball or during the re-creation of the lie, there is no penalty. The ball must be replaced and the lie re-created.

However, despite help from his caddie and fellow-competitors, Grace could not find the ball within the five minutes permitted for search. He was required to return to the tee to play another ball under stroke and distance (Rule 27-1). He hit his next shot to four feet and carded a bogey 4.

Martin Laird incurred a one-stroke penalty during the third round of the 2013 Open Championship at Muirfield for failing to announce his intention to his marker or fellow-competitor that he wished to lift a ball to identify it.

Previously, Laird had hit his ball into the rough and had identified the ball by gently parting the grass to see the identification mark. This is permissible, as a player may touch or bend long grass but only to the extent necessary to find or identify the ball (Rule 12-1). Laird played his ball but it remained in the rough. To ensure he had the correct ball again, this time he marked the position of the ball and touched it, moving it slightly to see the identification mark before playing on.

Rule 12-2 specifies in part that, "Before lifting the ball, the player must announce his intention to his opponent in match play, marker or fellow-competitor in stroke play and mark the position of the ball." While Laird had marked the position of the ball, he did not inform his fellow-competitor and marker, Dustin Johnson, or the referee that was assigned to the group that he wished to lift the ball for identification. By failing to comply with this procedure, he incurred a penalty of one stroke.

It is worth noting that a referee can fulfil the responsibilities of an opponent, marker or fellow-competitor when a player wishes to lift his ball for identification. This is sometimes useful if a marker, opponent or fellow-competitor is out of range and is unable to witness the procedure.

Martin Laird plays from the rough on the 17th hole during the 142nd Open Championship at Muirfield. Laird incurred a one-stroke penalty for failing to announce his intention that he wished to lift a ball to identify it.

Spain's Alvaro Quiros stormed to an eventful victory in the Dubai Desert Classic in 2011. A wayward drive on the par-4, eighth hole at the Emirates Golf Club found a bad lie in a bush, forcing him to take a penalty drop for an unplayable ball. When he dropped his ball it plugged slightly in the soft sandy ground, making his third stroke over palm trees even trickier. His ball then came to rest in one the many palm trees bordering the fairway.

Quiros could see a Callaway ball with two identification dots similar to his identification mark in the tree but was still not 100 per cent sure that it was his ball. A referee was on hand and with the help of a pair of binoculars, Quiros was able to positively identify the ball visible in the palm tree as his ball.

As the ball was not lost, Quiros chose to declare the ball unplayable and take relief under Rule 28c. As a ball may be substituted under this Rule, he proceeded by dropping another ball, under penalty of one stroke, within two club-lengths of the point on the ground immediately below the place where the ball lay in the tree, as provided in Decision 28/11. A short chip and two putts later, he walked off the green with a triple-bogey seven. However, he made up for the costly score with a hole-in-one at the par-3, 11th hole taking him straight back into contention for the title.

Rule 13 BALL PLAYED AS IT LIES

DEFINITIONS
All defined terms are
in *italics* and are listed in
the Definitions section –
see pages 13–23.

13-1 General

The ball must be played as it lies, except as otherwise provided in the *Rules*.
(Ball at rest moved – see Rule 18)

13-2 Improving Lie, Area of Intended Stance or Swing, or Line of Play

A player must not improve or allow to be improved:

o   the position or lie of his ball,
o   the area of his intended *stance* or swing,
o   his *line of play* or a reasonable extension of that line beyond the *hole*, or
o   the area in which he is to drop or place a ball,

by any of the following actions:

o   pressing a club on the ground,
o   moving, bending or breaking anything growing or fixed (including immovable *obstructions* and objects defining *out of bounds*),
o   creating or eliminating irregularities of surface,
o   removing or pressing down sand, loose soil, replaced divots or other cut turf placed in position, or
o   removing dew, frost or water.

However, the player incurs no penalty if the action occurs:

o   in grounding the club lightly when *addressing the ball*,
o   in fairly taking his *stance*,
o   in making a *stroke* or the backward movement of his club for a *stroke* and the *stroke* is made,
o   in creating or eliminating irregularities of surface within the *teeing ground* or in removing dew, frost or water from the *teeing ground*, or
o   on the *putting green* in removing sand and loose soil or in repairing damage (Rule 16-1).

Exception

Ball in *hazard* – see Rule 13-4.

13-3 Building Stance

A player is entitled to place his feet firmly in taking his *stance*, but he must not build a *stance*.

13-4 Ball in Hazard; Prohibited Actions

Except as provided in the *Rules*, before making a *stroke* at a ball that is in a *hazard* (whether a *bunker* or a *water hazard*) or that, having been lifted from a *hazard*, may be dropped or placed in the *hazard*, the player must not:

a.   Test the condition of the *hazard* or any similar *hazard*;
b.   Touch the ground in the *hazard* or water in the *water hazard* with his hand or a club; or
c.   Touch or move a *loose impediment* lying in or touching the *hazard*.

Exceptions

1   Provided nothing is done that constitutes testing the condition of the *hazard* or improves the lie of the ball, there is no penalty if the player (a) touches the ground or *loose impediments* in any *hazard* or water in a *water hazard* as a result of or to prevent falling, in removing an *obstruction*, in measuring or in marking the position of, retrieving,

IMPROVING LINE OF PLAY

A player must not remove sand that lies off the putting green on the line of play. Sand is only a loose impediment when it lies on the putting green.

ELIMINATING IRREGULARITIES OF SURFACE

A player must not replace a divot to eliminate an irregularity of surface on his line of play.

13

lifting, placing or replacing a ball under any Rule or (b) places his clubs in a *hazard*.

2 At any time, the player may smooth sand or soil in a *hazard* provided this is for the sole purpose of caring for the course and nothing is done to breach Rule 13-2 with respect to his next *stroke*. If a ball played from a *hazard* is outside the *hazard* after the *stroke*, the player may smooth sand or soil in the *hazard* without restriction.

3 If the player makes a *stroke* from a *hazard* and the ball comes to rest in another *hazard*, Rule 13-4a does not apply to any subsequent actions taken in the *hazard* from which the *stroke* was made.

NOTE

At any time, including at *address* or in the backward movement for the *stroke*, the player may touch, with a club or otherwise, any *obstruction*, any construction declared by the *Committee* to be an integral part of the *course* or any grass, bush, tree or other growing thing.

PENALTY

For breach of Rule:

Match play – Loss of hole;

Stroke play – Two strokes.

(Searching for ball – see Rule 12-1)

(Relief for ball in water hazard – see Rule 26)

PLACING CLUBS IN HAZARD

The player may place his clubs in the hazard provided he does not test the condition of the hazard or improve the lie of the ball.

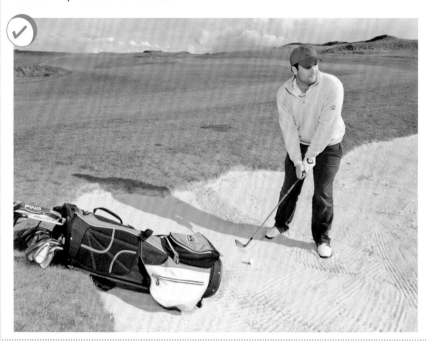

TOUCHING HAZARD TO PREVENT FALLING

The player may use a club to enter or leave a hazard if there is a risk of falling, provided she does not test the condition of the hazard or improve the lie of the ball.

BALL IN A BUNKER

Before making a stroke at a ball that is in a bunker the player must not:

... touch the ground with his club;

... touch a loose impediment with his club at address or on his backswing;

... remove loose impediments;

... or smooth sand that would improve the lie, area of intended stance or swing or line of play for the next stroke.

BALL IN A BUNKER: SMOOTHING PRIOR TO STROKE

At any time, including prior to making a stroke, a player may smooth sand in the hazard provided nothing is done to improve the lie of the ball, the area of intended stance or intended swing or line of play for the next stroke and it is for the sole purpose of caring for the course.

GROUNDING CLUB ON BRIDGE IN WATER HAZARD

In a hazard, a player may touch an obstruction, such as a bridge, at any time (see Note to Rule 13-4).

RULE 13 INCIDENTS

Rory McIlroy incurred a two-stroke penalty during the second round of the Abu Dhabi Championship in 2012 as a result of brushing aside some sand that lay on his line of play on the fringe of the putting green on the 9th hole.

Sand and loose soil are loose impediments when they lie on the putting green, so the key to this ruling was the position of the sand. As the sand was lying on the fringe and not on the putting green, McIlroy was not entitled to brush it away. Consequently, he was in breach of Rule 13-2 for improving his line of play.

The actions of her caddie cost Stacey Lewis a two-stroke penalty during the third round of the LPGA Founders Cup in 2013. Her caddie, Travis Wilson, tested the surface of the bunker with his right foot when he walked into the fairway bunker on the 16th hole. During a stipulated round, for any breach of the Rules by her caddie, the player incurs the applicable penalty. Both the player and the caddie are responsible for knowing the Rules.

Before signing for her score, Lewis watched a video of the situation to confirm her understanding. "We looked at the video, and you have to zoom in on his foot, but he walks into the bunker, he kind of pushes, he kind of bounces his knees a little bit and his foot turns," Lewis said. "They were the big indicators that his foot turned and you could kind of hear the sand crunch a bit. So that was deemed to be testing the sand."

The term "testing the condition of the hazard" is clarified in Decision 13-4/0.5. This term covers all actions by which the player could gain more information about the hazard than could be gained from taking the stance for the stroke to be made. While a certain amount of digging in with the feet in the sand is permissible when taking the stance, Lewis' caddie's actions had gone further than this, resulting in the breach of Rule 13-4a.

Sun Ju Ahn was penalised for building a stance at the Women's British Open at Royal Birkdale in 2014. Playing the last hole of the third round of the Women's Open, Ahn hit her second shot into the bunker on the right of the green. The ball came to rest close to the face of the bunker. In an effort to get her feet into position for the stroke and to provide a firm base to play from, she scraped the sand down from the side of the bunker several times.

Rather than simply placing her feet in the bunker, the action of scraping the sand down with several deliberate movements of the foot constituted building a stance. The penalty for a breach of Rule 13-3 is loss of hole in match play or two strokes in stroke play.

Carl Pettersen incurred a two-stroke penalty during the final round of the 2012 US PGA Championship at Kiawah Island for touching a loose impediment with his club in a lateral water hazard.

Pettersen's ball had come to rest just inside the margin of a hazard on the 1st hole of the final round. Before

Q & A

Can I repair pitch-marks on my line of play?

Pitch-marks that are on the putting green may be repaired, whether or not the ball lies on the putting green (see Rule 16-1).

Pitch-marks that lie elsewhere on the course may not be repaired if doing so would improve the lie, area of intended stance or swing or line of play. However, if the pitch-mark was created after the ball came to rest in equity (Rule 1-4), you may repair the pitch-mark. A player is entitled to the lie his stroke gave him.

If my ball lands in a bunker can I rake it before I play my shot?

Yes, provided nothing is done to breach Rule 13-2 with respect to the next stroke and it is for the sole purpose of caring for the course. For example, your ball lies on the right-hand side of a large bunker. The rake has been left on the left-hand side and after retrieving the rake you smooth your footprints in order to keep the bunker tidy before moving to your ball. Because the smoothing does not improve the lie of the ball, the area of your intended stance or swing or your line of play for your next stroke and it is for the purpose of caring for the course, there is no breach (see Exception 2 to Rule 13-4).

making the stroke, Pettersen asked the referee if he was allowed to touch the grass in the hazard with his club prior to the stroke. The referee confirmed that this was permissible, as the Note to Rule 13-4 permits the player to touch grass or a growing thing in the hazard at any time, including the backward movement of the club for the stroke but without grounding the club.

In making the backward movement for the stroke, Pettersen brushed the grass behind the ball with his club, which in itself was not a breach of the Rules, but his club also moved a small leaf. Rule 13-4c provides that a player cannot touch or move a loose impediment lying in the same hazard that his ball is in prior to the stroke. As the Definition of "Stroke" clarifies, the stroke begins only once the player has begun the forward movement of the club with the intention of striking at and moving the ball. The backswing is not part of the stroke, so in touching the small leaf before the stroke, Pettersen was in breach of the Rule.

After a close examination of the television coverage to confirm the facts, Pettersen was advised of the penalty as he left the 4th tee, turning his opening par into a double-bogey 6.

Graeme McDowell incurred a similar penalty in the 2012 BMW Championship at Crooked Stick for touching a leaf in a bunker at the 9th hole. "It's a very unusual situation when I've got a small branch behind my ball with a leaf attached to it, and in the process of prepar-

ing to play, I grazed the top of the leaf," McDowell said. "I'm deemed to have touched a loose impediment in a hazard, which is a two-stroke penalty. I just didn't give the branch enough respect."

"I just felt that perhaps I had turned my club on the way back as I made my backswing, and as soon as I did it I kind of felt like something was up," said McDowell. He signed for a double-bogey seven and instead found himself in fifth place, three strokes behind the leader.

Sun-Ju Ahn of South Korea plays from the greenside bunker on the 18th hole during the third round of the Ricoh Women's British Open at Royal Birkdale. She was later penalised for building a stance in the bunker.

Rule 14 STRIKING THE BALL

DEFINITIONS
All defined terms are in *italics* and are listed in the Definitions section – see pages 13–23.

14-1 General
14-1 a Fairly Striking the Ball
The ball must be fairly struck at with the head of the club and must not be pushed, scraped or spooned.

BALL TO BE FAIRLY STRUCK AT WITH CLUBHEAD

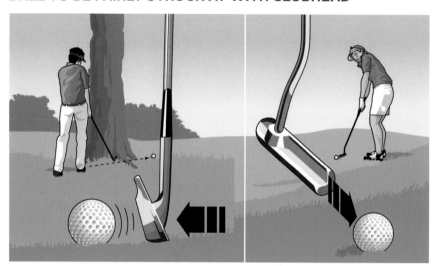

A player may strike the ball with the back or toe of the clubhead.

14-1 b Anchoring the Club
In making a stroke, the player must not anchor the club, either "directly" or by use of an "anchor point."

NOTE 1

The club is anchored "directly" when the player intentionally holds the club or a gripping hand in contact with any part of his body, except that the player may hold the club or a gripping hand against a hand or forearm.

NOTE 2

An "anchor point" exists when the player intentionally holds a forearm in contact with any part of his body to establish a gripping hand as a stable point around which the other hand may swing the club.

PROHIBITED STROKES

In making a stroke, the player must not anchor the club, either directly or by use of an anchor point.

PERMITTED STROKES

Rule 14-1b only applies to strokes made with the club anchored, either directly or through the use of a forearm to establish an anchor point. Longer than standard putters can still be used provided there is no such anchoring.

14-2 Assistance
14-2 a Physical Assistance and Protection from Elements

A player omust not make a stroke while accepting physical assistance or protection from the elements.

14-2 b Positioning of Caddie or Partner Behind Ball

A player must not make a *stroke* with his *caddie*, his *partner* or his *partner's caddie* positioned on or close to an extension of the *line of play* or *line of putt* behind the ball.

Jim Furyk's caddie "Fluff" holds an umbrella over his head whilst he prepares to putt in the 2006 Ryder Cup. Furyk would have incurred a loss of hole penalty under Rule 14-2 if he had allowed his caddie to remain in this position when he made the stroke.

Exception

There is no penalty if the player's *caddie*, his *partner* or his *partner's caddie* is inadvertently located on or close to an extension of the *line of play* or *line of putt* behind the ball.

PENALTY

For breach of Rule 14-1 or 14-2:

Match play – Loss of hole;

Stroke play – Two strokes.

14-3 Artificial Devices, Unusual Equipment; Abnormal Use of Equipment

Rule 14-3 governs the use of *equipment* and devices (including electronic devices) that might assist a player in making a specific *stroke* or generally in his play.

Golf is a challenging game in which success should depend on the judgement, skills and abilities of the player. This principle guides The *R&A* in determining whether the use of any item is in breach of Rule 14-3.

For detailed specifications and interpretations on the conformity of *equipment* and devices under Rule 14-3 and the process for consultation and submission regarding *equipment* and devices, see Appendix IV.

Except as provided in the *Rules*, during a *stipulated round* the player must not use any artificial device or unusual *equipment*, or use any *equipment* in an abnormal manner:

a. That might assist him in making a *stroke* or in his play; or

b. For the purpose of gauging or measuring distance or conditions that might affect his play; or

c. That might assist him in gripping the club, except that:

   (i) gloves may be worn provided that they are plain gloves;

   (ii) resin, powder and drying or moisturising agents may be used; and

   (iii) a towel or handkerchief may be wrapped around the grip.

Exceptions

1   A player is not in breach of this Rule if (a) the *equipment* or device is designed for or

CADDIE POSITIONED ON EXTENSION OF LINE OF PLAY BEHIND BALL

A caddie may assist a player with alignment prior to a stroke but a player must not make a stroke with the caddie positioned on or close to an extension of the line of putt.

has the effect of alleviating a medical condition, (b) the player has a legitimate medical reason to use the *equipment* or device, and (c) the *Committee* is satisfied that its use does not give the player any undue advantage over other players.

2 A player is not in breach of this Rule if he uses *equipment* in a traditionally accepted manner.

PENALTY

For breach of Rule 14-3:

Match play – Loss of hole;

Stroke play – Two strokes.

For subsequent offence – Disqualification.

In the event of a breach between the play of two holes, the penalty applies to the next hole.

NOTE

The Committee may make a Local Rule allowing players to use a distance-measuring device.

14-4 Striking the Ball More Than Once

If a player's club strikes the ball more than once in the course of a *stroke*, the player must count the *stroke* and add a *penalty stroke*, making two *strokes* in all.

14-5 Playing Moving Ball

A player must not make a *stroke* at his ball while it is moving.

Exceptions

o Ball falling off tee – Rule 11-3
o Striking the ball more than once – Rule 14-4
o Ball moving in water – Rule 14-6

When the ball begins to move only after the player has begun the *stroke* or the backward movement of his club for the *stroke*, he incurs no penalty under this Rule for playing a moving ball, but he is not exempt from any penalty under Rule 18-2 (Ball at rest moved by player).

(Ball purposely deflected or stopped by player, partner or caddie – see Rule 1-2)

14-6 Ball Moving in Water

When a ball is moving in water in a *water hazard*, the player may, without penalty, make a *stroke*, but he must not delay making his *stroke* in order to allow the wind or current to improve the position of the ball. A ball moving in water in a *water hazard* may be lifted if the player elects to invoke Rule 26.

PENALTY

For breach of Rule 14-5 or 14-6:

Match play – Loss of hole;

Stroke play – Two strokes.

RULE 14 INCIDENTS

Jeff Overton was disqualified from the 2013 Invitational held at the Colonial Country Club. Midway through the third round he used an alignment putting aid in breach of Rule 14-3.

During a back-up in play, Overton asked a referee if he could putt and chip during the delay on a nearby practice putting green. Under Rule 7-2, between the play of two holes, a player may practise chipping or putting on or near such a facility.

Once on the putting green, Overton decided to use an alignment device to check his putting stroke, which ultimately led to the disqualification. "It's unfortunate," PGA Tour's Mark Russell said. "We don't like to disqualify players, but our Rules are clear on this."

At the time, the use of an artificial device during the stipulated round resulted in automatic disqualification, as Overton found to his cost. However, as of 1 January 2016, the penalty for a breach of this Rule is revised. If this incident happened today, the player would incur a two-stroke penalty in stroke play or a loss of hole penalty in match play for the use of the artificial device. For any subsequent offences, the penalty would still be disqualification.

Justin Rose called a penalty on himself at the 2014 Memorial Tournament in Ohio for striking his ball more than once. His chip shot from behind the green on the 12th hole was in a "shocking" lie. "I knew double hitting it was a possibility and tried to just let the club stay in the ground, but it bounced up and caught it," said Rose. "It was pretty obvious; I wanted them to verify that it wasn't a triple hit. I wanted to make sure."

If a player's ball strikes the club more than once in the course of a stroke, the player must count the stroke and add a penalty stroke, making two strokes in all (Rule 14-4). The fact that the player may have connected with the ball more than twice is immaterial. Rose added the penalty to his score and continued to play the ball from where it had come to rest.

Q & A

If I make a stroke with my club and my hand touches my clothing, am I in breach of Rule 14-1b?

If you merely touch an article of clothing with the club or gripping hand in making the stroke, generally there is no penalty. This might occur if you are wearing loose-fitting clothes or rain gear and are holding the club close to your body, and the club inadvertently touches the clothing in making the stroke.

The answer would be different if you intentionally used the club or a gripping hand to press an article of clothing against any part of the body, other than a forearm or gripping hand. Intentionally using a gripping hand to hold an article of clothing is a breach of Rule 14-3.

SUBSTITUTED BALL; WRONG BALL

DEFINITIONS
All defined terms are in *italics* and are listed in the Definitions section – see pages 13–23.

15-1 General

A player must hole out with the ball played from the *teeing ground*, unless the ball is *lost* or *out of bounds* or the player *substitutes* another ball, whether or not substitution is permitted (see Rule 15-2). If a player plays a *wrong ball*, see Rule 15-3.

15-2 Substituted Ball

A player may *substitute* a ball when proceeding under a *Rule* that permits the player to play, drop or place another ball in completing the play of a hole. The *substituted ball* becomes the *ball in play*.

If a player *substitutes* a ball when not permitted to do so under the Rules (including an unintentional *substitution* when a wrong ball is dropped or placed by the player), that *substituted ball* is not a *wrong* ball; it becomes the *ball in play*. If the mistake is not corrected as provided in Rule 20-6 and the player makes a *stroke* at an incorrectly *substituted ball*, he loses the hole in match play or incurs a penalty of two strokes in stroke play under the applicable *Rule* and, in stroke play, must play out the hole with the *substituted* ball.

Exception

If a player incurs a penalty for making a *stroke* from a wrong place, there is no additional penalty for substituting a ball when not permitted.
(Playing from wrong place – see Rule 20-7)

15-3 Wrong Ball
15-3 a Match Play

If a player makes a *stroke* at a *wrong ball*, he loses the hole.

If the *wrong ball* belongs to another player, its owner must place a ball on the spot from which the *wrong ball* was first played.

If the player and *opponent* exchange balls during the play of a hole, the first to make a *stroke* at a *wrong ball* loses the hole; when this cannot be determined, the hole must be played out with the balls exchanged.

Exception

There is no penalty if a player makes a *stroke* at a *wrong ball* that is moving in water in a *water hazard*. Any *strokes* made at a *wrong ball* moving in water in a *water hazard* do not count in the player's score. The player must correct his mistake by playing the correct ball or by proceeding under the *Rules*.
(Placing and Replacing – see Rule 20-3)

15-3 b Stroke Play

If a *competitor* makes a *stroke* or *strokes* at a *wrong ball*, he incurs a penalty of two strokes.

The *competitor* must correct his mistake by playing the correct ball or by proceeding under the *Rules*. If he fails to correct his mistake before making a *stroke* on the next *teeing ground* or, in the case of the last hole of the round, fails to declare his intention to correct his mistake before leaving the *putting green*, he is disqualified.

Strokes made by a *competitor* with a *wrong ball* do not count in his score. If the *wrong ball* belongs to another *competitor*, its owner must place a ball on the spot from which the *wrong ball* was first played.

PLAYING A WRONG BALL IN STROKE PLAY

Exception

There is no penalty if a *competitor* makes a *stroke* at a *wrong ball* that is moving in water in a *water hazard*. Any *strokes* made at a *wrong ball* moving in water in a *water hazard* do not count in the *competitor's* score.

(Placing and Replacing – see Rule 20-3)

Q & A

Must a player announce to his opponent(s) or fellow-competitor(s) that he intends to change his ball between the play of two holes?

Although such an announcement would be courteous, and could help avoid any possible confusion, a player is not required by the Rules to inform anyone what type of ball he intends to play at a hole.

RULE 15 INCIDENTS

Hunter Mahan and Jamie Donaldson suffered a rare two-stroke penalty at the 2014 US Open after they played each other's golf ball by mistake during their second round. Both players were playing a Titleist golf ball with a similar slash through the number. The responsibility for playing the proper ball rests with the player (Rule 12-2).

Mahan played his tee shot first on the 18th hole, which he hit straight, while Donaldson's ball took a visible kick to the left when it landed. Mahan's caddie approached the ball on the fairway and established the yardage for Mahan. Meanwhile, Donaldson and his caddie ventured over to the other ball on the left.

Mahan played first and Donaldson followed. It was not until the two players reached the putting green that they realised their mistake of playing each other's ball. Both players incurred a penalty of two strokes for playing a wrong ball (Rule 15-3) and were required to correct the mistake by playing the correct ball. Fortunately, this error was picked up before either player had played from the next teeing ground. Failure to correct the mistake would have resulted in disqualification under this Rule.

Mahan and Donaldson were able to return to the fairway, where they dropped the balls as near as possible to the places where they originally lay and continued play of the hole.

Nathan Smith was not so fortunate at the Arnold Palmer Invitational in 2014. He violated Rule 15-3 on the par 4, 5th hole, by playing his ball from a spot that was out of bounds. His tee shot had landed to the right of the fairway on the wrong side of the line of white stakes defining the out of bounds.

A ball lying out of bounds is no longer in play and thus is a wrong ball – see Definition of Ball in Play and Wrong Ball. Accordingly, Smith incurred a two-stroke penalty and was required to proceed under stroke and distance (Rule 27-1). But as he did not correct his mistake before playing from the next teeing ground, Smith was disqualified from the competition.

Hunter Mahan of the United States waits with his caddie John Wood for a ruling. Mahan and Donaldson both played a wrong ball in breach of Rule 15-3b during the US Open at Pinehurst Resort & Country Club.

Rule 16 THE PUTTING GREEN

16-1 General
16-1 a Touching Line of Putt
The *line of putt* must not be touched except:

(i) the player may remove *loose impediments*, provided he does not press anything down;

(ii) the player may place the club in front of the ball when *addressing* it, provided he does not press anything down;

(iii) in measuring – Rule 18-6;

(iv) in lifting or replacing the ball – Rule 16-1b;

(v) in pressing down a ball-marker;

(vi) in repairing old *hole* plugs or ball marks on the *putting green* – Rule 16-1c; and

(vii) in removing movable *obstructions* – Rule 24-1.

(Indicating line of putt on *putting green* – see Rule 8-2b)

16-1 b Lifting and Cleaning Ball
A ball on the *putting green* may be lifted and, if desired, cleaned. The position of the ball must be marked before it is lifted and the ball must be replaced (see Rule 20-1). When another ball is in motion, a ball that might influence the movement of the ball in motion must not be lifted.

16-1 c Repair of Hole Plugs, Ball Marks and Other Damage
The player may repair an old *hole* plug or damage to the *putting green* caused by the impact of a ball, whether or not the player's ball lies on the *putting green*. If a ball or

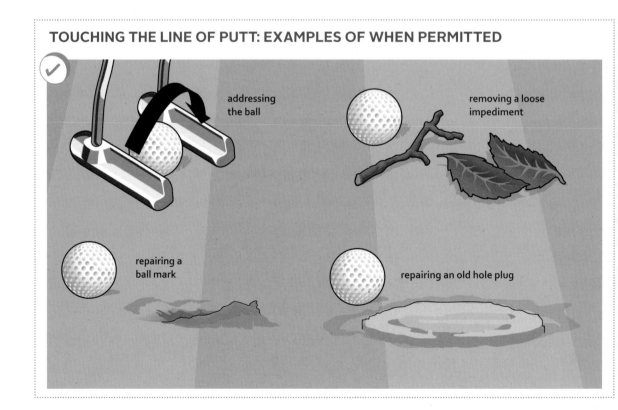

TOUCHING THE LINE OF PUTT: EXAMPLES OF WHEN PERMITTED

addressing the ball

removing a loose impediment

repairing a ball mark

repairing an old hole plug

REPAIRING DAMAGE

A player may not repair spike damage if it might subsequently assist him in his play of the hole.

ball-marker is accidentally *moved* in the process of the repair, the ball or ball-marker must be replaced. There is no penalty, provided the movement of the ball or ball-marker is directly attributable to the specific act of repairing an old *hole* plug or damage to the *putting green* caused by the impact of a ball. Otherwise, Rule 18 applies.

Any other damage to the *putting green* must not be repaired if it might assist the player in his subsequent play of the hole.

16-1 d Testing Surface

During the *stipulated round*, a player must not test the surface of any *putting green* by rolling a ball or roughening or scraping the surface.

Exception

Between the play of two holes, a player may test the surface of any practice *putting green* and the *putting green* of the hole last played, unless the *Committee* has prohibited such action (see Note 2 to Rule 7-2).

16-1 e Standing Astride or on Line of Putt

The player must not make a *stroke* on the *putting green* from a *stance* astride, or with either foot touching, the *line of putt* or an extension of that line behind the ball.

Exception

There is no penalty if the *stance* is inadvertently taken on or astride the *line of putt* (or an extension of that line behind the ball) or is taken to avoid standing on another player's *line of putt* or prospective *line of putt*.

REMOVING LOOSE IMPEDIMENTS FROM THE LINE OF PUTT

Loose impediments can be removed from the line of putt by any means provided nothing is pressed down.

STANDING ON THE LINE OF PUTT

There is no penalty for standing on the line of putt if it is done inadvertently or to avoid standing on another player's line of putt.

BALL OVERHANGING HOLE

A player may wait 10 seconds to see if the ball will fall into the hole. After that time the ball is deemed to be at rest. If the ball then falls into the hole, the player has holed out with the last stroke but a penalty stroke must be added.

16-1 f Making Stroke While Another Ball in Motion

The player must not make a *stroke* while another ball is in motion after a *stroke* from the *putting green*, except that if a player does so, there is no penalty if it was his turn to play.

(Lifting ball assisting or interfering with play while another ball in motion – see Rule 22)

PENALTY

For breach of Rule 16-1:

Match play – Loss of hole;

Stroke play – Two strokes.

(Position of *caddie* or *partner* – see Rule 14-2)

(Wrong *putting green* – see Rule 25-3)

16-2 Ball Overhanging Hole

When any part of the ball overhangs the lip of the *hole*, the player is allowed enough time to reach the *hole* without unreasonable delay and an additional ten seconds to determine whether the ball is at rest. If by then the ball has not fallen into the *hole*, it is deemed to be at rest. If the ball subsequently falls into the *hole*, the player is deemed to have *holed* out with his last *stroke*, and must add a penalty stroke to his score for the hole; otherwise, there is no penalty under this Rule.

(Undue delay – see Rule 6-7)

RULE 16 INCIDENTS

Nick Watney and his caddie, Chad Reynolds, were involved in a potential Rules incident during the first round of the 2012 Hyundai Tournament of Champions in Kapalua. Watney was lining up a putt on the 7th hole when Reynolds bent down behind him to assist with the line of putt. While crouching down to look at the line, the caddie moved his hand back and forth in a swiping motion several times, as if he were checking the grain on the green.

At first it was clear that he was not touching the surface of the green, but as Reynolds continued with the motion, his hand moved closer to the ground and it was difficult to tell if it was touching the putting green or not. Under Rule 16-1d, a player must not test the surface of any putting green by rolling a ball or roughening or scraping the surface. The reference to the player in Rule 16-1d includes his caddie, so the Rule prohibits the caddie, as well as the player, from testing the surface of the putting green.

However, in Watney's case, it was not clear if Reynolds had actually touched the surface of the putting green with his hand. PGA Tour referee Slugger White reviewed video evidence of the alleged incident and spoke with Watney and Reynolds before Watney signed his score card.

After scrutinsing all the evidence, officials determined that Reynolds had not touched the putting green, so Watney posted his even-par 73 for the first round. "I fully support Chad," Watney said. "He's one of the best caddies out there, and I didn't think he would do something like that." Reynolds said, "I didn't touch the ground and had no intention to do so, but it was worth checking."

K. J. Choi raised a few eyebrows at the 2010 Open Championship at St Andrews when he started to putt using a croquet-style of stroke from just off the putting green. Choi took the view that, although it was unconventional, facing the hole helped him to play the right kind of stroke required for the Scottish links terrain.

His plan was to use a regular putting stroke on the putting green but for shots from off the green up to 70 feet he was practising the new style in the hope to put it to good effect during the Championship. His friend and mentor had helped him to design a new putter to accommodate the new stroke, dubbing it the "JuanPutt".

Rule 16-1e prevents a player from making a stroke on the putting green with a stance astride the line of putt. However, this prohibition applies only when the ball

K. J. Choi of South Korea practices his new style of stroke during the 139th Open Championship on the Old Course using a stance astride the line of play.

lies on the putting green and does not apply when playing from any other part of the course. Provided the ball is fairly struck at (Rule 14-1), a player may make a stroke from a stance on or astride an extension of the line of play behind the ball.

"Facing the hole simply makes sense," claimed Choi. "It is easier to stay focused on the line of play." However, Choi's 2010 Open campaign was cut short when he missed the cut after opening rounds of 76 and 74.

Q & A

What are the Rules concerning the location of the hole on the putting green?

The location of the hole on the putting green is not a matter covered under the Rules of Golf. However, when setting such locations, various specific points should be considered.

There must be sufficient putting surface between the hole and the front and the sides of the green to accommodate the required shot. For example, if the hole requires a long iron- or wood-shot to the green, the hole should be placed deeper in the green and farther from its sides than would be the case if the hole requires a short pitch-shot.

It is recommended that the hole should be positioned at least four paces from any edge of the green. In addition, an area of 2–3 feet (0.6–0.9 metres) in radius around the hole should be as nearly level as possible. Every effort should be made to ensure that holes are not positioned within three paces of a very severe slope or ridge or of a recently used hole. In general, there should be a balanced selection of hole positions for the entire course with respect to left, right, central, front and back positions. Six quite difficult, six moderately difficult and six relatively easy positions are recommended. One should also try to keep a balance of using the left and right of the green: for example, on the first nine, there should be four hole positions to the left, four to the right and one in the centre. The second nine should be similar.

Finally, in order to observe the Rules of Golf, the greenkeeper who cuts the hole must make sure that any hole-liner does not exceed 4¼ inches (108 mm) in outer diameter, and if possible any liner must be sunk at least 1 inch (25.4 mm) below the putting green surface.

Additional guidance regarding hole positions is contained in The R&A's Guidance on Running a Competition (available via The R&A website, www.randa.org).

May a player clean his ball by rubbing it on the putting green?

Yes, provided the act is not for the purpose of testing the surface of the putting green (Rule 16-1d). It is recommended that a ball be cleaned in other ways to eliminate any question as to the player's intentions.

It is recommended that the hole should be positioned at least four paces from any edge of the green.

Rule 17 THE FLAGSTICK

17-1 Flagstick Attended, Removed or Held Up

Before making a *stroke* from anywhere on the *course*, the player may have the *flagstick* attended, removed or held up to indicate the position of the *hole*.

If the *flagstick* is not attended, removed or held up before the player makes a *stroke*, it must not be attended, removed or held up during the *stroke* or while the player's ball is in motion if doing so might influence the movement of the ball.

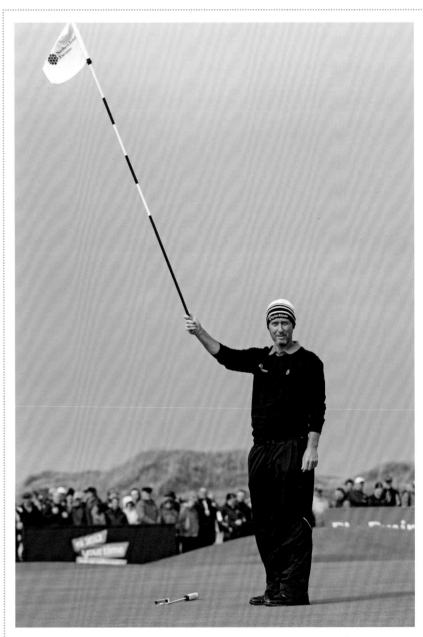

The flagstick can be attended, removed or held up before making a stroke from anywhere on the course.

BALL STRIKING ATTENDED FLAGSTICK IN STROKE PLAY

A player is penalised two strokes if he strikes the flagstick while it is being attended (see Rule 17-3a).

NOTE 1

If the *flagstick* is in the *hole* and anyone stands near it while a *stroke* is being made, he is deemed to be attending the *flagstick*.

NOTE 2

If, prior to the *stroke*, the *flagstick* is attended, removed or held up by anyone with the player's knowledge and he makes no objection, the player is deemed to have authorised it.

NOTE 3

If anyone attends or holds up the *flagstick* while a *stroke* is being made, he is deemed to be attending the *flagstick* until the ball comes to rest.
(Moving attended, removed or held-up flagstick while ball in motion – see Rule 24-1)

17-2 Unauthorised Attendance

If an *opponent* or his *caddie* in match play or a *fellow-competitor* or his *caddie* in stroke play, without the player's authority or prior knowledge, attends, removes or holds up the *flagstick* during the *stroke* or while the ball is in motion, and the act might influence the movement of the ball, the *opponent* or *fellow-competitor* incurs the applicable penalty.

BALL STRIKES FLAGSTICK LYING ON GREEN

When the flagstick has been removed, the player's ball must not strike it.

* PENALTY

For breach of Rule 17-1 or 17-2:

Match play – Loss of hole;

Stroke play – Two strokes.

*In stroke play, if a breach of Rule 17-2 occurs and the *competitor's* ball subsequently strikes the *flagstick*, the person attending or holding it or anything carried by him, the *competitor* incurs no penalty. The ball is played as it lies, except that if the *stroke* was made on the *putting green*, the *stroke* is cancelled and the ball must be replaced and replayed.

17-3 Ball Striking Flagstick or Attendant

The player's ball must not strike:

a. The *flagstick* when it is attended, removed or held up;

b. The person attending or holding up the *flagstick* or anything carried by him; or

c. The *flagstick* in the *hole*, unattended, when the *stroke* has been made on the *putting green*.

Exception

When the *flagstick* is attended, removed or held up without the player's authority – see Rule 17-2.

PENALTY

For breach of Rule 17-3:

Match play – Loss of hole;

Stroke play – Two strokes and the ball must be played as it lies.

17-4 Ball Resting Against Flagstick

When a player's ball rests against the *flagstick* in the *hole* and the ball is not *holed*, the player or another person authorised by him may move or remove the *flagstick*, and if the ball falls into the *hole*, the player is deemed to have *holed* out with his last *stroke*; otherwise, the ball, if *moved*, must be placed on the lip of the *hole*, without penalty.

Rule 17 Incidents

During the 2000 Open at St Andrews, Jack Nicklaus hit his approach to the 2nd green well left. His ball ended up on the 16th-hole portion of this dual green, with a bunker between himself and the hole. He floated up a perfect wedge shot that almost went in the hole. The referee accompanying the group was unsighted by the bunker and assumed that Nicklaus had played his shot from the fairway beyond the green.

As they walked to the next tee Nicklaus admitted that he was unsure if his ball was on the green or not and the referee reminded him that if he had played from the green he should have had the flagstick attended. "I had a 40-yard pitch shot over a bunker," said Nicklaus after the round. "You don't think much about having the pin attended. I've never done that before. It never entered my mind."

Another very uncommon incident in professional golf occurred with Phillip Price during the 2004 Dubai Desert Classic. Having played his second shot just on to the green at the par-5 3rd hole, his caddie was about to attend the flagstick prior to the Welshman putting. At this point, Price asked his caddie to take a look at the line of putt from behind his ball.

After conferring on the line, Price and his caddie forgot to have the flagstick attended and the player putted from the green with the flagstick in the hole, which, of itself, is not a breach of the Rules. Unfortunately, Price's putt was perfect and the ball rolled into the hole. Rule 17-3c provides that the player's ball must not strike the flagstick in the hole when a stroke has been made from the putting green and the resultant two-stroke penalty meant that Price's eagle three became a par 5.

In the 2007 Arnold Palmer Invitational, Boo Weekley found himself incurring a two-stroke penalty after trying to save his fellow-competitor, Tom Johnson, from a penalty during their third round. At the par-3 2nd hole, Johnson hit his tee shot on to the right side of the green, 85 feet from the hole. Because of the steep slope on the green and the back-left hole location, he determined that the best way to get the ball close to the hole was to chip from the green, which is permitted, and try to land it in the back fringe so the ball could run down to the hole. However, as Johnson later said, "I spaced out and forgot to tell my caddie to attend the pin." Johnson played the perfect shot and the ball was rolling down slowly towards the hole when Weekley noticed that the ball might strike the flagstick in the hole. He therefore ran over and pulled the flagstick out.

Someone in the gallery mentioned what he had seen to a referee, and the matter was raised with the players in the scoring area before they returned their score cards. "They asked me if I had authorised Boo to pull the pin," Johnson said. "And I didn't." This meant that Weekley had removed the flagstick without authorisation while a ball was in motion. As the act could have influenced the movement of Johnson's ball, Weekley was subject to a penalty of two strokes under Rule 17-2.

Weekley, whose 67 was turned into a 69, was reported as having said, "Thanks, I learned something," to the Rules officials. Johnson said, "I just put my arm around him and told him he handles adversity better than anyone I've ever played with."

Q & A

May the player have the flagstick attended even if his ball is not on the putting green?
Yes. Rule 17-1 states that, before making a stroke from anywhere on the course, the player may have the flagstick attended, removed or held up.

May a player putt with one hand while holding the flagstick with the other?
Yes, provided the flagstick has been removed from the hole and the ball therefore does not strike it. If the ball were to strike the flagstick, a breach of Rule 17-3a would occur. The player must not lean on the flagstick in order to steady himself whilst he putts, as that would be contrary to Rule 14-3.

Rule 18 BALL AT REST MOVED

DEFINITIONS
All defined terms are in *italics* and are listed in the Definitions section – see pages 13–23.

18-1 By Outside Agency

If a ball at rest is *moved* by an *outside agency*, there is no penalty and the ball must be replaced.

> **NOTE**
> It is a question of fact whether a ball has been *moved* by an *outside agency*. In order to apply this Rule, it must be known or virtually certain that an *outside agency* has *moved* the ball. In the absence of such knowledge or certainty, the player must play the ball as it lies or, if the ball is not found, proceed under Rule 27-1.
> (Player's ball at rest moved by another ball – see Rule 18-5)

18-2 By Player, Partner, Caddie or Equipment

Except as permitted by the Rules, when a player's ball is *in play*, if
(i) the player, his *partner* or either of their *caddies:*
o lifts or *moves* the ball,
o touches it purposely (except with a club in the act of *addressing the ball*), or
o causes the ball to *move*, or
(ii) the equipment of the player or his *partner* causes the ball to *move*,
the player incurs a penalty of one stroke.

   If the ball is moved, it must be replaced, unless the movement of the ball occurs after the player has begun the *stroke* or the backward movement of the club for the *stroke* and the *stroke* is made.

   Under the *Rules* there is no penalty if a player accidentally causes his ball to *move* in the following circumstances:
o In searching for a ball covered by sand or in re-creating the lie of a ball that has been altered during such a process, in the replacement of *loose impediments* moved in a *hazard* while finding or identifying a ball, in probing for a ball lying in water in a *water hazard* or in searching for a ball in an *obstruction* or an *abnormal ground condition* – Rule 12-1
o In repairing a *hole* plug or ball mark – Rule 16-1c
o In measuring – Rule 18-6
o In lifting a ball under a *Rule* – Rule 20-1

BALL AT REST MOVED

By Outside Agency – no penalty and replace ball (Rule 18-1).

By Player, Partner, Caddie or Equipment – one-stroke penalty and replace ball (Rule 18-2).

By Opponent, Caddie or Equipment During Search – no penalty and replace ball (Rule 18-3a).

By Opponent, Caddie or Equipment Not During Search – opponent incurs one-stroke penalty and replace ball (Rule 18-3b).

By Fellow-Competitor, Caddie or Equipment – no penalty and replace ball (Rule 18-4).

By Another Ball – replace moved ball (Rule 18-5).

In Measuring – no penalty and replace ball (Rule 18-6).

o   In placing or replacing a ball under a *Rule* – Rule 20-3a

o   In removing a *loose impediment* on the *putting green* – Rule 23-1

o   In removing movable *obstructions* – Rule 24-1

18-3 By Opponent, Caddie or Equipment in Match Play
18-3 a During Search

If, during search for a player's ball, an *opponent*, his *caddie* or his *equipment moves* the ball, touches it or causes it to *move*, there is no penalty. If the ball is *moved*, it must be replaced.

18-3 b Other Than During Search

If, other than during search for a player's ball, an *opponent*, his *caddie* or his *equipment moves* the ball, touches it purposely or causes it to *move*, except as otherwise provided in the *Rules*, the *opponent* incurs a penalty of one stroke. If the ball is *moved*, it must be replaced.

(Playing a wrong ball – see Rule 15-3)

(Ball moved in measuring – see Rule 18-6)

18-4 By Fellow-Competitor, Caddie or Equipment in Stroke Play

If a *fellow-competitor*, his *caddie* or his *equipment moves* the player's ball, touches it or causes it to *move*, there is no penalty. If the ball is *moved*, it must be replaced.

(Playing a wrong ball – see Rule 15-3)

18-5 By Another Ball

If a *ball in play* and at rest is *moved* by another ball in motion after a *stroke*, the *moved* ball must be replaced.

18-6 Ball Moved in Measuring

If a ball or ball-marker is *moved* in measuring while proceeding under or in determining the application of a *Rule*, the ball or ball-marker must be replaced. There is no penalty, provided the movement of the ball or ball-marker is directly attributable to the specific act of measuring. Otherwise, the provisions of Rule 18-2, 18-3b or 18-4 apply.

---

* PENALTY

For breach of Rule:

Match play – Loss of hole;

Stroke play – Two strokes.

*If a player who is required to replace a ball fails to do so, or if he makes a stroke at a ball substituted under Rule 18 when such substitution is not permitted, he incurs the general penalty for breach of Rule 18, but there is no additional penalty under this Rule.

NOTE 1

If a ball to be replaced under this Rule is not immediately recoverable, another ball may be *substituted*.

NOTE 2

If the original lie of a ball to be placed or replaced has been altered, see Rule 20-3b.

NOTE 3

If it is impossible to determine the spot on which a ball is to be placed or replaced, see Rule 20-3c.

Q & A

A player's ball is lying on the fairway and, in taking a practice swing, he accidentally moves the ball. Does he incur a penalty?
The player did not make a stroke as he had no intention of making a stroke (see the definition of "Stroke"); however, the ball was in play and the player has moved his ball (which was at rest). The player incurs a penalty of one stroke and must replace the ball (Rule 18-2).

After the player has addressed his ball on the fairway and stepped away, the ball moves. Is there a penalty?
The answer depends on the player's actions and if these caused the ball at rest to move. All relevant information must be considered and the weight of evidence must be elevated. For further guidance, see Decision 18-2/0.5.

RULE 18 INCIDENTS

Paul Casey faced a new challenger while lining up an eagle putt on the 12th green at Kingsbarns Golf Links during the 2012 Alfred Dunhill Cup.

While Casey was lining up his putt, a dog ran on to the green and ran off with his golf ball. The terrier made it as far as the 13th tee, where a spectator stopped him in his tracks and retrieved the golf ball for Casey.

A dog is an outside agency – see Definition of Outside Agency. If a ball at rest is moved by an outside agency, there is no penalty and the ball must be replaced (Rule 18-1). As it was known that the dog had moved the ball, Casey was entitled to replace his ball on the spot from which the dog had picked it up from the putting green.

Had the original ball not been recoverable or if it had been damaged by the dog, Casey could have been entitled to substitute another ball. On examination, the golf ball was found to be in perfect condition, so Casey was able to continue with the original ball and putted out for a birdie.

"It's the weirdest thing I've ever had happen to me on a golf course," said Casey. "I noticed the dog on the 12th tee and he sort of followed us down the fairway before taking a real liking to my golf ball!"

A playful dog picks up Paul Casey's ball. The dog is an outside agency and Rule 18-1 was applied to allow Casey to continue play.

Justin Rose found himself in an unusual situation at the 2014 Players Championship after the two-stroke penalty issued to him at the end of the third round was rescinded.

Rose incurred a penalty for moving his ball at rest and failing to replace it. The player was aware that the ball had oscillated when he had put the club down close to it on the springy grass, but he did not think that the ball had come to rest in a different spot and played out the 18th hole. Before Rose signed his score card, it was brought to his attention that the ball may have moved, and after a review of high-definition television coverage with officials, it was determined that his ball had definitely moved.

However, the Definition of "Moved" – when a ball "leaves its position and comes to rest in any other place" – does not contemplate movements of the ball that are only discernible through the use of high-definition television or any other form of sophisticated technology.

Decision 18/4 in particular contemplates cases where television evidence shows that a ball at rest changes position by an amount not noticeable to the naked eye. When determining whether or not a ball at rest has moved, a player must make that judgment based on all the information readily available to him at the time, so that he can determine whether the ball must be replaced under Rule 18-2. When it is not reasonably discernible to the naked eye, a player's determination that the ball has not moved will be deemed to be conclusive, even if that determination is later shown to be incorrect through the use of sophisticated technology.

In reviewing the case, the officials focused on how large a part the television close-ups had played in the original ruling being made. It was resolved that the only way to confirm whether and how much the ball had in fact changed position was as a result of using sophisticated technology. It was not discernible to the naked eye, so there was really no way Rose could have known that the ball had come to rest in another place.

Rose stressed his belief at the time that the ball had oscillated rather than moved. "I went down to the trailer and, again, we looked at it, everyone was pretty happy that it didn't move; and then we looked at it in another trailer, where they really zoomed in. And, I mean, the movement was virtually not visible."

The two-stroke penalty was rescinded based on the principle outlined in Decision 18/4 and Rose's 73 was adjusted to 71 before he commenced his final round of the Championship.

Justin Rose had another encounter with Rule 18-2 at the 2013 BMW Championship. While preparing for an approach shot at Conway Farms, he made a practice swing near his ball and took a divot, which landed on his ball and caused it to move.

Although Rose had no intention to move the ball, by creating the divot he had caused his ball at rest to move. In such circumstances, the player is in breach of Rule 18-2 and incurs a one-stroke penalty and must replace the ball.

Justin Rose of England had a two-stroke penalty rescinded at The Players Championship in 2014 due to the role TV evidence played in the original determination of the ruling.

Rule 19

DEFINITIONS
All defined terms are in *italics* and are listed in the Definitions section – see pages 13–23.

BALL IN MOTION DEFLECTED OR STOPPED

19-1 By Outside Agency

If a player's ball in motion is accidentally deflected or stopped by any *outside agency*, it is a *rub of the green*, there is no penalty and the ball must be played as it lies, except:

a. If a player's ball in motion after a *stroke* other than on the *putting green* comes to rest in or on any moving or animate *outside agency*, the ball must *through the green* or in a *hazard* be dropped, or on the *putting green* be placed, as near as possible to the spot directly under the place where the ball came to rest in or on the *outside agency*, but not nearer the *hole*, and

b. If a player's ball in motion after a *stroke* on the *putting green* is deflected or stopped by, or comes to rest in or on, any moving or animate *outside agency*, except a worm, insect or the like, the *stroke* is cancelled. The ball must be replaced and replayed.

If the ball is not immediately recoverable, another ball may be *substituted*.

Exception

Ball striking person attending or holding up *flagstick* or anything carried by him – see Rule 17-3b.

NOTE

If a player's ball in motion has been deliberately deflected or stopped by an *outside agency*:

(a) after a *stroke* from anywhere other than on the *putting green*, the spot where the ball would have come to rest must be estimated. If that spot is:

  (i) *through the green* or in a *hazard*, the ball must be dropped as near as possible to that spot;

  (ii) *out of bounds*, the player must proceed under Rule 27-1; or

  (iii) on the *putting green*, the ball must be placed on that spot.

(b) after a *stroke* on the *putting green*, the *stroke* is cancelled. The ball must be replaced and replayed.

If the outside agency is a *fellow-competitor* or his *caddie*, Rule 1-2 applies to the *fellow-competitor*.

(Player's ball deflected or stopped by another ball – see Rule 19-5)

19-2 By Player, Partner, Caddie or Equipment

If a player's ball is accidentally deflected or stopped by himself, his *partner* or either of their *caddies* or *equipment*, the player incurs a penalty of one stroke. The ball must be played as it lies, except when it comes to rest in or on the player's, his *partner's* or either of their *caddies'* clothes or *equipment*, in which case the ball must *through the green* or in a *hazard* be dropped, or on the *putting green* be placed, as near as possible to the spot directly under the place where the ball came to rest in or on the article, but not nearer the *hole*.

Exceptions

1 Ball striking person attending or holding up *flagstick* or anything carried by him – see Rule 17-3b.

2 Dropped ball – see Rule 20-2a.

(Ball purposely deflected or stopped by player, partner or caddie – see Rule 1-2)

BALL IN MOTION DEFLECTED OR STOPPED

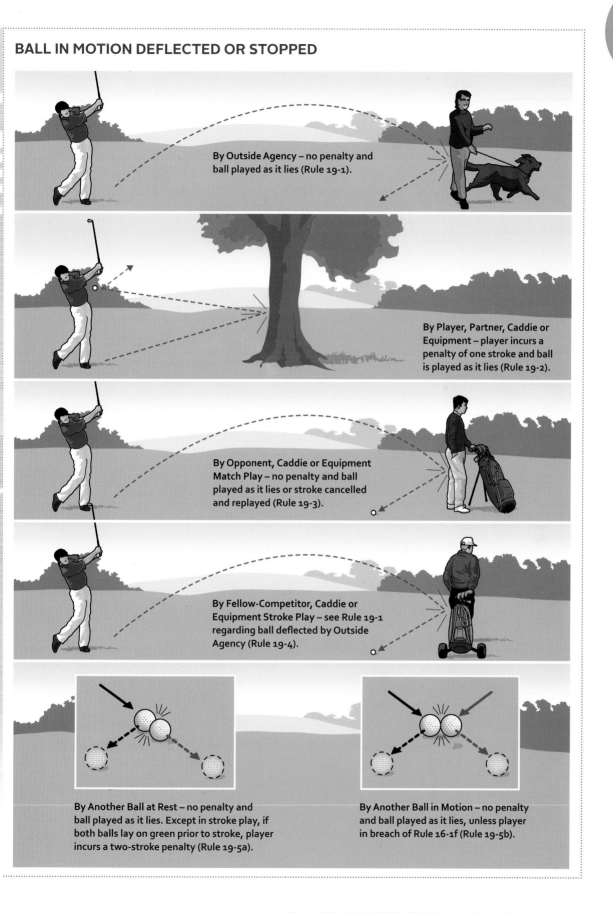

By Outside Agency – no penalty and ball played as it lies (Rule 19-1).

By Player, Partner, Caddie or Equipment – player incurs a penalty of one stroke and ball is played as it lies (Rule 19-2).

By Opponent, Caddie or Equipment Match Play – no penalty and ball played as it lies or stroke cancelled and replayed (Rule 19-3).

By Fellow-Competitor, Caddie or Equipment Stroke Play – see Rule 19-1 regarding ball deflected by Outside Agency (Rule 19-4).

By Another Ball at Rest – no penalty and ball played as it lies. Except in stroke play, if both balls lay on green prior to stroke, player incurs a two-stroke penalty (Rule 19-5a).

By Another Ball in Motion – no penalty and ball played as it lies, unless player in breach of Rule 16-1f (Rule 19-5b).

19

Ross Fisher retrieves his ball in order to proceed under Rule 19-1 after his tee-shot was stopped by a spectator's umbrella. The spectator and the umbrella are outside agencies.

19-3 By Opponent, Caddie or Equipment in Match Play

If a player's ball is accidentally deflected or stopped by an *opponent*, his *caddie* or his *equipment*, there is no penalty. The player may, before another *stroke* is made by either *side*, cancel the *stroke* and play a ball, without penalty, as nearly as possible at the spot from which the original ball was last played (Rule 20-5) or he may play the ball as it lies. However, if the player elects not to cancel the *stroke* and the ball has come to rest in or on the *opponent's* or his *caddie's* clothes or *equipment*, the ball must *through the green* or in a *hazard* be dropped, or on the *putting green* be placed, as near as possible to the spot directly under the place where the ball came to rest in or on the article, but not nearer the hole.

Exception

Ball striking person attending or holding up *flagstick* or anything carried by him – see Rule 17-3b. (Ball purposely deflected or stopped by opponent or caddie – see Rule 1-2)

19-4 By Fellow-Competitor, Caddie or Equipment in Stroke Play

See Rule 19-1 regarding ball deflected by *outside agency*.

Exception

Ball striking person attending or holding up *flagstick* or anything carried by him – see Rule 17-3b.

19-5 By Another Ball
19-5 a At Rest

If a player's ball in motion after a *stroke* is deflected or stopped by a *ball in play* and at rest, the player must play his ball as it lies. In match play, there is no penalty. In stroke play, there is no penalty, unless both balls lay on the *putting green* prior to the *stroke*, in which case the player incurs a penalty of two strokes.

19-5 b In Motion

If a player's ball in motion after a *stroke* other than on the *putting green* is deflected or stopped by another ball in motion after a *stroke*, the player must play his ball as it lies, without penalty.

If a player's ball in motion after a *stroke* on the *putting green* is deflected or stopped by another ball in motion after a *stroke*, the player's *stroke* is cancelled. The ball must be replaced and replayed, without penalty.

NOTE

Nothing in this Rule overrides the provisions of Rule 10-1 (Order of Play in Match Play) or Rule 16-1f (Making Stroke While Another Ball in Motion).

PENALTY

For breach of Rule:

Match play – Loss of hole;

Stroke play – Two strokes.

RULE 19 INCIDENTS

During the 2014 Tour Championship, Rory McIlroy required the help of the Rules of Golf to help him get out of a spot of bother. McIlroy's tee shot at East Lake's 14th hole hit a tree and somehow ended up in a spectator's pocket!

"I hit it up on the tree and it ricocheted straight into his pocket," McIlroy said after shooting a 5-under-par 65.

Rule 19-1a clarifies that if a player's ball in motion after a stroke, other than on the putting green, comes to rest in or on any moving or animate outside agency, the ball through the green must be dropped, as near as possible to the spot directly under the place where the ball came to rest in or on the animate outside agency, but not nearer the hole.

Fortunately, the spectator remained in the same position under the tree until McIlroy made his way to him. McIlroy was therefore able drop his ball as near as possible to the spot where the spectator had been standing when the ball entered his pocket.

Wales' Jamie Donaldson found himself three shots clear of the field at the halfway point of the Nedbank Golf Chal-lenge in 2013, although his advantage could have been even greater if not for an unfortunate deflection when playing from the fairway bunker on the par-5 10th hole.

"It was mad, I just pushed my tee shot a little bit into the bunker and tried to move it about 100 yards down the fairway," explained Donaldson. "But it clipped the lip, and as the ball came back it collided with the shaft of the club and my shoulder."

If a player's ball is accidentally deflected or stopped by the player himself or his equipment, the player incurs a penalty of one stroke. The ball is played as it lies, except when it comes to rest in or on the player or his equipment, in which case the ball must be dropped, as near as possible to the spot directly under the place where the ball came to rest in or on the article, but not nearer the hole (Rule 19-2).

Donaldson therefore incurred the one-stroke penalty and had to play the ball from the place where it had come to rest in the bunker.

Q & A

What do I do if my ball strikes a tee-marker or a direction post?

If a ball strikes a tee-marker, water hazard post, direction post or similar, it is simply a rub of the green and the ball must be played as it lies, without penalty (Rule 19-1).

What penalty do I incur if I strike my ball and it hits my golf bag as a result?

In match play or stroke play, the player incurs a penalty of one stroke for a breach and must play the ball as it lies (Rule 19-2).

What do I do if my ball is stopped or deflected by a rake held by my caddie?

A rake that is being carried or held by a player's caddie is considered to be the equipment of the player at that time (see Note 2 to the Definition of "Equipment"). The player incurs a penalty of one stroke and must play the ball as it lies.

Rule 20 LIFTING, DROPPING AND PLACING; PLAYING FROM WRONG PLACE

DEFINITIONS
All defined terms are in *italics* and are listed in the Definitions section – see pages 13–23.

20-1 Lifting and Marking

A ball to be lifted under the *Rules* may be lifted by the player, his *partner* or another person authorised by the player. In any such case, the player is responsible for any breach of the *Rules*.

The position of the ball must be marked before it is lifted under a *Rule* that requires it to be replaced. If it is not marked, the player incurs a penalty of one stroke and the ball must be replaced. If it is not replaced, the player incurs the general penalty for breach of this Rule but there is no additional penalty under Rule 20-1.

If a ball or ball-marker is accidentally *moved* in the process of lifting the ball under a *Rule* or marking its position, the ball or ball-marker must be replaced. There is no penalty, provided the movement of the ball or ball-marker is directly attributable to the specific act of marking the position of or lifting the ball. Otherwise, the player incurs a penalty of one stroke under this Rule or Rule 18-2.

Exception

If a player incurs a penalty for failing to act in accordance with Rule 5-3 or 12-2, there is no additional penalty under Rule 20-1.

NOTE

The position of a ball to be lifted should be marked by placing a ball-marker, a small coin or other similar object immediately behind the ball. If the ball-marker interferes with the play, *stance* or *stroke* of another player, it should be placed one or more clubhead-lengths to one side.

20-2 Dropping and Re-Dropping
20-2 a By Whom and How

A ball to be dropped under the *Rules* must be dropped by the player himself. He must stand erect, hold the ball at shoulder height and arm's length and drop it. If a ball is dropped by any other person or in any other manner and the error is not corrected as provided in Rule 20-6, the player incurs a penalty of one stroke.

If the ball, when dropped, touches any person or the *equipment* of any player before or after it strikes a part of the *course* and before it comes to rest, the ball must be re-dropped, without penalty. There is no limit to the number of times a ball must be re-dropped in these circumstances.

(Taking action to influence position or movement of ball – see Rule 1-2)

20-2 b Where to Drop

When a ball is to be dropped as near as possible to a specific spot, it must be dropped not nearer the *hole* than the specific spot which, if it is not precisely known to the player, must be estimated.

A ball when dropped must first strike a part of the *course* where the applicable *Rule* requires it to be dropped. If it is not so dropped, Rules 20-6 and 20-7 apply.

PROCEDURE FOR LIFTING BALL

When a ball is lifted anywhere on the course and it has to be replaced, for example when it interferes with the play of another competitor (Rule 22-2), the position of the ball must be marked before it is lifted.

20-2 c When to Re-Drop

A dropped ball must be re-dropped, without penalty, if it:

(i)   rolls into and comes to rest in a *hazard*;

(ii) rolls out of and comes to rest outside a *hazard*;

(iii) rolls onto and comes to rest on a *putting green*;

(iv) rolls and comes to rest *out of bounds*;

(v)   rolls to and comes to rest in a position where there is interference by the condition from which relief was taken under Rule 24-2b (immovable obstruction), Rule 25-1 (abnormal ground conditions), Rule 25-3 (wrong putting green) or a Local Rule (Rule 33-8a), or rolls back into the pitch-mark from which it was lifted under Rule 25-2 (embedded ball);

(vi) rolls and comes to rest more than two club-lengths from where it first struck a part of the *course*; or

(vii) rolls and comes to rest nearer the *hole* than:

(a) its original position or estimated position (see Rule 20-2b) unless otherwise permitted by the *Rules*; or

(b) the *nearest point of relief* or maximum available relief (Rule 24-2, 25-1 or 25-3); or

(c) the point where the original ball last crossed the margin of the *water hazard* or *lateral water hazard* (Rule 26-1).

If the ball when re-dropped rolls into any position listed above, it must be placed as near as possible to the spot where it first struck a part of the *course* when re-dropped.

NOTE 1

If a ball when dropped or re-dropped comes to rest and subsequently *moves*, the ball must be played as it lies, unless the provisions of any other *Rule* apply.

NOTE 2

If a ball to be re-dropped or placed under this Rule is not immediately recoverable, another ball may be *substituted*.

(Use of dropping zone – see Appendix 1, Part A, Section 6)

20-3 Placing and Replacing
20-3 a By Whom and Where

A ball to be placed under the *Rules* must be placed by the player or his *partner*.

A ball to be replaced under the *Rules* must be replaced by any one of the following: (i) the person who lifted or *moved* the ball, (ii) the player, or (iii) the player's *partner*. The ball must be placed on the spot from which it was lifted or *moved*. If the ball is placed or replaced by any other person and the error is not corrected as provided in Rule 20-6, the player incurs a penalty of one stroke. In any such case, the player is responsible for any other breach of the *Rules* that occurs as a result of the placing or replacing of the ball.

If a ball or ball-marker is accidentally *moved* in the process of placing or replacing the ball, the ball or ball-marker must be replaced. There is no penalty, provided the movement

K. J. Choi drops his ball under the watchful eye of a referee. The player shall stand up straight, hold the ball at shoulder height and arm's length and drop it.

WHEN TO RE-DROP BALL

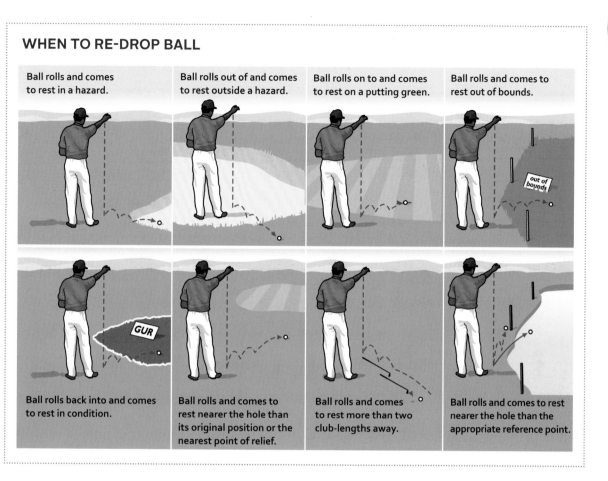

| Ball rolls and comes to rest in a hazard. | Ball rolls out of and comes to rest outside a hazard. | Ball rolls on to and comes to rest on a putting green. | Ball rolls and comes to rest out of bounds. |

| Ball rolls back into and comes to rest in condition. | Ball rolls and comes to rest nearer the hole than its original position or the nearest point of relief. | Ball rolls and comes to rest more than two club-lengths away. | Ball rolls and comes to rest nearer the hole than the appropriate reference point. |

of the ball or ball-marker is directly attributable to the specific act of placing or replacing the ball or removing the ball-marker. Otherwise, the player incurs a penalty of one stroke under Rule 18-2 or 20-1.

If a ball to be replaced is placed other than on the spot from which it was lifted or *moved* and the error is not corrected as provided in Rule 20-6, the player incurs the general penalty, loss of hole in match play or two strokes in stroke play, for a breach of the applicable Rule.

20-3 b Lie of Ball to be Placed or Replaced Altered

If the original lie of a ball to be placed or replaced has been altered:

(i) except in a *hazard*, the ball must be placed in the nearest lie most similar to the original lie that is not more than one club-length from the original lie, not nearer the *hole* and not in a *hazard*;

(ii) in a *water hazard*, the ball must be placed in accordance with Clause (i) above, except that the ball must be placed in the *water hazard*;

(iii) in a *bunker*, the original lie must be re-created as nearly as possible and the ball must be placed in that lie.

NOTE

If the original lie of a ball to be placed or replaced has been altered and it is impossible to determine the spot where the ball is to be placed or replaced, Rule 20-3b applies if the original lie is known, and Rule 20-3c applies if the original lie is not known.

Exception
If the player is searching for or identifying a ball covered by sand – see Rule 12-1a.

20-3 c Spot Not Determinable
If it is impossible to determine the spot where the ball is to be placed or replaced:
(i) *through the green,* the ball must be dropped as near as possible to the place where it lay but not in a *hazard* or on a *putting green*;
(ii) in a *hazard,* the ball must be dropped in the *hazard* as near as possible to the place where it lay;
(iii) on the *putting green,* the ball must be placed as near as possible to the place where it lay but not in a *hazard.*

Exception
When resuming play (Rule 6-8d), if the spot where the ball is to be placed is impossible to determine, it must be estimated and the ball placed on the estimated spot.

20-3 d Ball Fails to Come to Rest on Spot
If a ball when placed fails to come to rest on the spot on which it was placed, there is no penalty and the ball must be replaced. If it still fails to come to rest on that spot:
(i) except in a *hazard,* it must be placed at the nearest spot where it can be placed at rest that is not nearer the *hole* and not in a *hazard*;
(ii) in a *hazard,* it must be placed in the *hazard* at the nearest spot where it can be placed at rest that is not nearer the *hole.*

If a ball when placed comes to rest on the spot on which it is placed, and it subsequently *moves,* there is no penalty and the ball must be played as it lies, unless the provisions of any other *Rule* apply.

LIE OF BALL ALTERED

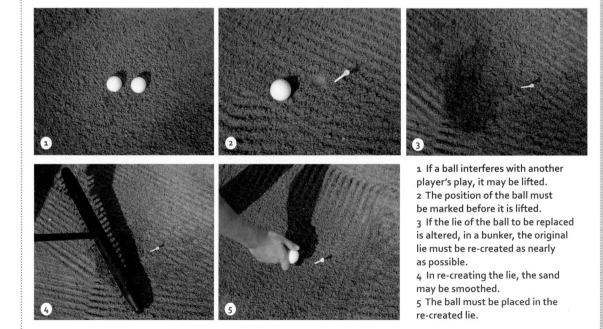

1 If a ball interferes with another player's play, it may be lifted.
2 The position of the ball must be marked before it is lifted.
3 If the lie of the ball to be replaced is altered, in a bunker, the original lie must be re-created as nearly as possible.
4 In re-creating the lie, the sand may be smoothed.
5 The ball must be placed in the re-created lie.

* PENALTY

For breach of Rule 20-1, 20-2 or 20-3:

Match play – Loss of hole;

Stroke play – Two strokes.

*If a player makes a *stroke* at a ball *substituted* under one of these Rules when such *substitution* is not permitted, he incurs the general penalty for breach of that Rule, but there is no additional penalty under that Rule. If a player drops a ball in an improper manner and plays from a wrong place or if the ball has been put into play by a person not permitted by the *Rules* and then played from a wrong place, see Note 3 to Rule 20-7c.

20-4 When Ball Dropped, Placed or Replaced is in Play

If the player's *ball in play* has been lifted, it is again in *play* when dropped or placed. A ball that has been replaced is *in play* whether or not the ball-marker has been removed.

A substituted ball becomes the *ball in play* when it has been dropped or placed.

(Ball incorrectly substituted – see Rule 15-2)

(Lifting ball incorrectly substituted, dropped or placed – see Rule 20-6)

20-5 Making Next Stroke from Where Previous Stroke Made

When a player elects or is required to make his next *stroke* from where a previous *stroke* was made, he must proceed as follows:

(a) **On the Teeing Ground:** The ball to be played must be played from within the *teeing ground*. It may be played from anywhere within the *teeing ground* and may be teed.

(b) **Through the Green:** The ball to be played must be dropped and when dropped must first strike a part of the *course through the green*.

(c) **In a Hazard:** The ball to be played must be dropped and when dropped must first strike a part of the *course* in the *hazard*.

(d) **On the Putting Green:** The ball to be played must be placed on the *putting green*.

PENALTY

For breach of Rule 20-5:

Match play – Loss of hole;

Stroke play – Two strokes.

20-6 Lifting Ball Incorrectly Substituted, Dropped or Placed

A ball incorrectly *substituted*, dropped or placed in a wrong place or otherwise not in accordance with the *Rules* but not played may be lifted, without penalty, and the player must then proceed correctly.

20-7 Playing from Wrong Place
20-7 a General

A player has played from a wrong place if he makes a *stroke* at his *ball in play*:

(i) on a part of the *course* where the *Rules* do not permit a *stroke* to be made or a ball to be dropped or placed; or

(ii) when the *Rules* require a dropped ball to be re-dropped or a *moved* ball to be replaced.

NOTE

For a ball played from outside the *teeing ground* or from a wrong *teeing ground* – see Rule 11-4.

20-7 b Match Play

If a player makes a *stroke* from a wrong place, he loses the hole.

20-7 c Stroke Play

If a *competitor* makes a *stroke* from a wrong place, he incurs a penalty of two strokes under the applicable Rule. He must play out the hole with the ball played from the wrong place, without correcting his error, provided he has not committed a serious breach (see Note 1).

If a *competitor* becomes aware that he has played from a wrong place and believes that he may have committed a serious breach, he must, before making a *stroke* on the next *teeing ground*, play out the hole with a second ball played in accordance with the *Rules*. If the hole being played is the last hole of the round, he must declare, before leaving the *putting green*, that he will play out the hole with a second ball played in accordance with the *Rules*.

If the *competitor* has played a second ball, he must report the facts to the *Committee* before returning his score card; if he fails to do so, he is disqualified. The *Committee* must determine whether the *competitor* has committed a serious breach of the applicable *Rule*. If he has, the score with the second ball counts and the competitor must add two *penalty strokes* to his score with that ball. If the *competitor* has committed a serious breach and has failed to correct it as outlined above, he is disqualified.

NOTE 1

A *competitor* is deemed to have committed a serious breach of the applicable Rule if the *Committee* considers he has gained a significant advantage as a result of playing from a wrong place.

NOTE 2

If a *competitor* plays a second ball under Rule 20-7c and it is ruled not to count, *strokes* made with that ball and *penalty strokes* incurred solely by playing that ball are disregarded. If the second ball is ruled to count, the *stroke* made from the wrong place and any *strokes* subsequently taken with the original ball including *penalty strokes* incurred solely by playing that ball are disregarded.

NOTE 3

If a player incurs a penalty for making a *stroke* from a wrong place, there is no additional penalty for:

(a)   *substituting* a ball when not permitted;

(b)   dropping a ball when the *Rules* require it to be placed, or placing a ball when the *Rules* require it to be dropped;

(c)   dropping a ball in an improper manner; or

(d)   a ball being put into play by a person not permitted to do so under the *Rules*.

PLAYING FROM THE WRONG PLACE

If a player moves her ball-marker a putter head-length to one side, she must remember to put it back before she makes her next stroke. Otherwise the player will be penalised for playing from a wrong place.

Q & A

Must a player use a small coin or similar object to mark the position of his ball before lifting it?

The Note to Rule 20-1 states in part that the position of the ball should be marked by placing a ball-marker, small coin or other small object immediately behind the ball. When the word "should" is used in the Rules of Golf it is a recommendation only and failure to comply does not result in a penalty – see the section entitled "How to Use the Rule Book" on page 5. The intention is to emphasise that use of a ball-marker or other small object (such as a coin) is considered to be the best way to mark a ball.

Is the person who lifted the player's ball the only person who may replace it?

No. Up to a maximum of three different people may replace a ball, depending on the circumstances, that is the player, his partner or the person who lifted it. For example, in a four-ball match, if a player were to authorise his caddie to lift his ball, the caddie, the player or the player's partner could replace it. However, if the player lifts the ball himself, only the player or his partner may replace it – see Rule 20-3a.

Must the position of the ball be marked when taking a drop from an immovable obstruction, an abnormal ground condition or because the ball is considered unplayable?

The original position of the ball need only be marked when it is lifted under a Rule that requires it to be replaced on the same spot (e.g. marking and lifting a ball on the putting green under Rule 16-1b). If the ball is to be dropped or placed in any other position, such as taking a free drop from an immovable obstruction, ground under repair or relief under the unplayable ball Rule, the original position of the ball does not need to be marked, but it is considered good practice to do so.

RULE 20 INCIDENTS

Finishing tied after 72 holes, Ian Poulter and Robert Karlsson went head-to-head for the 2010 Dubai World Championship title. The pair halved the first extra hole in the play-off with birdies and both found the putting green on the second play-off hole. Poulter had left himself a 30-foot birdie putt and had marked and lifted the ball. After assessing the putt, he bent down with the intention of replacing his ball, when the ball slipped out of his hand and moved his ball-marker.

Rule 20-3a provides that if a ball-marker is accidentally moved in the process of replacing the ball, the ball or ball-marker must be replaced and there is no penalty, provided the movement of the ball-marker is directly attributable to the specific act of replacing the ball. But if the movement of the ball-marker is not in the specific act of replacing the ball, the player incurs a penalty of one stroke and must replace the ball or ball-marker.

Decision 20-1/15 provides that in order for the movement of the ball-marker to be considered directly attributable to the specific act of replacing the ball, the movement has to occur when the ball was actually placed in front of the ball-marker such that the player's hand or the placement of the ball causes the ball-marker to move. The Decision also clarifies that any accidental movement of the ball-marker that occurs before the specific act, such as dropping the ball, regardless of the height from which

it was dropped, is not considered directly attributable to the specific act of replacing the ball.

Consequently, in Poulter's case as he had dropped his ball prior to the specific act of replacing it, he was penalised one stroke for the accidental movement of the ball-marker. He then replaced his ball on the original spot from which it was lifted, composed himself and attempted the putt for what was now a par, but it wasn't to be. Poulter missed out on the title, world ranking points and over €300,000 in earnings for his accidental error.

After the event, Poulter commented that he had the ball-marker (a platinum coin) specially made at the beginning of 2010. "It has my kids' names on it and it's my lucky coin," he said. "After the year I've had, I still consider it lucky."

Former Open Champion Paul Lawrie had a similar experience at the Qatar Masters in 2012. He dropped his ball on a coin that was marking the position of his ball on the 10th green during the second round and the coin moved. Lawrie went on to win despite his fumble with the ball.

"It was one of those freak things," said Lawrie. "Nobody purposely throws a ball on the coin to move it but it did move." Again, Decision 20-1/15 was applied to Lawrie, as the movement of the coin was not directly attributable to the specific act of replacing the ball.

Ian Poulter receives a ruling from Andy McFee, Senior Referee on the European Tour. Poulter incurred a one-shot penalty for a breach of Rule 20-1 during the play-off for the Dubai World Championship in 2010.

Rule 21 CLEANING BALL

DEFINITIONS
All defined terms are in *italics* and are listed in the Definitions section – see pages 13–23.

A ball on the *putting green* may be cleaned when lifted under Rule 16-1b. Elsewhere, a ball may be cleaned when lifted, except when it has been lifted:

a. To determine if it is unfit for play (Rule 5-3);

b. For identification (Rule 12-2), in which case it may be cleaned only to the extent necessary for identification; or

c. Because it is assisting or interfering with play (Rule 22).

If a player cleans his ball during play of a hole except as provided in this Rule, he incurs a penalty of one stroke and the ball, if lifted, must be replaced.

If a player who is required to replace a ball fails to do so, he incurs the general penalty under the applicable Rule, but there is no additional penalty under Rule 21.

Exception

If a player incurs a penalty for failing to act in accordance with Rule 5-3, 12-2 or 22, there is no additional penalty under Rule 21.

Q & A

A player is asked to lift his ball because it is interfering with the play of a fellow-competitor (Rule 22-2) and puts it in his pocket. Is he deemed to have cleaned it?

Whether the ball is cleaned is a question of fact. The action of putting the ball into a pocket can result in the ball being cleaned and any doubt should be resolved against the player. In both match play and stroke play, the player would incur a one-stroke penalty if it were considered that he had cleaned his ball.

Rule 22 BALL ASSISTING OR INTERFERING WITH PLAY

DEFINITIONS
All defined terms are in *italics* and are listed in the Definitions section – see pages 13–23.

22-1 Ball Assisting Play

Except when a ball is in motion, if a player considers that a ball might assist any other player, he may:

a. Lift the ball if it is his ball; or

b. Have any other ball lifted.

A ball lifted under this Rule must be replaced (see Rule 20-3). The ball must not be cleaned, unless it lies on the *putting green* (see Rule 21).

In stroke play, a player required to lift his ball may play first rather than lift the ball.

In stroke play, if the *Committee* determines that *competitors* have agreed not to lift a ball that might assist any *competitor*, they are disqualified.

NOTE

When another ball is in motion, a ball that might influence the movement of the ball in motion must not be lifted.

22-2 Ball Interfering with Play

Except when a ball is in motion, if a player considers that another ball might interfere with his play, he may have it lifted.

A ball lifted under this Rule must be replaced (see Rule 20-3). The ball must not be cleaned, unless it lies on the *putting green* (see Rule 21).

In stroke play, a player required to lift his ball may play first rather than lift the ball.

NOTE 1

Except on the *putting green*, a player may not lift his ball solely because he considers that it might interfere with the play of another player. If a player lifts his ball without being asked to do so, he incurs a penalty of one stroke for a breach of Rule 18-2, but there is no additional penalty under Rule 22.

NOTE 2

When another ball is in motion, a ball that might influence the movement of the ball in motion must not be lifted.

PENALTY

For breach of Rule:

Match play – Loss of hole;

Stroke play – Two strokes.

BALL INTERFERING WITH OR ASSISTING PLAY

If a player considers that his ball might assist another player, he is entitled to mark and lift his ball.

Q & A

What is the procedure if my ball lies close to another ball in a bunker?

When your ball interferes with the play of another player, you may lift your ball (see Rule 22-2). The position of the ball must be marked before lifting it and the ball must not be cleaned. If the lie of the ball is altered when the other player plays, you are required to re-create the original lie as nearly as possible and the ball must be replaced in that lie (Rule 20-3b). The lie may be created using a rake, hand or a club, etc. See also page 106.

RULE 22 INCIDENTS

At the 2008 Open Championship at Royal Birkdale, Spain's Pablo Larrazábal and Australia's Adam Scott required the assistance of the referee when playing the par-4 13th hole. Both had found the bunker front left of the green and as it was, both balls had come to rest very close to one another. Scott's ball was further away from the hole and lying nicely but Larrazábal had a slightly plugged lie just a couple of inches in front of Scott's.

Rule 22 allows any player to lift his ball if he believes it will assist another player, or have any ball lifted that might interfere with his play or assist any other player. The ball must not be cleaned, unless it lies on the putting green. Scott asked Larrazábal to move his ball as it was certainly going to interfere with his stroke.

Under the referee's watchful eye, Larrazábal marked the ball with a tee peg, lifted it and set it aside on the ground outside the bunker, having been advised not to clean the ball. However, his tee peg was now interfering with Scott's swing, so Larrazábal was asked to move it. Hovering his club above the sand, he moved the tee peg two clubhead-lengths to the side out of the way.

It is worth noting that had Larrazábal touched the sand with his club when he was measuring the two clubhead-lengths, he would not have been penalised. As it is difficult to "hover" the club above the sand when measuring, Exception 1 to Rule 13-4 permits the player to touch the ground in the hazard with a club or hand without penalty if it is as a result of measuring or in marking the position of the ball.

Scott was then able to play his stroke out of the bunker. In doing so he significantly altered the original lie of Larrazábal's ball. Rule 20-3b covers these situations where the lie of a ball to be replaced has been altered. In a bunker, the original lie must be re-created as nearly as possible and the ball must be placed in that lie.

The bunker was restored to its original condition and the referee then guided Larrazábal in first replacing the tee peg to its original spot and then replacing the ball. As the ball had been in a slightly plugged lie, Larrazábal was required to press the ball into the sand to ensure he replicated the plugged nature of the original lie. Decision 20-3b/1 clarifies that the lie must be re-created as nearly as possible, including any irregularities, such as a depression or heel mark that the ball may have come to rest in. Larrazábal then played his stroke from the bunker and found the putting green like Scott.

Rule 23 LOOSE IMPEDIMENTS

DEFINITIONS
All defined terms are
in *italics* and are listed in
the Definitions section –
see pages 13–23.

23-1 Relief

Except when both the *loose impediment* and the ball lie in or touch the same *hazard*, any *loose impediment* may be removed without penalty.

If the ball lies anywhere other than on the *putting green* and the removal of a *loose impediment* by the player causes the ball to *move*, Rule 18-2 applies.

On the putting green, if the ball or ball-marker is accidentally moved in the process of the player removing a loose impediment, the ball or ball-marker must be replaced. There is no penalty, provided the movement of the ball or ball-marker is directly attributable to the removal of the loose impediment. Otherwise, the player incurs a penalty of one stroke under Rule 18-2.

When a ball is in motion, a *loose impediment* that might influence the movement of the ball must not be removed.

NOTE

If the ball lies in a *hazard*, the player must not touch or move any *loose impediment* lying in or touching the same *hazard* – see Rule 13-4c.

PENALTY

For breach of Rule:

Match play – Loss of hole;

Stroke play – Two strokes.

(Searching for ball in hazard – see Rule 12-1)

(Touching line of putt – see Rule 16-1a)

Through the green, the player is entitled to remove loose impediments without penalty. If the player causes the ball to move, Rule 18-2 applies.

Q & A

Can I use my putter, hand, cap or towel to remove loose impediments?

Yes. Loose impediments may be removed by any means. In removing loose impediments on the line of putt, the player must not press anything down.

Can I remove stones from bunkers?

Stones are, by definition, loose impediments. Generally, it is not permitted to remove a loose impediment that lies in the same hazard as your ball (Rule 13-4c); however, a Committee can introduce a Local Rule stating that stones in bunkers are movable obstructions (Appendix 1, Part A, 3f).

Can I remove sand that lies on the putting green even though my ball lies off the putting green?

Except when the ball lies in a hazard, Rule 23-1 allows the player to remove loose impediments without penalty regardless of where the ball lies. However, as sand and loose soils are loose impediments only when they lie on the putting green, it is the position of the sand and loose soil that is key. Provided the sand or loose soil lie on the putting green, it may be removed.

Zach Johnson brushes aside loose impediments on the putting green using a towel. Loose impediments may be removed by any means, except that, on the line of putt, the player must not press anything down (Rule 16-1a).

RULE 23 INCIDENTS

During the 2013 World Challenge at Sherwood Country Club, Lee Westwood's ball came to rest on a large leaf on the putting green at the 4th hole. Having never encountered this situation, Westwood called in a referee.

As Westwood's ball lay on the putting green, he was entitled to mark and lift his ball under Rule 16-1a. The loose impediment was then removed and the ball replaced without the leaf interfering.

However, as the ball was on the putting green, had Westwood simply removed the leaf instead of marking the ball, and the ball had accidentally moved in the process of removing the leaf, there would have been no penalty, provided the movement of the ball was directly attributable to the removal of the loose impediment – see Rule 23-1.

Camilo Villegas was disqualified ultimately for a breach of Rule 6-6d from the season-opening 2010 Hyundi Tournament of Champions for signing for a wrong score. This was as a result of a penalty incurred under Rule 23-1 that he failed to include in his score before signing and submitting his first round score card.

The situation that gave rise to the penalty happened when Villegas was playing the 15th hole at the Plantation course at Kapalua. His chip to the elevated green on the par-5 failed to make it to the top of the slope and began to roll back down towards his feet. When Villegas saw the ball rolling back down the hill, he used his club to sweep away the debris that was caused by his divot. Small clumps of turf had been dislodged when he hit the stroke and were no longer attached to the ground but were still lying in the area where he had played from. The ball eventually came to rest in the same area.

Rule 23-1 states "When a ball is in motion, a loose impediment that might influence the movement of the ball must not be moved". As the ball was clearly in motion and potentially returning to the same area when he removed the loose impediments, Villegas had breached Rule 23-1, the penalty for which is two strokes in stroke play.

Villegas did not realise he had breached the Rule and signed for a 7 for the 15th hole when it should have included the two-stroke penalty for a 9. The breach of the Rules went unnoticed until later that day when a viewer, who had been watching a replay of the tournament on television, spotted it and contacted the PGA Tour. However, it was too late to include the penalty in his score as Villegas had already signed and submitted his score card so he was disqualified.

If this situation were to happen today, the outcome would be different. The introduction of the Exception to Rule 6-6d for 2016 provides a two-stroke penalty, rather than disqualification, for a competitor who returns a score lower than actually taken due to failure to include a penalty which he did not know he had incurred.

Villegas failed to include the penalty, as he was not aware that he had breached the Rules, nor was he aware that any of his actions were in question at the time he returned his score card. Consequently, under this new Exception, Villegas would avoid disqualification but would be penalised two strokes for the breach of Rule 23-1 and incur an additional penalty of two strokes for signing for a score lower than actually taken (Rule 6-6d), resulting in a total score of 11 for that hole – a big number but better than being disqualified!

Lee Westwood putts after removing the leaf that his ball had come to rest on top of during play of the 4th hole. He was able to remove the leaf without penalty.

Rule 24 OBSTRUCTIONS

DEFINITIONS
All defined terms are
in *italics* and are listed in
the Definitions section –
see pages 13–23.

24-1 Movable Obstruction

A player may take relief, without penalty, from a movable *obstruction* as follows:

a. If the ball does not lie in or on the *obstruction*, the *obstruction* may be removed. If the ball *moves*, it must be replaced, and there is no penalty, provided that the movement of the ball is directly attributable to the removal of the *obstruction*. Otherwise, Rule 18-2 applies.

MOVABLE OBSTRUCTION

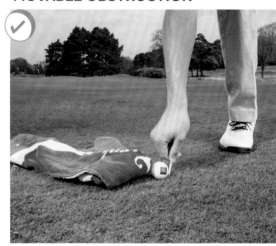

It is recommended to place a mark next to the ball before removing the obstruction. If the ball moves as a result of moving the obstruction, it can then be replaced on the same spot.

BALL AGAINST RAKE ROLLS INTO BUNKER WHEN RAKE REMOVED

The ball must be replaced if it moves when the rake is removed. If the ball does not come to rest on the original spot when replaced a second time, the player must place it at the nearest spot, not nearer the hole nor in the bunker, where it will come to rest.

b. If the ball lies in or on the *obstruction*, the ball may be lifted and the *obstruction* removed. The ball must *through the green* or in a *hazard* be dropped, or on the *putting green* be placed, as near as possible to the spot directly under the place where the ball lay in or on the *obstruction*, but not nearer the *hole*.

The ball may be cleaned when lifted under this Rule.

When a ball is in motion, an *obstruction* that might influence the movement of the ball, other than *equipment* of any player or the *flagstick* when attended, removed or held up, must not be moved.

(Exerting influence on ball – see Rule 1-2)

NOTE

If a ball to be dropped or placed under this Rule is not immediately recoverable, another ball may be *substituted*.

24-2 Immovable Obstruction
24-2 a Interference

Interference by an immovable *obstruction* occurs when a ball lies in or on the *obstruction*, or when the *obstruction* interferes with the player's *stance* or the area of his intended swing. If the player's ball lies on the *putting green*, interference also occurs if an immovable *obstruction* on the *putting green* intervenes on his *line of putt*. Otherwise, intervention on the *line of play* is not, of itself, interference under this Rule.

FLAGSTICK REMOVED WHEN BALL IN MOTION

When a ball is in motion it is permissible to move a flagstick that has been removed and that might influence the movement of the ball. See Rule 24-1.

24-2 bRelief

Except when the ball is in a *water hazard* or a *lateral water hazard*, a player may take relief from interference by an immovable *obstruction* as follows:

(i) **Through the Green:** If the ball lies *through the green*, the player must lift the ball and drop it, without penalty, within one club-length of and not nearer the *hole* than the *nearest point of relief*. The *nearest point of relief* must not be in a *hazard* or on a *putting green*. When the ball is dropped within one club-length of the *nearest point of relief*, the ball must first strike a part of the *course* at a spot that avoids interference by the immovable *obstruction* and is not in a *hazard* and not on a *putting green*.

(ii) **In a Bunker:** If the ball is in a *bunker*, the player must lift the ball and drop it either:

    (a) Without penalty, in accordance with Clause (i) above, except that the *nearest point of relief* must be in the *bunker* and the ball must be dropped in the *bunker*; or

    (b) Under penalty of one stroke, outside the *bunker* keeping the point where the ball lay directly between the *hole* and the spot on which the ball is dropped, with no limit to how far behind the *bunker* the ball may be dropped.

(iii) **On the Putting Green:** If the ball lies on the *putting green*, the player must lift the ball and place it, without penalty, at the *nearest point of relief* that is not in a *hazard*. The *nearest point of relief* may be off the *putting green*.

(iv) **On the Teeing Ground:** If the ball lies on the *teeing ground*, the player must lift the ball and drop it, without penalty, in accordance with Clause (i) above.

The ball may be cleaned when lifted under this Rule.

(Ball rolling to a position where there is interference by the condition from which relief was taken – see Rule 20-2c(v))

BALL BEHIND IMMOVABLE OBSTRUCTION

There is no relief from an immovable obstruction on the line of play. The shelter would have to interfere with the player's stance or swing, or the lie of the ball, for Rule 24-2 to apply.

ROADS AND PATHS

Relief without penalty is available from an immovable obstruction. The nearest point of relief here will be in bushes. Relief is optional so the player can, of course, play the ball as it lies.

DIRECTION OF PLAY

IMMOVABLE OBSTRUCTION IN BUNKER

The player is entitled to relief from an immovable obstruction when the ball is in a bunker. The nearest point of relief must be in the bunker and the ball must be dropped in the bunker. Alternatively, the ball may be dropped outside of the bunker, under penalty of one stroke.

RELIEF FOR SIDEWAYS STROKE

A player is entitled to relief from an immovable obstruction for a sideways stroke that is reasonable. A sideways stroke away from a fence surrounding a tree nursery would be considered, in the circumstances, reasonable.

Exception

A player may not take relief under this Rule if (a) interference by anything other than an immovable *obstruction* makes the *stroke* clearly impracticable or (b) interference by an immovable *obstruction* would occur only through use of a clearly unreasonable *stroke* or an unnecessarily abnormal *stance*, swing or direction of play.

NOTE 1

If a ball is in a *water hazard* (including a *lateral water hazard*), the player may not take relief from interference by an immovable *obstruction*. The player must play the ball as it lies or proceed under Rule 26-1.

NOTE 2

If a ball to be dropped or placed under this Rule is not immediately recoverable, another ball may be *substituted*.

NOTE 3

The *Committee* may make a Local Rule stating that the player must determine the *nearest point of relief* without crossing over, through or under the *obstruction*.

24-3 Ball in Obstruction Not Found

It is a question of fact whether a ball that has not been found after having been struck toward an *obstruction* is in the *obstruction*. In order to apply this Rule, it must be known or virtually certain that the ball is in the *obstruction*. In the absence of such knowledge or certainty, the player must proceed under Rule 27-1.

24-3 a Ball in Movable Obstruction Not Found

If it is known or virtually certain that a ball that has not been found is in a movable *obstruction*, the player may *substitute* another ball and take relief, without penalty, under this Rule. If he elects to do so, he must remove the *obstruction* and *through the green* or in a *hazard* drop a ball, or on the *putting green* place a ball, as near as possible to the spot directly under the place where the ball last crossed the outermost limits of the movable *obstruction*, but not nearer the hole.

24-3 b Ball in Immovable Obstruction Not Found

If it is known or virtually certain that a ball that has not been found is in an immovable *obstruction*, the player may take relief under this Rule. If he elects to do so, the spot where the ball last crossed the outermost limits of the *obstruction* must be determined and, for the purpose of applying this Rule, the ball is deemed to lie at this spot and the player must proceed as follows:

RELIEF FROM OBSTRUCTION GIVES RELIEF FOR LINE OF PLAY

After taking relief from an immovable obstruction, the player is permitted by the Rules to play in any direction. It is the player's good fortune if the bush no longer hinders a stroke towards the green.

(i) **Through the Green:** If the ball last crossed the outermost limits of the immovable *obstruction* at a spot *through the green*, the player may *substitute* another ball, without penalty, and take relief as prescribed in Rule 24-2b(i).

(ii) **In a Bunker:** If the ball last crossed the outermost limits of the immovable *obstruction* at a spot in a *bunker*, the player may *substitute* another ball, without penalty, and take relief as prescribed in Rule 24-2b(ii).

(iii) **In a Water Hazard (including a Lateral Water Hazard):** If the ball last crossed the outermost limits of the immovable *obstruction* at a spot in a *water hazard*, the player is not entitled to relief without penalty. The player must proceed under Rule 26-1.

(iv) **On the Putting Green:** If the ball last crossed the outermost limits of the immovable *obstruction* at a spot on the *putting green*, the player may *substitute* another ball, without penalty, and take relief as prescribed in Rule 24-2b(iii).

PENALTY

For breach of Rule:

Match play – Loss of hole;

Stroke play – Two strokes.

STILE IN BOUNDARY FENCE

Although a boundary fence is not an immovable obstruction, the stile is. The player may take relief from the stile under Rule 24-2.

NO RELIEF WITHOUT PENALTY IN WATER HAZARD

There is no free relief from an immovable obstruction in a water hazard, even if the ball is playable. The player must play the ball as it lies or proceed under the water hazard Rule (see Rule 26).

Ball on bridge above hazard
The ball is in the water hazard because the margins of a water hazard are deemed to extend vertically upwards. The bridge is an immovable obstruction but there is no relief without penalty from an immovable obstruction when the ball lies in or touches a water hazard. If the ball is played from the bridge the club may be grounded.

Q & A

My ball lies in a water hazard but in a playable position. When I take my stance, I have interference from an immovable obstruction in the water hazard. Am I entitled to relief without penalty from the immovable obstruction?

When a ball lies in a water hazard, you are not entitled to relief without penalty from an immovable obstruction, regardless of whether the obstruction is in the water hazard or outside it. You must play the ball as it lies or proceed under Rule 26-1.

However, if the ball lies outside the water hazard, a player may take relief from the immovable obstruction under Rule 24-2, irrespective of whether the immovable obstruction is inside the water hazard or outside it.

May stakes defining a water hazard or lateral water hazard be moved?

A water hazard stake is an obstruction – see Definition of "obstruction". Consequently, if such a stake is movable, it may be removed without penalty, in accordance with Rule 24-1. A player may remove a movable obstruction anywhere on the course, irrespective of whether his ball lies in a water hazard or not.

RULE 24 INCIDENTS

Ian Poulter incurred a two-stroke penalty for dropping a ball incorrectly under Rule 24-2 after taking relief from a cart path during his second round of the Volvo China Open in Shenzhen in 2014.

Poulter had hit his drive into a lateral water hazard which consisted of some dense trees. Poulter correctly established the point where his ball last crossed the margin of the lateral water hazard and measured two club-lengths from this point under Rule 26-1c. The two club-length measurement resulted in him dropping the ball on the cart path, an immovable obstruction.

Now that the ball was back in play, Poulter was entitled to take relief from the immovable obstruction and he decided to do so. If a player elects to take relief from an immovable obstruction, the player must lift the ball and drop it, without penalty, within one club-length of and not nearer the hole than the nearest point of relief.

Poulter correctly established his nearest point of relief and began to measure the area in which to drop the ball. But, instead of measuring the permissible one club-length from the nearest point of relief, in the heat of the moment and confusing it with the lateral water hazard relief, he measured two club-lengths.

He then went on to drop his ball within the second club-length and played from this spot. Had he realised his error before playing his shot, he would have been able to correct his error under Rule 20-6. But playing the incorrectly dropped ball resulted in him playing from a wrong place. As per Rule 20-7, if a competitor makes a stroke from a wrong place, he incurs a penalty of two strokes under the applicable Rule. In this case it was a breach of Rule 24-2.

"It was a schoolboy error," Poulter said after the round. "I just made a mistake. We make them and I guess that was a fun one. I took two club-lengths as opposed to one and it's a two-shot penalty, which turned a bad six into a really bad eight, so not the best of holes. I guess I need to get the Rule book back out and start chewing it."

Ian Poulter contemplates his options when taking relief, first from the lateral water hazard, and then second from the cart path, an immovable obstruction.

Rule 25 ABNORMAL GROUND CONDITIONS, EMBEDDED BALL AND WRONG PUTTING GREEN

DEFINITIONS
All defined terms are
in *italics* and are listed in
the Definitions section –
see pages 13–23.

25-1 Abnormal Ground Conditions
25-1 a Interference

Interference by an *abnormal ground condition* occurs when a ball lies in or touches the condition or when the condition interferes with the player's *stance* or the area of his intended swing. If the player's ball lies on the *putting green*, interference also occurs if an *abnormal ground condition* on the *putting green* intervenes on his *line of putt*. Otherwise, intervention on the *line of play* is not, of itself, interference under this Rule.

NOTE

The *Committee* may make a Local Rule stating that interference by an *abnormal ground condition* with a player's *stance* is deemed not to be, of itself, interference under this Rule.

A fallen tree still attached to its stump is not ground under repair, but it can be so declared by the Committee.

A rut made by a tractor is not ground under repair, but the Committee would be justified in declaring a deep rut to be ground under repair.

AREAS REQUIRING PRESERVATION

If there is an area of the course, such as a plantation of young trees, which requires preservation, the Committee should declare it "Ground Under Repair – Play Prohibited" unitl such time that the trees mature.

25-1 b Relief

Except when the ball is in a *water hazard* or a *lateral water hazard*, a player may take relief from interference by an *abnormal ground condition* as follows:

(i) **Through the Green:** If the ball lies *through the green*, the player must lift the ball and drop it, without penalty, within one club-length of and not nearer the *hole* than the *nearest point of relief*. The *nearest point of relief* must not be in a *hazard* or on a *putting green*. When the ball is dropped within one club-length of the *nearest point of relief*, the ball must first strike a part of the *course* at a spot that avoids interference by the condition and is not in a *hazard* and not on a *putting green*.

(ii) **In a Bunker:** If the ball is in a *bunker*, the player must lift the ball and drop it either:

    (a) Without penalty, in accordance with Clause (i) above, except that the *nearest point of relief* must be in the *bunker* and the ball must be dropped in the *bunker* or, if complete relief is impossible, as near as possible to the spot where the ball lay, but not nearer the *hole*, on a part of the *course* in the *bunker* that affords maximum available relief from the condition; or

    (b) Under penalty of one stroke, outside the *bunker* keeping the point where the ball lay directly between the *hole* and the spot on which the ball is dropped, with no limit to how far behind the *bunker* the ball may be dropped.

(iii) **On the Putting Green:** If the ball lies on the *putting green*, the player must lift the ball and place it, without penalty, at the *nearest point of relief* that is not in a *hazard* or, if complete relief is impossible, at the nearest position to where it lay that affords maximum available relief from the condition, but not nearer the *hole* and not in a *hazard*. The *nearest point of relief* or maximum available relief may be off the *putting green*.

(iv) **On the Teeing Ground:** If the ball lies on the *teeing ground*, the player must lift the ball and drop it, without penalty, in accordance with Clause (i) above.

CASUAL WATER ON PUTTING GREEN

In both illustrations the player's ball lies on the putting green at Point 1. In illustration A his ball is in casual water, while in illustration B casual water intervenes on his line of putt. In either case, if relief is required, the player must place the ball at Point 3, the "nearest point of relief" even though it is not on the putting green. Point 2 still has interference from the casual water and Point 4, while it is still on the putting green, is further from the ball than Point 3.

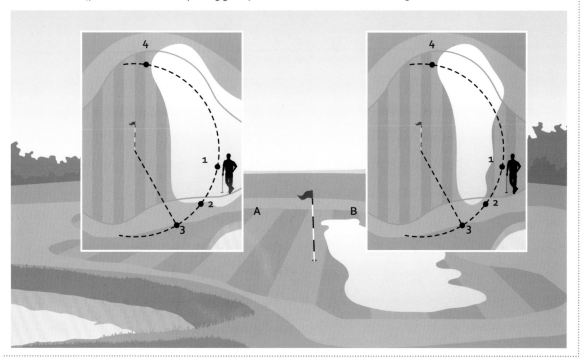

BALL CLOSE TO CASUAL WATER: LEFT-HANDED STROKE NOT REASONABLE

A right-handed player cannot choose to play left-handed in order to obtain relief from the casual water if there is no other reason to play left-handed. A left-handed stroke is not reasonable in these circumstances.

BALL CLOSE TO CASUAL WATER: LEFT-HANDED STROKE REASONABLE

1 A player who can't play a normal right-handed stroke because of a tree, may decide to play left-handed, in which case she would be standing in casual water.

DIRECTION OF PLAY

2

3 She is entitled to relief from the casual water for a left-handed stroke and having dropped the ball, she may then play right-handed or left-handed.

4

BALL IN CASUAL WATER IN BUNKER: FREE RELIEF

As the player is able to take complete relief from the casual water, if the player wishes to take free relief the ball must be dropped within one club-length of the nearest point of relief in the bunker. If complete relief is not possible, the ball must be dropped on the spot that gives the player maximum available relief in the bunker (see Rule 25-1b (ii)).

STANCE INTERFERED WITH BY BURROWING ANIMAL HOLE: BALL UNPLAYABLE BECAUSE OF OTHER CONDITION

As the ball is clearly unplayable due to the tree, the player is not entitled to free relief from a rabbit scrape because, in this situation, it is clearly impracticable for the player to make a stroke at the ball. See the Exception to Rule 25-1b.

The ball may be cleaned when lifted under Rule 25-1b.

(Ball rolling to a position where there is interference by the condition from which relief was taken – see Rule 20-2c(v))

Exception

A player may not take relief under this Rule if (a) interference by anything other than an *abnormal ground condition* makes the *stroke* clearly impracticable or (b) interference by an *abnormal ground condition* would occur only through use of a clearly unreasonable stroke or an unnecessarily abnormal *stance*, swing or direction of play.

NOTE 1

If a ball is in a *water hazard* (including a *lateral water hazard*), the player is not entitled to relief, without penalty, from interference by an *abnormal ground condition*. The player must play the ball as it lies (unless prohibited by Local Rule) or proceed under Rule 26-1.

NOTE 2

If a ball to be dropped or placed under this Rule is not immediately recoverable, another ball may be *substituted*.

25-1 c Ball in Abnormal Ground Condition Not Found

It is a question of fact whether a ball that has not been found after having been struck toward an *abnormal ground condition* is in such a condition. In order to apply this Rule, it must be known or virtually certain that the ball is in the *abnormal ground condition*. In the absence of such knowledge or certainty, the player must proceed under Rule 27-1.

If it is known or virtually certain that a ball that has not been found is in an *abnormal ground condition*, the player may take relief under this Rule. If he elects to do so, the spot where the ball last crossed the outermost limits of the *abnormal ground condition* must be determined and, for the purpose of applying this Rule, the ball is deemed to lie at this spot and the player must proceed as follows:

(i) **Through the Green:** If the ball last crossed the outermost limits of the *abnormal ground condition* at a spot *through the green*, the player may *substitute* another ball, without penalty, and take relief as prescribed in Rule 25-1b(i).

(ii) **In a Bunker:** If the ball last crossed the outermost limits of the *abnormal ground condition* at a spot in a *bunker*, the player may *substitute* another ball, without penalty, and take relief as prescribed in Rule 25-1b(ii).

(iii) **In a Water Hazard (including a Lateral Water Hazard):** If the ball last crossed the outermost limits of the *abnormal ground condition* at a spot in a *water hazard*, the player is not entitled to relief without penalty. The player must proceed under Rule 26-1.

(iv) **On the Putting Green:** If the ball last crossed the outermost limits of the *abnormal ground condition* at a spot on the *putting green*, the player may *substitute* another ball, without penalty, and take relief as prescribed in Rule 25-1b(iii).

25-2 Embedded Ball

If a player's ball is embedded in any closely-mown area *through the green*, it may be lifted, cleaned and dropped, without penalty, as near as possible to the spot where it lay but not nearer the hole. The ball when dropped must first strike a part of the *course through the green*.

NOTE 1

A ball is "embedded" when it is in its own pitch-mark and part of the ball is below the level of the ground. A ball does not necessarily have to touch the soil to be embedded (e.g. grass, *loose impediments* and the like may intervene between the ball and the soil).

EMBEDDED BALL

Grass-covered ground bordering a bunker is not part of the bunker. As the grass is not "closely mown" there is no relief for an embedded ball. The ball must be played as it lies or declared unplayable.

RELIEF FROM A WRONG PUTTING GREEN

Relief from a wrong putting green is only available if the ball lies on a wrong putting green. There is no relief for interference to stance. The player must not play a ball that lies on a wrong putting green.

NOTE 2
"Closely-mown area" means any area of the course, including paths through the rough, cut to fairway height or less.

NOTE 3
The Committee may adopt the Local Rule as provided for in Appendix I allowing a player relief, without penalty, for a ball embedded anywhere *through the green*.

25-3 Wrong Putting Green
25-3 a Interference

Interference by a *wrong putting green* occurs when a ball is on the *wrong putting green*.
Interference to a player's *stance* or the area of his intended swing is not, of itself, interference under this Rule.

25-3 b Relief

If a player's ball lies on a *wrong putting green*, he must not play the ball as it lies. He must take relief, without penalty, as follows:
The player must lift the ball and drop it within one club-length of and not nearer the *hole* than the *nearest point of relief*. The *nearest point of relief* must not be in a *hazard* or on

a *putting green*. When dropping the ball within one club-length of the *nearest point of relief*, the ball must first strike a part of the *course* at a spot that avoids interference by the *wrong putting green* and is not in a *hazard* and not on a *putting green*. The ball may be cleaned when lifted under this Rule.

PENALTY
For breach of Rule:
Match play – Loss of hole;
Stroke play – Two strokes.

RULE 25 INCIDENTS

In January 2014, Rory McIlroy was left regretting a two-stroke penalty he incurred in the third round of the Abu Dhabi Golf Championship, which eventually saw him finish one stroke behind winner Pablo Larrazábal.

It is common at Tour events for the spectator crossing points to be outlined with white paint and declared by Local Rule to be ground under repair (GUR). This is because over the duration of the tournament, these areas can become damaged by the volume of spectator traffic crossing the fairways.

Interference by an abnormal ground condition, such as GUR or casual water, occurs when a ball lies in or touches the condition or when the condition interferes with the player's stance or area of his intended swing. McIlroy's ball had come to rest within the margins of one of these spectator crossing points on the 2nd hole and he elected to take relief without penalty under Rule 25-1b.

McIlroy dropped the ball within one club-length of the nearest point of relief and not nearer the hole, and then played the ball. However, a fellow-competitor's caddie noticed that McIlroy's left foot was still in the GUR when he made the stroke.

The caddie mentioned this to McIlroy before he signed and returned his score card so that they could check it out. It is worth remembering that no alteration can be made to your score card once you have returned it to the Committee (Rule 6-6c), so this gave McIlroy the chance to discuss it with the European Tour's Chief Referee, John Paramor, before submitting his score for the third round.

Paramor said, "When he stood to the ball, his left foot was standing on or just over the line demarking the area of ground under repair which is part of the ground under repair. When taking relief you must take complete relief. That is, you cannot choose to take relief from the lie of the ball only – you must take relief from everything that is 'interference'."

Therefore, the player must take relief for the lie of the ball, the stance and the area of intended swing. By having one foot in the GUR, McIlroy technically still had interference from the GUR and by subsequently playing the ball he played from the wrong place, incurring a two-stroke penalty.

McIlroy commented, "I knew the Rule. I knew you have to take full relief. I just didn't know where my foot was."

Keegan Bradley withdrew from the 2014 BMW Championship prior to the third round, citing uneasiness about a potential Rules breach in the first round.

When playing the 18th hole, Bradley found the water hazard and had to take a penalty drop. His third shot came up short of the green and embedded in the steep grass face just above the greenside bunker.

A ball that is embedded in its own pitch-mark in the ground in any closely mown area through the green may be lifted, cleaned and dropped, without penalty, as near as possible to the spot where it lay but not nearer the hole. The ball when dropped must first strike a part of the course through the green.

Q & A

Can I get relief without penalty from a bunker that is completely covered by casual water?

No. The player may play the ball as it lies, or:

o   take relief in accordance with Rule 25-1b(ii)(a), or

o   drop the ball behind the bunker under penalty of one stroke as in Rule 25-1b(ii)(b), or

o   deem the ball unplayable and proceed in accordance with Rule 28 (see Decision 25-1b/8). However, prior to a competition commencing, a Committee can declare specific flooded bunkers as ground under repair and automatically the bunker is classified as "through the green" (see Decision 33-8/27). This permits relief without penalty to be taken outside the specified bunkers under Rule 25-1b(i).

If I step heavily around my ball, water is forced to the surface. Can I take relief for casual water?

Casual water does not exist in this situation. Casual water is water that is visible before or after the player takes his stance (see Definition of Casual Water). The player must not jump up and down or try to force the water up in order to prove the existence of casual water.

Believing the ball to be embedded, Bradley took relief under Rule 25-2 and chipped on to the green and putted out for a double bogey. After his round, Bradley had a conversation with a fan, who told the player that he had seen the ball bounce before coming to rest. If the ball had bounced, could it really have embedded in the ground? Concerned, Bradley met with the chief referee the next day to discuss the situation. They returned to the spot at the bunker and examined the area, trying to locate the pitch-mark to assist in determining the facts. After further consideration, the referee absolved Bradley of any violation.

However, Bradley remained troubled with the situation and decided to withdraw from the tournament. "I just feel withdrawing is the right thing to do to protect the field in the BMW Championship and the Tour Championship next week," Bradley said in a statement released after his withdrawal. "It's eating me alive. I didn't call my fellow-competitors for help in the first place and that bothers me. I know the referee approved the drop, but I just can't be absolutely sure it was the right spot."

Robert Rock was granted relief after his drive embedded in the soft fairway during the Open de Portugal in 2010. Rock's tee shot had pitched on the fairway, jumped forwards a foot and then rolled back into the very same pitch-mark.

For a ball to be considered embedded, it must be embedded in its own pitch-mark with part of the ball below the level of the ground. Decision 25-2/1 goes further to clarify that if a ball spins back into its own pitch-mark, it is considered to be embedded in the pitch-mark.

However, Rock and his fellow competitors did not see the ball land from the tee so were not entirely sure if the ball had landed in its own pitch-mark or that of another player. Rock called for the assistance of a referee.

The referee, Matts Lanner, had not been present when the ball landed so he asked those walking with the group if anyone had spotted the ball coming to rest. TV commentator Wayne Riley had been walking ahead of Rock's group in preparation to provide commentary for the coverage of their second shots to the green, and witnessed the ball pitch and zip back into its own pitch-mark. He was able to confirm this to Rock and the referee.

With this knowledge, Rock was able to apply Rule 25-2 since the ball was effectively embedded in its own pitch-mark. Without penalty, he lifted and dropped the ball as close to the spot where it lay but not nearer the hole. Had Rock dropped the ball and it had embedded in the soft ground conditions again, he would have been entitled to proceed under Rule 25-2 for a second time (Decision 25-2/2).

Rule 26 WATER HAZARDS (INCLUDING LATERAL WATER HAZARDS)

DEFINITIONS
All defined terms are
in *italics* and are listed in
the Definitions section –
see pages 13–23.

26-1 Relief for Ball in Water Hazard

It is a question of fact whether a ball that has not been found after having been struck toward a *water hazard* is in the *hazard*. In the absence of knowledge or virtual certainty that a ball struck toward a *water hazard*, but not found, is in the *hazard*, the player must proceed under Rule 27-1.

If a ball is found in a *water hazard* or if it is known or virtually certain that a ball that has not been found is in the *water hazard* (whether the ball lies in water or not), the player may under penalty of one stroke:

a. Proceed under the stroke and distance provision of Rule 27-1 by playing a ball as nearly as possible at the spot from which the original ball was last played (see Rule 20-5); or

b. Drop a ball behind the *water hazard*, keeping the point at which the original ball last crossed the margin of the *water hazard* directly between the *hole* and the spot on which the ball is dropped, with no limit to how far behind the *water hazard* the ball may be dropped; or

c. As additional options available only if the ball last crossed the margin of a *lateral water hazard*, drop a ball outside the *water hazard* within two club-lengths of and not nearer

Padraig Harrington and a referee discuss his options for relief after his ball entered the Swilcan Burn on the 1st hole of the Old Course during the 2010 Open Championship. The point where the ball last crossed the margin of the hazard is the key to applying Rule 26-1b or 26-1c.

KNOWN OR VIRTUALLY CERTAIN THAT BALL IS IN WATER HAZARD

The player cannot assume his ball is in the hazard. There has to be almost no doubt that it is in the hazard. If it is not known or there is doubt, the player must proceed under the lost ball Rule (see Rule 27-1).

the *hole* than (i) the point where the original ball last crossed the margin of the *water hazard* or (ii) a point on the opposite margin of the *water hazard* equidistant from the *hole*. When proceeding under this Rule, the player may lift and clean his ball or *substitute* a ball.

(Prohibited actions when ball is in a hazard – see Rule 13-4)

(Ball moving in water in a water hazard – see Rule 14-6)

26-2 Ball Played Within Water Hazard
26-2 a Ball Comes to Rest in Same or Another Water Hazard

If a ball played from within a *water hazard* comes to rest in the same or another *water hazard* after the *stroke*, the player may:

(i) under penalty of one stroke, play a ball as nearly as possible at the spot from which the last stroke from outside a *water hazard* was made (see Rule 20-5); or

BALL CROSSING MARGIN OF WATER HAZARD: OPTIONS FOR RELIEF

Under penalty of one stroke, you may play a ball from where you last played, or you may drop a ball behind the hazard on an extension of the line from the hole to the point at which the ball last crossed the margin (Point B). The point at which the ball first crossed the margin (Point A) is irrelevant.

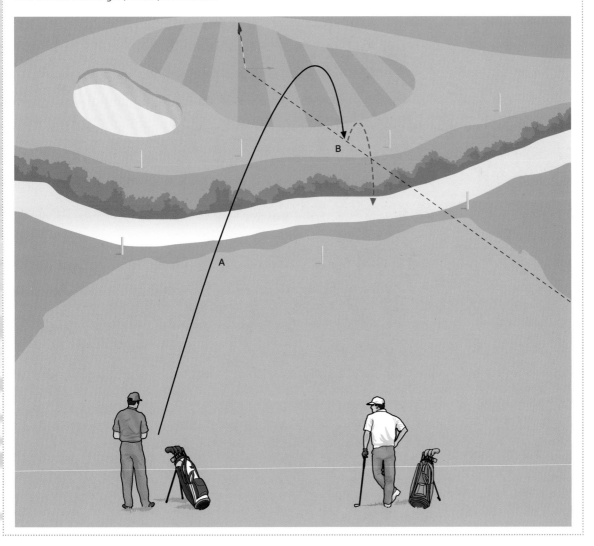

RELIEF FROM LATERAL WATER HAZARD

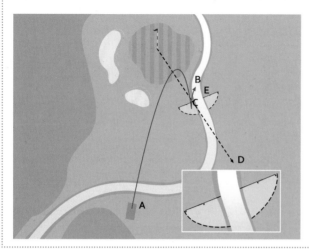

The player has played a ball from the tee (Point A) into the lateral water hazard at Point B. It last crossed the margin of the hazard at Point C and the point on the opposite margin, equidistant from the hole is Point E. He may play the ball as it lies or, under penalty of one stroke:
(i) play another ball from the tee – Rule 26-1a; (ii) drop a ball anywhere on the far side of the hazard on the dotted line from the hole through Point C, e.g. Point D – Rule 26-1b; (iii) drop a ball in the area on the near side of the hazard, which is all ground within two club-lengths of Point C – Rule 26-1c(i); or (iv) drop a ball in the area on the far side of the hazard, which is all ground within two club-lengths of Point E – Rule 26-1c(ii).

BALL PLAYED FROM WITHIN WATER HAZARD

The player's tee-shot at a par-3 hole comes to rest in a water hazard. He plays from the hazard, but fails to get his ball out. He may play the ball as it lies or, under penalty of one stroke:
(i) drop a ball at the spot from which he's just played his second stroke and play again from there; (ii) drop a ball behind the hazard, anywhere on the dotted line, and play from there; or (iii) play another ball from the tee.

(ii) proceed under Rule 26-1a, 26-1b or, if applicable, 26-1c, incurring the penalty of one stroke under that Rule. For purposes of applying Rule 26-1b or 26-1c, the reference point is the point where the original ball last crossed the margin of the *hazard* in which it lies.

NOTE

If the player proceeds under Rule 26-1a by dropping a ball in the *hazard* as near as possible to the spot from which the original ball was last played, but elects not to play the dropped ball, he may then proceed under Clause (i) above, Rule 26-1b or, if applicable, Rule 26-1c. If he does so, he incurs a total of two penalty strokes: the penalty of one stroke for proceeding under Rule 26-1a, and an additional penalty of one stroke for then proceeding under Clause (i) above, Rule 26-1b or Rule 26-1c.

Oliver Fisher plays his ball, which had stopped short of the hazard. Stakes and lines used to define the margin of or identify a lateral water hazard must be red.

26-2 bBall Lost or Unplayable Outside Hazard or Out of Bounds

If a ball played from within a *water hazard* is lost or deemed unplayable outside the *hazard* or is *out of bounds*, the player may, after taking a penalty of one stroke under Rule 27-1 or 28a, play a ball as nearly as possible at the spot in the *hazard* from which the original ball was last played (see Rule 20-5).

If the player elects not to play a ball from that spot, he may:

(i) add an additional penalty of one stroke (making a total of two *penalty strokes*) and play a ball as nearly as possible at the spot from which the last stroke from outside a *water hazard* was made (see Rule 20-5); or

(ii) proceed under Rule 26-1b or, if applicable, Rule 26-1c, adding the additional penalty of one stroke prescribed by the Rule (making a total of two *penalty strokes*) and using as the reference point the point where the original ball last crossed the margin of the *hazard* before it came to rest in the *hazard*.

NOTE 1

When proceeding under Rule 26-2b, the player is not required to drop a ball under Rule 27-1 or 28a. If he does drop a ball, he is not required to play it. He may alternatively proceed under Clause (i) or (ii) above. If he does so, he incurs a total of two penalty strokes: the penalty of one stroke under Rule 27-1 or 28a, and an additional penalty of one stroke for then proceeding under Clause (i) or (ii) above.

NOTE 2

If a ball played from within a *water hazard* is deemed unplayable outside the *hazard*, nothing in Rule 26-2b precludes the player from proceeding under Rule 28b or c.

PENALTY

For breach of Rule:
Match play – Loss of hole;
Stroke play – Two strokes.

RULE 26 INCIDENTS

Suzann Pettersen and Carlota Ciganda were drawn to play against Stacy Lewis and Lexi Thompson on the first day of the 2013 Solheim Cup at Colorado Golf Club in Denver. The format was four-ball better ball and the match was all square after 14 holes.

At the par-5 15th hole, Pettersen and Ciganda both hit their second shots into the lateral water hazard on the right-hand side of the hole. Ciganda was determined to find her ball in case it was playable, so a ball search commenced. Right before the five-minute search time expired, the ball was found in the hazard but it was not playable.

Ciganda then had to consider her options for relief. As returning to where she last played from was not attractive, a long discussion with the referee commenced as to where the ball last crossed the margin of the hazard. This was important, as Ciganda's line to the green was obscured by trees so selecting her best option for relief was imperative. However, determining where the ball last crossed into the hazard was proving difficult, as no one had actually witnessed it crossing the margin into the hazard.

After further discussion, including the involvement of team members and vice-captains, the referee decided to call for a second opinion to establish the correct point of entry. The option to drop two club-lengths on the opposite side of the hazard (Rule 26-1c) was appealing to Ciganda as the opposite side eliminated some of the challenge of the trees that she was faced with.

After consideration, the point on the opposite margin of the lateral water hazard was correctly identified and confirmed by the second referee. However, Ciganda was then given the option of dropping a ball back on a line from that point, rather than dropping it within two club-lengths. The option to drop a ball back on a line must be assessed from the original point of entry and not from the equidistant point on the opposite side of the lateral water hazard.

Ciganda dropped the ball 40 yards behind the hazard and went on to find the green with her fourth shot. She holed a 15-foot putt to save par and halve the hole with the US side.

"The point the ball last crossed the margin of the hazard was accurately established and one of the options, under Rule 26-1c, is for the player to drop her ball on the opposite margin of the hazard, equidistant from the hole," Brad Alexander, joint chief referee at the Solheim Cup, explained in the subsequent press conference. "That point was also accurately established. The Rule allows the player to drop within two club lengths of that point, on the equal and opposite margin. However, a mistake was made, and the player was allowed to drop behind that point, in line with the flagstick."

Carlota Ciganda drops her ball after getting assistance to determine the point where the original ball last crossed the margin of the lateral water hazard on the 15th hole during the 2013 Solheim Cup.

Q & A

What differentiates a water hazard from a lateral water hazard?

A water hazard is any sea, lake, pond, river, ditch, surface drainage ditch or other open water course (whether or not containing water) and anything of a similar nature – see the Definition of "water hazard". If a player's ball lies in a water hazard, he may play the ball as it lies or proceed under Rule 26-1a or b.

A lateral water hazard is a water hazard or that part of a water hazard so situated that it is not possible or is deemed by the Committee to be impracticable to drop a ball behind the water hazard in accordance with Rule 26-1b – see Definition of "lateral water hazard" – for example, if the area behind the water hazard is out of bounds or is thick with trees. If a player's ball lies in a lateral water hazard, he may, in addition to the options available when in a water hazard, proceed under Rule 26-1c. Stakes and lines defining a water hazard must be yellow. Stakes and lines defining a lateral water hazard must be red.

Rule 27 BALL LOST OR OUT OF BOUNDS; PROVISIONAL BALL

DEFINITIONS
All defined terms are
in *italics* and are listed in
the Definitions section –
see pages 13–23.

27-1 Stroke and Distance; Ball Out of Bounds; Ball Not Found Within Five Minutes

27-1 a Proceeding Under Stroke and Distance

At any time, a player may, under penalty of one stroke, play a ball as nearly as possible at the spot from which the original ball was last played (see Rule 20-5), i.e. proceed under penalty of stroke and distance.

Except as otherwise provided in the *Rules*, if a player makes a *stroke* at a ball from the spot at which the original ball was last played, he is deemed to have proceeded under penalty of stroke and distance.

27-1 b Ball Out of Bounds

If a ball is *out of bounds,* the player must play a ball, under penalty of one stroke, as nearly as possible at the spot from which the original ball was last played (see Rule 20-5).

27-1 c Ball Not Found Within Five Minutes

If a ball is *lost* as a result of not being found or identified as his by the player within five minutes after the player's *side* or his or their *caddies* have begun to search for it, the player must play a ball, under penalty of one stroke, as nearly as possible at the spot from which the original ball was last played (see Rule 20-5).

Exception

If it is known or virtually certain that the original ball, that has not been found, has been moved by an *outside agency* (Rule 18-1), is in an *obstruction* (Rule 24-3), is in an *abnormal ground condition* (Rule 25-1) or is in a *water hazard* (Rule 26-1), the player may proceed under the applicable Rule.

PENALTY
For breach of Rule 27-1:
  Match play – Loss of hole;
  Stroke play – Two strokes.

BALL NOT FOUND WITHIN FIVE MINUTES

A ball is lost as a result of not being found or identified as his by the player within five minutes after the player's side or their caddies have begun to search for it.

PLAYERS UNABLE TO IDENTIFY THEIR BALLS

If two players are unable to distinguish which ball is which, both balls are lost (see Definition of Lost Ball).

27-2 Provisional Ball
27-2 a Procedure

If a ball may be lost outside a *water hazard* or may be *out of bounds*, to save time the player may play another ball provisionally in accordance with Rule 27-1. The player must:

(i) announce to his *opponent* in match play or his *marker* or a *fellow-competitor* in stroke play that he intends to play a provisional ball; and

(ii) play the provisional ball before he or his *partner* goes forward to search for the original ball.

If a player fails to meet the above requirements prior to playing another ball, that ball is not a *provisional ball* and becomes the *ball in play* under penalty of stroke and distance (Rule 27-1); the original ball is lost.

(Order of play from teeing ground – see Rule 10-3)

NOTE

If a *provisional ball* played under Rule 27-2a might be *lost* outside a *water hazard* or *out of bounds*, the player may play another *provisional ball*. If another *provisional ball* is played, it bears the same relationship to the previous *provisional ball* as the first *provisional ball* bears to the original ball.

27-2 b When Provisional Ball Becomes Ball in Play

The player may play a *provisional ball* until he reaches the place where the original ball is likely to be. If he makes a *stroke* with the *provisional ball* from the place where the original ball is likely to be or from a point nearer the *hole* than that place, the original ball is *lost* and the *provisional ball* becomes the *ball in play* under penalty of stroke and distance (Rule 27-1).

If the original ball is *lost* outside a *water hazard* or is *out of bounds*, the *provisional ball* becomes the *ball in play*, under penalty of stroke and distance (Rule 27-1).

A ball is not "lost" merely because the player returns to the tee with the intention to play another ball before the five minutes search is up. However, if the player plays another ball, the second ball becomes the ball in play and the original ball must be abandoned if it is subsequently found.

PROVISIONAL BALL BECOMES BALL IN PLAY

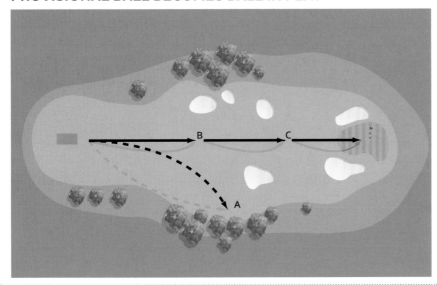

The player has played from the tee and his ball may be lost at A. He plays a provisional ball to B and then from B to C. The player decides not to look for his original ball at A and plays his provisional ball from C to the green. Consequently, the provisional ball becomes the ball in play, under penalty of stroke and distance and the original ball is by definition lost. This is because the player has played a stroke with the provisional ball from a point nearer the hole than the place where the original ball is likely to be.

Exception

If it is known or virtually certain that the original ball, that has not been found, has been moved by an *outside agency* (Rule 18-1), or is in an *obstruction* (Rule 24-3) or an *abnormal ground condition* (Rule 25-1c), the player may proceed under the applicable Rule.

27-2 c When Provisional Ball to be Abandoned

If the original ball is neither *lost* nor *out of bounds*, the player must abandon the *provisional ball* and continue playing the original ball. If it is known or virtually certain that the original ball is in a *water hazard*, the player may proceed in accordance with Rule 26-1. In either situation, if the player makes any further *strokes* at the *provisional ball*, he is playing a *wrong ball* and the provisions of Rule 15-3 apply.

NOTE

If a player plays a *provisional ball* under Rule 27-2a, the *strokes* made after this Rule has been invoked with a *provisional ball* subsequently abandoned under Rule 27-2c and penalties incurred solely by playing that ball are disregarded.

PROVISIONAL BALL

If a ball may be lost outside of a water hazard or out of bounds, to save time the player may play another ball provisionally.

The player must inform his opponent, marker or fellow-competitor that he intends to play a provisional ball.
The player's statement must specifically mention the words "provisional ball" or must make it clear that he is proceeding under Rule 27-2a. He must play it before going forward to search for the original ball.

RULE 27 INCIDENTS

During the final day's play of the 141st Open Championship at Royal Lytham & St Annes, several players lost balls due to a stiff breeze blowing. It was not surprising that a few tee shots found unwanted locations.

If a ball may be lost outside a water hazard or may be out of bounds, to save time the player may play a provisional ball (Rule 27-2a). Brandt Snedeker, John Daly, Brandon Grace and Jeev Milkha Singh all chose to play a provisional ball in the event that their original balls were not found. In all cases, the players decided that it would be to their advantage not to find the original ball.

Accordingly, each player did not search for the original ball and walked directly towards his provisional ball and played it. If a player plays a stroke with the provisional ball from a point that is nearer the hole than the place where the original ball is likely to be, this renders the original ball lost (see Definition of Lost Ball and Rule 27-2b).

The player is entitled to play such a stroke. However, in the meantime if anyone – a spectator, a fellow-competitor or an opponent - finds the original ball within five minutes and before the player makes a stroke at the provisional ball, the player must inspect the ball that has been found. If it is the player's original ball, he must continue play with it (or proceed under the unplayable ball Rule). The provisional ball must be abandoned (Rule 27-2c).

As Snedeker, Daly, Grace and Singh had all played the provisional ball from a spot nearer to the hole than where the original was likely to be, the original ball was no longer the ball in play. The provisional ball became the ball in play under penalty of stroke and distance (Rule 27-1).

Q & A

May a player, after going forward to search for his ball that was struck approximately 200 yards, return to where he last played in order to play a provisional ball?
No. If the player did so the second ball would become the ball in play and the original ball would be lost (see Rule 27-2a and Definition "Lost Ball"). He must play a provisional ball "before going forward to search" as the principle behind the provisional ball Rule is saving time.

A player hits his ball into some long grass and is unable to find it. May he drop a ball in the area where he thinks his original ball is lost?
No. The player must return to where he last played and put a ball into play under penalty of stroke and distance – see Rule 27-1.

After searching for five minutes, a player does not find his ball. He continues to search and finds and plays it. Is this permitted?
No. The ball was lost and therefore out of play when the five minute period allowed for search was up. By playing the ball, the player has played a wrong ball – see Rule 15-3.

Rule 28 BALL UNPLAYABLE

DEFINITIONS
All defined terms are
in *italics* and are listed in
the Definitions section –
see pages 13–23.

The player may deem his ball unplayable at any place on the *course*, except when the ball is in a *water hazard*. The player is the sole judge as to whether his ball is unplayable.

If the player deems his ball to be unplayable, he must, under penalty of one stroke:

a. Proceed under the stroke and distance provision of Rule 27-1 by playing a ball as nearly as possible at the spot from which the original ball was last played (see Rule 20-5); or

b. Drop a ball behind the point where the ball lay, keeping that point directly between the *hole* and the spot on which the ball is dropped, with no limit to how far behind that point the ball may be dropped; or

c. Drop a ball within two club-lengths of the spot where the ball lay, but not nearer the *hole*.

If the unplayable ball is in a *bunker*, the player may proceed under Clause a, b or c. If he elects to proceed under Clause b or c, a ball must be dropped in the *bunker*.

When proceeding under this Rule, the player may lift and clean his ball or *substitute* a ball.

PENALTY
For breach of Rule:
Match play – Loss of hole;
Stroke play – Two strokes.

BALL DEEMED UNPLAYABLE

Under option b of Rule 28 the player may go back as far as he likes but the ball must be dropped keeping the point where the ball lay directly between the hole and the spot on which the ball is dropped.

BALL UNPLAYABLE IN BUNKER: PLAYER'S OPTIONS

The player's tee-shot comes to rest in a bunker, in an unplayable position. Under penalty of one stroke he may: (a) play again from where he last played (i.e. the tee); or (b) drop a ball in the bunker behind the point where the ball lay (1), keeping that point directly between the hole and the spot on which the ball is dropped (i.e. line 1-2); or (c) drop a ball in the bunker within two club-lengths of where his ball lay (1) but not nearer the hole.

BALL UNPLAYABLE IN BUSH: PLACE FOR DROPPING

When dropping under option c of Rule 28, the ball must strike a part of the course within two club-lengths of where it lay.

RULE 28 INCIDENTS

During the first round of The Open Championship in 2012, Phil Mickelson had to employ one of the most frequently used Rules in the game of golf. Playing the 8th hole at Royal Lytham & St Annes, Mickelson struck his ball in the direction of a deep bunker on the left of the fairway with his tee shot. His ball came to rest in the bunker, leaving him with a difficult shot over the steep bunker face.

Due to the angle of the shot, the ball failed to clear the long grass at the top of the bunker. After a short ball search to locate the ball, it was found buried deep in the rough surrounding the edge of the bunker. Mickelson decided to proceed under the unplayable ball Rule.

Under this Rule, the player has three options for relief, each incurring a penalty of one stroke. The player can choose to proceed under the stroke and distance option by playing a ball as nearly as possible at the spot from which the original was last played from (Rule 28a). In Mickelson's case, this would have involved him dropping the ball back in the bunker and attempting the same shot again.

Alternatively, Mickelson could have dropped a ball within two club-lengths of where the ball lay but no nearer the hole (Rule 28c). For Mickelson, this option would see him drop the ball into thick long grass, potentially leaving him with a similar difficult lie in the rough.

Instead, Mickelson decided to proceed under Rule 28b. This option permits the player to drop a ball behind the point where it lay, keeping that point between the hole and the spot on which the ball is dropped, with no limit to how far back the ball may be dropped. This decision afforded Mickelson the best outcome and allowed him to drop the ball behind the bunker and on to the fairway under penalty of one stroke.

Phil Mickelson seeks the help of a referee to determine his options for relief after declaring his ball unplayable at the 2012 Open Championship.

Q & A

Where can a player deem his ball unplayable?

A player can deem his ball unplayable anywhere on the course except when the ball is in a water hazard. The player is the sole judge as to whether his ball is unplayable.

If I choose to take relief under Rule 28c – that is, drop a ball within two club-lengths but no nearer the hole, where do I measure the two club-lengths from?

The area in which to drop a ball under Rule 28c must be measured from where the ball lies, not from the outside edge of the perceived unplayable condition.

Rule 29 THREESOMES AND FOURSOMES

DEFINITIONS
All defined terms are in *italics* and are listed in the Definitions section – see pages 13–23.

29-1 General

In a *threesome* or a *foursome*, during any *stipulated round* the *partners* must play alternately from the *teeing grounds* and alternately during the play of each hole. *Penalty strokes* do not affect the order of play.

29-2 Match Play

If a player plays when his *partner* should have played, his *side* loses the hole.

29-3 Stroke Play

If the *partners* make a *stroke* or *strokes* in incorrect order, such *stroke* or *strokes* are cancelled and the side incurs a penalty of two strokes. The *side* must correct the error by playing a ball in correct order as nearly as possible at the spot from which it first played in incorrect order (see Rule 20-5). If the *side* makes a *stroke* on the next *teeing ground* without first correcting the error or, in the case of the last hole of the round, leaves the *putting green* without declaring its intention to correct the error, the side is disqualified.

FOURSOMES: ORDER OF PLAY WHEN A PARTNER DRIVES OUT OF BOUNDS

In foursomes, if one partner hits a ball out of bounds from the white tee, the other partner must play the side's third stroke from the same tee.

FOURSOMES: WHICH PARTNER DROPS THE BALL

See Rule 20-2a, which requires a ball to be dropped by the player himself.

If the ball is to be dropped under an applicable Rule the partner whose turn it is to play must drop the ball.

Q & A

Who plays the provisional ball in a foursome competition?

If there is doubt whether the original ball is out of bounds or lost and a provisional ball is to be played, the provisional ball must be played by the partner – that is, not by the player who played the original ball.

For example, Jane and John are playing in a mixed foursome competition. John hits his tee shot and there is doubt as to whether the ball is in or out of bounds, so they decide to play a provisional ball to save time. The provisional ball must be played by the partner. Therefore, Jane would play the provisional ball from the same teeing ground that John played from.

FOURSOMES: ORDER OF PLAY IN 36-HOLE COMPETITION

In a 36-hole competition when starting play of the second 18 holes, the order of play may be changed, provided there is no condition of competition to the contrary.

RULE 29 INCIDENTS

The practice putting green at the Old Course in St Andrews lies just off the course and only a few steps from the 1st tee. Paired together on the second day for the morning foursomes of the 1975 Walker Cup Match, the US side of veteran William C. Campbell and newcomer John Grace reported to the tee a little ahead of time. They had already decided that Grace would drive at the odd-numbered holes, so Campbell decided to use the extra time before the match began to walk to the practice green and hit a few putts.

As the visiting team, Campbell and Grace had the honour. The wind was blowing from the west off St Andrews Bay, which carried the announcement of the match's beginning beyond Campbell's earshot.

As the breeze momentarily died, Campbell heard "the click" of Grace's drive just before striking a practice putt, and he was unable to interrupt his stroke. He had practised during the play of the hole. Instantly and instinctively recognising his breach, Campbell walked on to the fairway and reported to the referee that the US had lost the 1st hole (Rule 7-2 and Rule 29).

The referee for the match accepted Campbell's report but made no immediate announcement to the other players. Because play of the hole had ended with the breach of Rule 7-2, Campbell was free to play his side's second from where Grace's good drive lay to the green, as simply more practice.

Walking across the Swilcan Burn, Campbell told Grace what had taken place. "He was incredulous, to say the least," Campbell recalls.

The Americans lost the 1st hole and eventually lost the match to Mark James and Richard Eyles.

Rule 30

30

DEFINITIONS

All defined terms are in *italics* and are listed in the Definitions section – see pages 13–23.

THREE-BALL, BEST-BALL AND FOUR-BALL MATCH PLAY

30-1 General

The Rules of Golf, so far as they are not at variance with the following specific Rules, apply to *three-ball*, *best-ball* and *four-ball* matches.

30-2 Three-Ball Match Play
30-2 a Ball at Rest Moved or Purposely Touched by an Opponent

If an *opponent* incurs a penalty stroke under Rule 18-3b, that penalty is incurred only in the match with the player whose ball was touched or moved. No penalty is incurred in his match with the other player.

30-2 b Ball Deflected or Stopped by an Opponent Accidentally

If a player's ball is accidentally deflected or stopped by an *opponent*, his *caddie* or *equipment*, there is no penalty. In his match with that *opponent* the player may, before another *stroke* is made by either *side*, cancel the *stroke* and play a ball, without penalty, as nearly as possible at the spot from which the original ball was last played (see Rule 20-5) or he may play the ball as it lies. In his match with the other *opponent*, the ball must be played as it lies.

Exception

Ball striking person attending or holding up *flagstick* or anything carried by him – see Rule 17-3b.

(Ball purposely deflected or stopped by opponent – see Rule 1-2)

30-3 Best-Ball and Four-Ball Match Play
30-3 a Representation of Side

A *side* may be represented by one *partner* for all or any part of a match; all *partners* need not be present. An absent *partner* may join a match between holes, but not during play of a hole.

30-3 b Order of Play

Balls belonging to the same *side* may be played in the order the *side* considers best.

30-3 c Wrong Ball

If a player incurs the loss of hole penalty under Rule 15-3a for making a *stroke* at a *wrong ball*, he is disqualified for that hole, but his *partner* incurs no penalty even if the *wrong ball* belongs to him. If the *wrong ball* belongs to another player, its owner must place a ball on the spot from which the *wrong ball* was first played.

(Placing and Replacing – see Rule 20-3)

30-3 d Penalty to Side

A *side* is penalised for a breach of any of the following by any *partner*:

○ **Rule 4** Clubs
○ **Rule 6-4** Caddie
○ Any Local Rule or Condition of Competition for which the penalty is an adjustment to the state of the match.

30-3 e Disqualification of Side

(i) A *side* is disqualified if any *partner* incurs a penalty of disqualification under any of the following:

- **Rule 1-3** Agreement to Waive Rules
- **Rule 4** Clubs
- **Rule 5-1 or 5-2** The Ball
- **Rule 6-2a** Handicap
- **Rule 6-4** Caddie
- **Rule 6-7** Undue Delay; Slow Play
- **Rule 11-1** Teeing
- **Rule 14-3** Artificial Devices, Unusual Equipment and Abnormal Use of Equipment
- **Rule 33-7** Disqualification Penalty Imposed by Committee

(ii) A *side* is disqualified if all *partners* incur a penalty of disqualification under any of the following:

- **Rule 6-3** Time of Starting and Groups
- **Rule 6-8** Discontinuance of Play

(iii) In all other cases where a breach of a *Rule* would result in disqualification, the player is disqualified for that hole only.

30-3 f Effect of Other Penalties

If a player's breach of a *Rule* assists his *partner's* play or adversely affects an *opponent's* play, the partner incurs the applicable penalty in addition to any penalty incurred by the player.

In all other cases where a player incurs a penalty for breach of a *Rule*, the penalty does not apply to his *partner*. Where the penalty is stated to be loss of hole, the effect is to disqualify the player for that hole.

FOUR-BALL MATCH PLAY: BREACH OF RULE BY ONE PARTNER

The removal of a loose impediment from the bunker would disqualify the player from the hole. Provided the breach does not assist the partner's play, the partner is not penalised – see Rule 30-3f.

THREE-BALL MATCH PLAY

FOUR-BALL: ONE PLAYER MAY REPRESENT SIDE

A "John, my ball has struck your bag. What do I do now?"
B "In your match with me you may either play the ball as it lies or cancel that stroke and replay it. In your match with Jim you must play your original ball as it lies."
A "That means I can have two balls in play at the same time at this hole."
B "That's right, one in your match against me and one in your match against Jim."

In four-ball match play, a partner may represent the side for some or all of the match. The absent partner may join in the match at the conclusion of a hole.

Ian Poulter confers with his partner, Rory McIlroy, at the 2014 Ryder Cup. Under Rule 30-3b, in match play it is up to each side to decide in which order they play.

Q & A

In a four-ball match, the player with the lowest handicap is unable to play. Should the absent partner be disregarded in determining the handicap allowances?
No. A side may be represented by one partner for all or any part of the match. In determining the handicap allowances, the handicaps of the three players should be reduced by the handicap of the absent player.

Rule 30 Incidents

During one of the 2006 Ryder Cup four-ball matches, the American duo Tiger Woods and Jim Furyk were up against Darren Clarke and Lee Westwood, for the European team. While playing the 7th hole at The K Club, Woods hit his second shot into the water behind the green and was not planning to continue the play of the hole, as permitted in match play. Of the remaining three balls, Clarke was farthest away from the hole but Jim Furyk wanted to play first. Although Woods was not going to complete the hole, his ball lying in the water was obviously the farthest away from the hole and, as Rule 30-3b provides that a side may play in the order it considers best, it was Tiger's "honour" and, therefore, Furyk was entitled to play first.

The American duo raised the question of whether Woods had to drop a ball first as he clearly could not play the one in the water. However, the referee with the match confirmed that the relevant point for determining the order of play is the spot where the ball lies in the water hazard, not where it might be dropped, so dropping was not necessary (see the Note to Rule 10-1b).

Rule 31 FOUR-BALL STROKE PLAY

DEFINITIONS
All defined terms are in *italics* and are listed in the Definitions section – see pages 13–23.

31-1 General
The Rules of Golf, so far as they are not at variance with the following specific Rules, apply to *four-ball* stroke play.

31-2 Representation of Side
A *side* may be represented by either *partner* for all or any part of a *stipulated round*; both *partners* need not be present. An absent *competitor* may join his *partner* between holes, but not during play of a hole.

31-3 Scoring
The *marker* is required to record for each hole only the gross score of whichever *partner's* score is to count. The gross scores to count must be individually identifiable; otherwise, the *side* is disqualified. Only one of the *partners* need be responsible for complying with Rule 6-6b. (Wrong score – see Rule 31-7a)

31-4 Order of Play
Balls belonging to the same *side* may be played in the order the *side* considers best.

31-5 Wrong Ball
If a *competitor* is in breach of Rule 15-3b for making a *stroke* at a *wrong ball*, he incurs a penalty

of two strokes and must correct his mistake by playing the correct ball or by proceeding under the *Rules*. His *partner* incurs no penalty, even if the *wrong ball* belongs to him.

If the *wrong ball* belongs to another *competitor*, its owner must place a ball on the spot from which the *wrong ball* was first played.

(Placing and Replacing – see Rule 20-3)

FOUR-BALL STROKE PLAY

Date __3RD APRIL 2015__

Competition __SPRING OPEN FOUR-BALL__

PLAYER A __J. SUTHERLAND__ Handicap __16__ Strokes __12__

PLAYER B __W.B. TAYLOR__ Handicap __12__ Strokes __9__

Hole	Length Yards	Par	Stroke Index	Gross Score A	Gross Score B	Net Score A	Net Score B	Won X Lost – Half O	Mar. Score
1	437	4	4		4		3		
2	320	4	14		4		4		
3	162	3	18		4		4		
4	504	5	7	6		5			
5	181	3	16	4		4			
6	443	4	2	5			4		
7	390	4	8	5			4		
8	346	4	12	5			4		
9	340	4	10	4			3		
Out	3123	35					35		

Hole	Length Yards	Par	Stroke Index	Gross Score A	Gross Score B	Net Score A	Net Score B	Won X Lost – Half O	Mar. Score
10	425	4	3	5			4		
11	141	3	17	3		3			
12	476	5	9	6			5		
13	211	3	11	4			4		
14	437	4	5	5			4		
15	460	4	1	5			4		
16	176	3	15	4		4			
17	340	4	13	4			4		
18	435	4	6	6		5			
In	3101	34					37		
Out	3123	35					35		
T'tl	6224	69					72		
Handicap									
Net Score									

Player's Signature __J. Sutherland__

Marker's Signature __R. J. Parker__

Partners' scores to be individually identified

1 The lower score of the *partners* is the score for the hole (Rule 31).

2 Only one of the *partners* need be responsible for complying with Rule 6-6b, i.e. recording scores, checking scores, countersigning and returning the card (Rule 31-3).

3 The *competitor* is solely responsible for the correctness of the gross score recorded. Although there is no objection to the *competitor* (or his *marker*) entering the net score, it is the *Committee's* responsibility to record the better-ball score for each hole, to add up the scores and to apply the handicaps recorded on the card (Rule 33-5). Thus there is no penalty for an error by the *competitor* (or his *marker*) for recording an incorrect net score.

4 Scores of the two *partners* must be kept in separate columns otherwise it is impossible for the *Committee* to apply the correct handicap. If the scores of both *partners*, having different handicaps, are recorded in the same column, the *Committee* has no alternative but to disqualify both *partners* (Rules 31-7 and 6-6 apply).

5 The *Committee* is responsible for laying down the conditions under which a competition is to be played (Rule 33-1), including the method of handicapping. In the above illustration the *Committee* laid down that ¾ handicaps would apply.

31-6 Penalty to Side

A *side* is penalised for a breach of any of the following by any *partner*:

- **Rule 4** Clubs
- **Rule 6-4** Caddie
- Any Local Rule or Condition of Competition for which there is a maximum penalty per round.

31-7 Disqualification Penalties
31-7 a Breach by One Partner

A *side* is disqualified from the competition if either *partner* incurs a penalty of disqualification under any of the following:

- **Rule 1-3** Agreement to Waive Rules
- **Rule 3-4** Refusal to Comply with a Rule
- **Rule 4** Clubs
- **Rule 5-1 or 5-2** The Ball
- **Rule 6-2b** Handicap
- **Rule 6-4** Caddie
- **Rule 6-6b** Signing and Returning Score Card
- **Rule 6-6d** Wrong Score for Hole
- **Rule 6-7** Undue Delay; Slow Play
- **Rule 7-1** Practice Before or Between Rounds
- **Rule 10-2c** Sides Agree to Play Out of Turn
- **Rule 11-1** Teeing
- **Rule 14-3** Artificial Devices, Unusual Equipment and Abnormal Use of Equipment
- **Rule 22-1** Ball Assisting Play
- **Rule 31-3** Gross Scores to Count Not Individually Identifiable
- **Rule 33-7** Disqualification Penalty Imposed by Committee

31-7 b Breach by Both Partners

A *side* is disqualified from the competition:

(i) if each *partner* incurs a penalty of disqualification for a breach of Rule 6-3 (Time of Starting and Groups) or Rule 6-8 (Discontinuance of Play), or

(ii) if, at the same hole, each *partner* is in breach of a *Rule* the penalty for which is disqualification from the competition or for a hole.

31-7 c For the Hole Only

In all other cases where a breach of a *Rule* would result in disqualification, the competitor is disqualified only for the hole at which the breach occurred.

31-8 Effect of Other Penalties

If a *competitor's* breach of a *Rule* assists his *partner's* play, the *partner* incurs the applicable penalty in addition to any penalty incurred by the *competitor*.

In all other cases where a *competitor* incurs a penalty for breach of a *Rule*, the penalty does not apply to his *partner*.

Q & A

Do both players have to sign the score card in a four-ball stroke play competition?
No. Only one of the partners need be responsible for complying with Rule 6-6b.

Rule 32

DEFINITIONS
All defined terms are
in *italics* and are listed in
the Definitions section –
see pages 13–23.

BOGEY, PAR AND STABLEFORD COMPETITIONS

32-1 Conditions

Bogey, par and Stableford competitions are forms of stroke play in which play is against a fixed score at each hole. The *Rules* for stroke play, so far as they are not at variance with the following specific Rules, apply.

In handicap bogey, par and Stableford competitions, the *competitor* with the lowest net score at a hole takes the *honour* at the next *teeing ground*.

32-1 a Bogey and Par Competitions

The scoring for bogey and par competitions is made as in match play.

Any hole for which a *competitor* makes no return is regarded as a loss. The winner is the *competitor* who is most successful in the aggregate of holes.

The *marker* is responsible for marking only the gross number of *strokes* for each hole where the *competitor* makes a net score equal to or less than the fixed score.

NOTE 1

The *competitor's* score is adjusted by deducting a hole or holes under the applicable Rule when a penalty other than disqualification is incurred under any of the following:

- Rule 4 Clubs
- Rule 6-4 Caddie
- Any Local Rule or Condition of Competition for which there is a maximum penalty per round.

The *competitor* is responsible for reporting the facts regarding such a breach to the *Committee* before he returns his score card so that the *Committee* may apply the penalty. If the *competitor* fails to report his breach to the *Committee*, he is disqualified.

NOTE 2

If the competitor is in breach of Rule 6-3a (Time of Starting) but arrives at his starting point, ready to play, within five minutes after his starting time, or is in breach of Rule 6-7 (Undue Delay; Slow Play), the *Committee* will deduct one hole from the aggregate of holes. For a repeated offence under Rule 6-7, see Rule 32-2a.

NOTE 3

If the competitor incurs the additional two-stroke penalty provided in the Exception to Rule 6-6d, that additional penalty is applied by deducting one hole from the aggregate of holes scored for the round. The penalty the competitor failed to include in his score is applied to the hole where the breach occurred. However, neither penalty applies when a breach of Rule 6-6d does not affect the result of the hole.

32-1 b Stableford Competitions

The scoring in Stableford competitions is made by points awarded in relation to a fixed score at each hole as follows:

Hole Played In	Points
More than one over fixed score or no score returned	0

One over fixed score	1
Fixed score	2
One under fixed score	3
Two under fixed score	4
Three under fixed score	5
Four under fixed score	6

The winner is the *competitor* who scores the highest number of points.

The *marker* is responsible for marking only the gross number of *strokes* at each hole where the *competitor's* net score earns one or more points.

NOTE 1

If a *competitor* is in breach of a *Rule* for which there is a maximum penalty per round, he must report the facts to the *Committee* before returning his score card; if he fails to do so, he is disqualified. The *Committee* will, from the total points scored for the round, deduct two points for each hole at which any breach occurred, with a maximum deduction per round of four points for each Rule breached.

NOTE 2

If the *competitor* is in breach of Rule 6-3a (Time of Starting) but arrives at his starting point, ready to play, within five minutes after his starting time, or is in breach of Rule 6-7 (Undue Delay; Slow Play), the *Committee* will deduct two points from the total points scored for the round. For a repeated offence under Rule 6-7, see Rule 32-2a.

NOTE 3

If the competitor incurs the additional two-stroke penalty provided in the Exception to Rule 6-6d, that additional penalty is applied by deducting two points from the total points scored for the round. The penalty the competitor failed to include in his score is applied to the hole where the breach occurred. However, neither penalty applies when a breach of Rule 6-6d does not affect the points scored on the hole.

NOTE 4

For the purpose of preventing slow play, the *Committee* may, in the conditions of a competition (Rule 33-1), establish pace of play guidelines, including maximum periods of time allowed to complete a *stipulated round*, a hole or a *stroke*.

The *Committee* may, in such a condition, modify the penalty for a breach of this Rule as follows:

First offence – Deduction of one point from the total points scored for the round;

Second offence – Deduction of a further two points from the total points scored for the round;

For subsequent offence – Disqualification.

32-2 Disqualification Penalties
32-2 a From the Competition

A *competitor* is disqualified from the competition if he incurs a penalty of disqualification under any of the following:

o **Rule 1-3** Agreement to Waive Rules
o **Rule 3-4** Refusal to Comply with a Rule
o **Rule 4** Clubs

- ○ **Rule 5-1 or 5-2** The Ball
- ○ **Rule 6-2b** Handicap
- ○ **Rule 6-3** Time of Starting and Groups
- ○ **Rule 6-4** Caddie
- ○ **Rule 6-6b** Signing and Returning Score Card
- ○ **Rule 6-6d** Wrong Score for Hole, i.e. when the recorded score is lower than actually taken, except that no penalty is incurred when a breach of this Rule does not affect the result of the hole
- ○ **Rule 6-7** Undue Delay; Slow Play
- ○ **Rule 6-8** Discontinuance of Play
- ○ **Rule 7-1** Practice Before or Between Rounds
- ○ **Rule 10-2c** Playing Out of Turn
- ○ **Rule 11-1** Teeing
- ○ **Rule 14-3** Artificial Devices, Unusual Equipment and Abnormal Use of Equipment
- ○ **Rule 22-1** Ball Assisting Play
- ○ **Rule 33-7** Disqualification Penalty Imposed by Committee

32-2 bFor a Hole

In all other cases where a breach of a *Rule* would result in disqualification, the competitor is disqualified only for the hole at which the breach occurred.

RULE 32 INCIDENTS

The Stableford format was invented in 1931 by Dr. Frank Barney Gorton Stableford. The now popular points scoring system was first played at Wallasey & Royal Liverpool Golf Clubs in 1932. A scratch golfer himself, Stableford's points system was developed through a desire to provide more fun for golfers playing in tough conditions on links courses in stroke play competitions. He wanted to avoid the situation in which a player tore the score card up after one bad score for a hole near the beginning of his round.

The result was the Stableford scoring system and the first competition held on 16 May 1932 was an instant success.

Q & A

In a handicap Stableford competition, how is the honour determined?
At the 1st hole, the honour is determined by the order of the draw. Thereafter, the honour is determined according to the lowest net score at each individual hole.

Rule 33 THE COMMITTEE

DEFINITIONS
All defined terms are in *italics* and are listed in the Definitions section – see pages 13–23.

33-1 Conditions; Waiving Rule

The *Committee* must establish the conditions under which a competition is to be played.

The *Committee* has no power to waive a Rule of Golf.

The number of holes of a *stipulated round* must not be reduced once play has commenced for that round.

Certain specific *Rules* governing stroke play are so substantially different from those governing match play that combining the two forms of play is not practicable and is not permitted. The result of a match played in these circumstances is null and void and, in the stroke play competition, the *competitors* are disqualified.

In stroke play, the *Committee* may limit a referee's duties.

33-2 The Course
33-2 a Defining Bounds and Margins

The *Committee* must define accurately:

(i)   the *course* and *out of bounds*,
(ii) the margins of *water hazards* and *lateral water hazards*,
(iii) *ground under repair*, and
(iv) *obstructions* and integral parts of the *course*.

33-2 b New Holes

New *holes* should be made on the day on which a stroke play competition begins and at such other times as the *Committee* considers necessary, provided all *competitors* in a single round play with each *hole* cut in the same position.

Exception

When it is impossible for a damaged *hole* to be repaired so that it conforms with the Definition, the *Committee* may make a new *hole* in a nearby similar position.

NOTE

Where a single round is to be played on more than one day, the *Committee* may provide, in the conditions of a competition (Rule 33-1), that the *holes* and *teeing grounds* may be differently situated on each day of the competition, provided that, on any one day, all *competitors* play with each *hole* and each *teeing ground* in the same position.

If the course is not in a playable condition, the Committee may have to temporarily suspend play. In stroke play only, if further play becomes impossible, the Committee may have to declare play null and void.

33-2 c Practice Ground

Where there is no practice ground available outside the area of a competition *course*, the *Committee* should establish the area on which players may practise on any day of a competition, if it is practicable to do so. On any day of a stroke play competition, the *Committee* should not normally permit practice on or to a *putting green* or from a *hazard* of the competition *course*.

33-2 d Course Unplayable

If the *Committee* or its authorised representative considers that for any reason the *course* is not in a playable condition or that there are circumstances that render the proper playing of the game impossible, it may, in match play or stroke play, order a temporary suspension of play or, in stroke play, declare play null and void and cancel all scores for the round in question. When a round is cancelled, all penalties incurred in that round are cancelled. (Procedure in discontinuing and resuming play – see Rule 6-8)

33-3 Times of Starting and Groups

The *Committee* must establish the times of starting and, in stroke play, arrange the groups in which *competitors* must play.

When a match play competition is played over an extended period, the *Committee* establishes the limit of time within which each round must be completed. When players are allowed to arrange the date of their match within these limits, the *Committee* should announce that the match must be played at a stated time on the last day of the period, unless the players agree to a prior date.

33-4 Handicap Stroke Table

The *Committee* must publish a table indicating the order of holes at which handicap strokes are to be given or received.

33-5 Score Card

In stroke play, the *Committee* must provide each *competitor* with a score card containing the date and the *competitor's* name or, in *foursome* or *four-ball* stroke play, the *competitors'* names.

In stroke play, the *Committee* is responsible for the addition of scores and application of the handicap recorded on the score card.

In *four-ball* stroke play, the *Committee* is responsible for recording the better-ball score for each hole and in the process applying the handicaps recorded on the score card, and adding the better-ball scores.

In bogey, par and Stableford competitions, the *Committee* is responsible for applying the handicap recorded on the score card and determining the result of each hole and the overall result or points total.

NOTE

The *Committee* may request that each *competitor* records the date and his name on his score card.

33-6 Decision of Ties

The *Committee* must announce the manner, day and time for the decision of a halved match or of a tie, whether played on level terms or under handicap.

A halved match must not be decided by stroke play. A tie in stroke play must not be decided by a match.

33-7 Disqualification Penalty; Committee Discretion

A penalty of disqualification may in exceptional individual cases be waived, modified or imposed if the *Committee* considers such action warranted.

Any penalty less than disqualification must not be waived or modified.

If a *Committee* considers that a player is guilty of a serious breach of etiquette, it may impose a penalty of disqualification under this Rule.

33-8 Local Rules
33-8 a Policy

The *Committee* may establish Local Rules for local abnormal conditions if they are consistent with the policy set forth in Appendix I.

33-8 b Waiving or Modifying a Rule

A Rule of Golf must not be waived by a Local Rule. However, if a *Committee* considers that local abnormal conditions interfere with the proper playing of the game to the extent that it is necessary to make a Local Rule that modifies the Rules of Golf, the Local Rule must be authorised by the *R&A*.

Q & A

Can a player be disqualified for an omission or error in adding his score or Stableford points on his score card?

A competitor is responsible only for the correctness of the score recorded for each hole (Rule 6-6d) and the Committee is responsible for the addition of scores or points (Rule 33-5). If a total recorded by a competitor is incorrect, it is the responsibility of the Committee to correct the error, without penalty to the competitor.

May a junior compete in adult club competitions and be eligible for prizes?

It is the responsibility of the Committee in charge of the competition to establish the conditions under which the competition is played (Rule 33-1). For example, who is eligible to play, handicap restrictions, age, gender, format, and so on. Therefore, it is for the Committee to decide whether juniors are eligible to enter and win any prizes in certain competitions.

Can I use a motorised cart?

Unless the use of a motorised cart is prohibited by the Committee in the conditions of competition (Rule 33-1), a player may use such equipment during a competition.

It is a policy of The R&A to encourage golfers with physical difficulties to play the game if at all possible. However, it is important that Clubs and Committees consider the issues surrounding the use of golf carts and any relevant legislation, as well as health and safety issues, weather and ground conditions. They should also decide whether the layout of the course dictates that the use of carts is impracticable.

If a Club or Committee does decide to permit the use of golf carts in competition, they may wish to consider putting restrictions on their use: for example, that golf carts would be permitted only for competitors with medical certificates or for competitors over a certain age who would otherwise be unable to participate due to physical limitations as a result of their age.

It is a matter for individual Clubs and Committees to decide and to be separately (continues on page 166)

RULE 33 INCIDENTS

Suspending play or cancelling rounds is one of the most difficult decisions a Committee has to make. The proper action depends on the circumstances in each case and must be left to the judgement of the Committee. If the Committee considers that for any reason the course is not in a playable condition or that there are circumstances that render the proper playing of the game impossible, it may order a temporary suspension of play or, in stroke play, declare play null and void and cancel all scores for the round in question (Rule 33-2d).

Severe winds forced play to be abandoned for the third straight day at the PGA Tour's season-opening Tournament of Champions in Hawaii in 2013. After play had finally got started on the Friday, it was soon suspended, leaving organisers hoping for a Saturday resumption. But with winds gusting up to 40 m.p.h. and balls moving on the greens, play was not possible. Just over an hour of golf was possible on Sunday before organisers called a halt and declared all scores up to that point null and void. Eventually, 36 holes were completed after the traditional weekend on Monday and a further

18 on Tuesday to get a 54-hole event played.

Players faced a similar situation at the 2012 Women's British Open at Royal Liverpool Golf Club. The second round scores were cancelled due to 60 m.p.h. winds when the organisers realised that it would have been unfair on those who had started not to cancel the round. Due to the exceptional circumstances and in an attempt to finish the tournament on Sunday as planned, the organisers decided to reduce the number of players who would make the cut so that the final two rounds could be played on the same day before darkness fell.

Storms had been forecast to delay the 2015 Honda Classic, but the last two days of the event at the PGA National in Florida saw weather that no one had anticipated. The second round was full of stops and starts, with a waterlogged course that needed time to drain. With four hours' worth of delays and a 90 per cent chance of storms on the Saturday, it looked like a Sunday finish was in jeopardy.

When it arrived, the predicted bad weather turned out to be more than an average thunderstorm. The course was completely waterlogged, palm trees swayed and a score-

board was blown into a nearby lake, from which it had to be retrieved.

With a Sunday finish out of the question, play continued into the Monday, which saw Padraig Harrington beat American rookie Daniel Berger in a play-off to win the rain-delayed event.

Situated on the shore of Lake Michigan, Whistling Straits is renowned for its bunkers. With reportedly over 1,200 on the course, the bunkers will be remembered for costing Dustin Johnson the chance of a play-off spot for the 2010 US PGA Championship.

Although many of the bunkers were positioned outside the gallery ropes, the Local Rules for the US PGA Championship clarified that all areas of the course that were designed and built as sand bunkers were to be played as bunkers. Consequently, if a ball lay in a bunker, the prohibited actions prescribed in Rule 13-4 applied. This was despite the fact that the bunkers outside the ropes were undoubtedly going to contain footprints and irregularities due to the huge volume of golf fans passing through them. The Local Rule clarified that there would be no free relief available from these irregularities in the bunker.

Due to the unique nature of the bunkers, the PGA Rules Committee was keen to highlight this Local Rule to ensure that all players were aware of the status of the bunkers. It was the first Local Rule listed on the Rules sheet, and copies were posted in prominent areas in and around the clubhouse as well as the starter handing a copy to each player on the 1st tee for each day of the Championship.

It was therefore very unfortunate that Dustin Johnson did not recognise that his pushed tee-shot on the 72nd hole had landed in one of these bunkers. By grounding his club in the sand, Johnson breached Rule 13-4b and incurred a two-stroke penalty, missing the chance of a play-off by one stroke.

Bad weather can lead to suspensions of play or even the need to cancel a round. The proper action depends on the circumstances and must be left to the judgement of the Committee.

After finishing their round, Dustin Johnson speaks with Co-chairman of the PGA of America Rules of Golf Committee, David Price, on the 18th green as Nick Watney looks on. Johnson was penalised after he grounded his club in a bunker on the 72nd hole. The sand in which his ball lay was a bunker, as had been clarified in a Local Rule.

(continued from page 163) legal position. It would be sensible for Clubs to ensure that they are aware of the relevant disability discrimination issues and of any guidance given by the Government or related bodies.

If a Club permits the use of golf carts, it would be prudent to ensure that appropriate insurance cover is in operation in the event of any accident or personal injury occurring as a result of their use.

Is the player responsible for completing the score card with the competition details, date, and so on?

It is the responsibility of the Committee to issue each competitor with a score card containing his name and the date of the competition (Rule 33-5). A Committee may ask the competitors to complete this information in order to assist in the administration of the event, but it cannot require players to do so. Ultimately it is the Committee's responsibility, and a player cannot be penalised for failing to do so.

Is it possible to play in a match play and stroke play competition during the same stipulated round?

No. Certain specific Rules governing stroke play are so substantially different from those governing match play that combining the two formats is not practicable and is prohibited by the Rules. The result of a match played in these circumstances is null and void and in the stroke play competition, the competitors are disqualified.

Rule 34 DISPUTES AND DECISIONS

DEFINITIONS
All defined terms are in *italics* and are listed in the Definitions section – see pages 13–23.

34-1 Claims and Penalties
34-1 a Match Play

If a claim is lodged with the *Committee* under Rule 2-5, a decision should be given as soon as possible so that the state of the match may, if necessary, be adjusted. If a claim is not made in accordance with Rule 2-5, it must not be considered by the *Committee*.

There is no time limit on applying the disqualification penalty for a breach of Rule 1-3.

34-1 b Stroke Play

In stroke play, a penalty must not be rescinded, modified or imposed after the competition has closed. A competition is closed when the result has been officially announced or, in stroke play qualifying followed by match play, when the player has teed off in his first match.

Exceptions

A penalty of disqualification must be imposed after the competition has closed if a *competitor*:

(i)   was in breach of Rule 1-3 (Agreement to Waive Rules); or

(ii) returned a score card on which he had recorded a handicap that, before the competition closed, he knew was higher than that to which he was entitled, and this affected the number of strokes received (Rule 6-2b); or

(iii) returned a score for any hole lower than actually taken (Rule 6-6d) for any reason other than failure to include one or more *penalty strokes* that, before the competition closed, he did not know he had incurred; or

When the Committee in charge of a competition appoints a referee, the referee's decision is final.

Q & A

What are the Rules for Greensomes and Texas Scrambles?

These are not recognised forms of play and thus are not covered by the Rules of Golf. Therefore, it is a matter for the Committee in charge of the competition to decide upon any matters that may arise and its decision shall be final (Rule 34-3).

When is a record score officially recognised as a "course record"?

The term "course record" is not defined in the Rules of Golf. Therefore it is a matter for the Committee in charge of the competition to decide whether it recognises a score as a course record. It is recommended that a record score should be recognised only if made in an individual stroke play competition (excluding a Stableford or a par/bogey competition) with the holes and tee-markers in their championship positions and when a Local Rule on preferred lies is not in operation.

A competition is closed when the result is officially announced. When is the result of a competition considered to be "officially announced"?

In order to avoid any confusion as to when the result is officially announced, it is recommended to have a condition of competition clarifying this matter. For example, it is common to consider the result of the competition officially announced and the competition closed when the trophy has been presented to the winner or when the results have been posted on the notice board.

(iv) knew, before the competition closed, that he had been in breach of any other *Rule* for which the penalty is disqualification.

34-2 Referee's Decision

If a *referee* has been appointed by the *Committee*, his decision is final.

34-3 Committee's Decision

In the absence of a *referee*, any dispute or doubtful point on the *Rules* must be referred to the *Committee*, whose decision is final.

If the *Committee* cannot come to a decision, it may refer the dispute or doubtful point to the Rules of Golf Committee of the *R&A*, whose decision is final.

If the dispute or doubtful point has not been referred to the Rules of Golf Committee, the player or players may request that an agreed statement be referred through a duly authorised representative of the *Committee* to the Rules of Golf Committee for an opinion as to the correctness of the decision given. The reply will be sent to this authorised representative.

If play is conducted other than in accordance with the Rules of Golf, the Rules of Golf Committee will not give a decision on any question.

RULE 34 INCIDENTS

On the 1st hole during the first round of the 2009 US Women's Open, it appeared from a review of the telecast following the event that Momoko Ueda's ball had moved after she had addressed it on the putting green. If this was the case, Ueda would have been subject to penalty under Rule 18-2 and would have been required to replace the ball.

The matter was brought to the attention of the USGA, organisers of the US Women's Open, the day after the competition had closed. Rule 34-1b stipulates that a penalty cannot be imposed after the competition has closed. However, if the Committee can establish that the player knew, before the competition closed, that a penalty should have been included in the competitor's score, then the penalty of disqualification can still be imposed.

The US Open Rules Committee was therefore obliged to ask Ueda whether she was aware, before the competition had closed, of the penalty for moving her ball after address. Ueda stated that she had only become aware of the situation and a possible breach the day after the event had finished and not before this time. Consequently, as she was not aware that she should have incurred a penalty before the competition had closed, no penalty could be imposed.

Momoko Ueda played in the 2009 US Open. It was not until the day after the results were announced that a possible breach came to the attention of the Committee.

APPENDICES

APPENDIX I

PART A
Local Rules 170

1 **Course – Defining Boundaries, Margins and Status of Objects** 170

2 **Course Protection** 170
a Ground Under Repair; Play Prohibited 170
b Protection of Young Trees 170
c Environmentally-Sensitive Areas 170

3 **Course Conditions** 171
a Embedded Ball 171
b "Preferred Lies" and "Winter Rules" 172
c Cleaning Ball 172
d Aeration Holes 172
e Seams of Cut Turf 172
f Stones in Bunkers 173

4 **Obstructions** 173
a Immovable Obstructions Close to Putting Green 173
b Temporary Immovable Obstructions 174
c Temporary Power Lines and Cables 175

5 **Water Hazards – Playing Ball Provisionally Under Rule 26-1** 176

6 **Dropping Zones** 176

7 **Distance-Measuring Devices** 177

PART B
Conditions of the Competition 177

1 **Specifications of Clubs and the Ball** 177
a List of Conforming Driver Heads 177
b List of Conforming Golf Balls 178
c One Ball Condition 178

2 **Caddie** 179

3 **Pace of Play** 179

4 **Suspension of Play Due to a Dangerous Situation** 179

5 **Practice** 179
a General 179
b Practice Between Holes 179

6 **Advice in Team Competitions** 180

7 **New Holes** 180

8 **Transportation** 180

9 **Anti-Doping** 180

10 **How to Decide Ties** 180

11 **Draw for Match Play** 181

APPENDIX II

Design of Clubs 184

1 **Clubs** 184
a General 184
b Adjustability 184
c Length 184
d Alignment 184

2 **Shaft** 186
a Straightness 186
b Bending and Twisting Properties 186
c Attachment to Clubhead 186

3 **Grip** 186

4 **Clubhead** 186
a Plain in Shape 186
b Dimensions, Volume and Moment of Inertia 186
c Spring Effect and Dynamic Properties 188
d Striking Faces 188

5 **Club Face** 188
a General 188
b Impact Area Roughness and Material 188
c Impact Area Markings 188
d Decorative Markings 190
e Non-Metallic Club Face Markings 190
f Putter Face Markings 190

APPENDIX III

The Ball 190

1 **General** 190

2 **Weight** 190

3 **Size** 190

4 **Spherical Symmetry** 190

5 **Initial Velocity** 190

6 **Overall Distance Standard** 190

APPENDIX IV

Devices and Other Equipment 191

1 **Tees (Rule 11)** 191

2 **Gloves (Rule 14-3)** 191

3 **Shoes (Rule 14-3)** 191

4 **Clothing (Rule 14-3)** 191

5 **Distance-Measuring Devices (Rule 14-3)** 191

APPENDIX I

PART A
Local Rules

Definitions
All defined terms are in *italics* and are listed alphabetically in the Definitions section – see pages 13-23.

General
As provided in Rule 33-8a, the *Committee* may make and publish Local Rules for local abnormal conditions if they are consistent with the policies established in this Appendix. In addition, detailed information regarding acceptable and prohibited Local Rules is provided in *Decisions on the Rules of Golf* under Rule 33-8 and in *Guidance on Running a Competition*.

If local abnormal conditions interfere with the proper playing of the game and the *Committee* considers it necessary to modify a Rule of Golf, authorisation from the *R&A* must be obtained.

Within the policies established in Appendix I, the *Committee* may adopt Specimen Local Rules by referring, on a score card or notice board, to the examples given below. However, Specimen Local Rules of a temporary nature should not be printed on a score card.

1 Course – Defining Boundaries, Margins and Status of Objects
The *Committee* may adopt Local Rules:
- Specifying means used to define *out of bounds*, *water hazards*, *lateral water hazards*, *ground under repair*, *obstructions* and integral parts of the *course* (Rule 33-2a).
- Clarifying the status of *water hazards* that may be *lateral water hazards* (Rule 26).
- Clarifying the status of objects that may be *obstructions* (Rule 24).
- Declaring any construction to be an integral part of the *course* and, accordingly, not an *obstruction*, e.g. built-up sides of *teeing grounds*, *putting greens* and *bunkers* (Rules 24 and 33-2a).
- Declaring artificial surfaces and sides of roads to be integral parts of the *course*.
- Providing relief of the type afforded under Rule 24-2b from roads and paths not having artificial surfaces and sides, if they could unfairly affect play.
- Defining temporary obstructions installed on or adjoining the *course* as movable, immovable or temporary immovable obstructions.

2 Course Protection
a Ground Under Repair; Play Prohibited
If the *Committee* wishes to protect any area of the *course*, including turf nurseries, young plantations and other parts of the *course* under cultivation, it should declare it to be *ground under repair* and prohibit play from within that area. The following Local Rule is recommended:

"The _____(defined by ____) is *ground under repair* from which play is prohibited. If a player's ball lies in the area, or if it interferes with the player's stance or the area of his intended swing, the player must take relief under Rule 25-1.

PENALTY FOR BREACH OF LOCAL RULE:
Match play – Loss of hole;
Stroke Play – Two strokes."

b Protection of Young Trees
When it is desired to prevent damage to young trees, the following Local Rule is recommended:

"Protection of young trees identified by _____ . If such a tree interferes with a player's *stance* or area of his intended swing, the ball must be lifted, without penalty, and dropped in accordance with the procedure prescribed in Rule 24-2b (Immovable Obstruction). If the ball lies in a *water hazard*, the player must lift and drop the ball in accordance with Rule 24-2b(i), except that the *nearest point of relief* must be in the *water hazard* and the ball must be dropped in the *water hazard*, or the player may proceed under Rule 26. The ball may be cleaned when lifted under this Local Rule.

Exception
A player may not obtain relief under this Local Rule if (a) interference by anything other than such a tree makes the *stroke* clearly impracticable or (b) interference by such a tree would occur only through the use of a clearly unreasonable *stroke* or an unnecessarily abnormal *stance*, swing or direction of play.

PENALTY FOR BREACH OF LOCAL RULE:
Match play – Loss of hole;
Stroke Play – Two strokes."

c Environmentally-Sensitive Areas
If an appropriate authority (i.e. a Government Agency or the like) prohibits entry into and/or play from an area on or adjoining the *course* for environmental reasons, the *Committee* should make a Local Rule clarifying the relief procedure. The *Committee* may not declare an area to be environmentally-sensitive.

The *Committee* has some discretion in terms of whether the area is defined as *ground under repair*, a *water hazard* or *out of bounds*. However, it may not simply define an area to be a *water hazard* if it does not meet the Definition of a "*Water Hazard*" and should attempt to preserve the character of the *hole*.
The following Local Rule is recommended:

1. Definition

n environmentally-sensitive area (ESA) is an area so declared
by an appropriate authority, entry into and/or play from which is
prohibited for environmental reasons.

The_____(defined by_____) are 'environmentally-
sensitive areas' (ESAs). These areas are to be played as (*ground
under repair – water hazards – out of bounds*).

2 Ball in Environmentally-Sensitive Area

Ground Under Repair:

If a ball is in an ESA defined as *ground under repair*, a ball must be
dropped in accordance with Rule 25-1b.

If it is known or virtually certain that a ball that has not been
found is in an ESA defined as *ground under repair*, the player may
take relief, without penalty, as prescribed in Rule 25-1c.

Water Hazards and Lateral Water Hazards:

If the ball is found in or if it is known or virtually certain that a ball
that has not been found is in an ESA defined as a *water hazard* or
lateral water hazard, the player must, under penalty of one stroke,
proceed under Rule 26-1.

NOTE

If a ball dropped in accordance with Rule 26 rolls into
a position where the ESA interferes with the player's
stance or the area of his intended swing, the player must
take relief as provided in Clause 3 of this Local Rule.

Out of Bounds:

If a ball is in an ESA defined as *out of bounds*, the player must play
a ball, under penalty of one stroke, as nearly as possible at the
spot from which the original ball was last played (see Rule 20-5).

3 Interference with Stance or Area of Intended Swing

Interference by an ESA occurs when the ESA interferes with the
player's *stance* or the area of his intended swing. If interference
exists, the player must take relief as follows:

(a) **Through the Green:** If the ball lies *through the green*,
the point on the *course* nearest to where the ball lies must be
determined that (a) is not nearer the *hole*, (b) avoids interference
by the ESA and (c) is not in a *hazard* or on a *putting green*. The
player must lift the ball and drop it, without penalty, within one
club-length of the point so determined on a part of the *course* that
fulfils (a), (b) and (c) above.

(b) **In a Hazard:** If the ball is in a *hazard*, the player must lift the
ball and drop it either:

(i) Without penalty, in the *hazard*, as near as possible to the
spot where the ball lay, but not nearer the *hole*, on a part of the
course that provides complete relief from the ESA; or

(ii) Under penalty of one *stroke*, outside the *hazard*, keeping
the point where the ball lay directly between the *hole* and the
spot on which the ball is dropped, with no limit to how far behind
the *hazard* the ball may be dropped. Additionally, the player may
proceed under Rule 26 or 28 if applicable.

(c) **On the Putting Green:** If the ball lies on the *putting green*,
the player must lift the ball and place it, without penalty, in the
nearest position to where it lay that affords complete relief from
the ESA, but not nearer the *hole* or in a *hazard*.

The ball may be cleaned when lifted under Clause 3 of this Local Rule.

Exception

A player must not take relief under Clause 3 of this Local Rule
if (a) interference by anything other than an ESA makes the
stroke clearly impracticable or (b) interference by an ESA would
occur only through the use of a clearly unreasonable *stroke* or an
unnecessarily abnormal stance, swing or direction of play.

PENALTY FOR BREACH OF LOCAL RULE:

Match play – Loss of hole;
Stroke Play – Two strokes.

NOTE

In the case of a serious breach of this Local Rule, the
Committee may impose a penalty of disqualification."

3 Course Conditions

a Embedded Ball

Course conditions, including mud and extreme wetness, may
interfere with proper playing of the game and warrant relief for an
embedded ball anywhere *through the green*.

Rule 25-2 provides relief, without penalty, for a ball embedded
in its own pitch-mark in any closely-mown area *through the green*.
On the *putting green*, a ball may be lifted and damage caused
by the impact of a ball may be repaired (Rules 16-1b and c).
When permission to take relief for an embedded ball anywhere
through the green would be warranted, the following Local Rule is
recommended:

"*Through the green*, a ball that is embedded may be lifted,
cleaned and dropped, without penalty, as near as possible to the
spot where it lay but not nearer the *hole*. The ball when dropped
must first strike a part of the *course through the green*.

NOTE

A ball is "embedded" when it is in its own pitch-mark
and part of the ball is below the level of the ground.
A ball does not necessarily have to touch the soil to be
embedded (e.g. grass, *loose impediments* and the like
may intervene between the ball and the soil).

Exceptions

1   A player may not take relief under this Local Rule if the ball is embedded in sand in an area that is not closely-mown.

2   A player may not take relief under this Local Rule if interference by anything other than the condition covered by this Local Rule makes the *stroke* clearly impracticable.

PENALTY FOR BREACH OF LOCAL RULE:

Match play – Loss of hole;
Stroke Play – Two strokes."

b   "Preferred Lies" and "Winter Rules"

Ground under repair is provided for in Rule 25, and occasional local abnormal conditions that might interfere with fair play and are not widespread should be defined as *ground under repair*.

However, adverse conditions, such as heavy snows, spring thaws, prolonged rains or extreme heat can make fairways unsatisfactory and sometimes prevent use of heavy mowing equipment. When these conditions are so general throughout a *course* that the *Committee* believes "preferred lies" or "winter rules" would promote fair play or help protect the *course*, the following Local Rule (which should be withdrawn as soon as conditions warrant) is recommended:

"A ball lying on a closely-mown area *through the green* (or specify a more restricted area, e.g. at the 6th hole) may be lifted without penalty and cleaned. Before lifting the ball, the player must mark its position. Having lifted the ball, he must place it on a spot within (specify area, e.g. six inches, one club-length, etc.) of and not nearer the *hole* than where it originally lay, that is not in a *hazard* and not on a *putting green*.

A player may place his ball only once, and it is in *play* when it has been placed (Rule 20-4). If the ball fails to come to rest on the spot on which it was placed, Rule 20-3d applies. If the ball when placed comes to rest on the spot on which it is placed and it subsequently *moves*, there is no penalty and the ball must be played as it lies, unless the provisions of any other *Rule* apply.

If the player fails to mark the position of the ball before lifting it, moves the ball-marker prior to putting the ball back into play or moves the ball in any other manner, such as rolling it with a club, he incurs a penalty of one stroke.

NOTE

"Closely-mown area" means any area of the course, including paths through the rough, cut to fairway height or less.

---

*PENALTY FOR BREACH OF LOCAL RULE:

Match play – Loss of hole;
Stroke play – Two strokes.

*If a player incurs the general penalty for a breach of this Local Rule, no additional penalty under the Local Rule is applied."

c   Cleaning Ball

Conditions, such as extreme wetness causing significant amounts of mud to adhere to the ball, may be such that permission to lift, clean and replace the ball would be appropriate. In these circumstances, the following Local Rule is recommended:

"(Specify area, e.g. at the 6th hole, on a closely-mown area, anywhere *through the green*, etc.) a ball may be lifted and cleaned without penalty. The ball must be replaced."

NOTE

The position of the ball must be marked before it is lifted under this Local Rule – see Rule 20-1.

PENALTY FOR BREACH OF LOCAL RULE:

Match play – Loss of hole;
Stroke Play – Two strokes."

d   Aeration Holes

When a *course* has been aerated, a Local Rule permitting relief, without penalty, from an aeration hole may be warranted. The following Local Rule is recommended:

"*Through the gree*n, a ball that comes to rest in or on an aeration hole may be lifted without penalty, cleaned and dropped as near as possible to the spot where it lay but not nearer the *hole*. The ball when dropped must first strike a part of the *course through the green*.

On the *putting green*, a ball that comes to rest in or on an aeration hole may be placed at the nearest spot not nearer the *hole* that avoids the situation.

PENALTY FOR BREACH OF LOCAL RULE:

Match play – Loss of hole;
Stroke Play – Two strokes."

e   Seams of Cut Turf

If a *Committee* wishes to allow relief from seams of cut turf, but not from the turf itself, the following Local Rule is recommended:

"*Through the green*, seams of cut turf (not the turf itself) are deemed to be *ground under repair*. However, interference by a seam with the player's *stance* is deemed not to be, of itself, interference under Rule 25-1. If the ball lies in or touches the seam or the seam interferes with the area of intended swing, relief is available under Rule 25-1. All seams within the cut turf area are considered the same seam.

RELIEF FROM STAKED TREES

If a staked tree interferes with a player's swing, the player must take relief in accordance with the Local Rule. If the nearest point of relief leaves the player blocked by the big tree, the player must just accept this.

PENALTY FOR BREACH OF LOCAL RULE:
Match play – Loss of hole;
Stroke Play – Two strokes."

Stones in Bunkers

Stones are, by definition, *loose impediments* and, when a player's ball is in a *hazard*, a stone lying in or touching the *hazard* may not be touched or moved (Rule 13-4). However, stones in *bunkers* may represent a danger to players (a player could be injured by a stone struck by the player's club in an attempt to play the ball) and they may interfere with the proper playing of the game.

When permission to lift a stone in a *bunker* is warranted, the following Local Rule is recommended:

"Stones in *bunkers* are movable *obstructions* (Rule 24-1 applies)."

4   Obstructions

a   Immovable Obstructions Close to Putting Green (e.g. Sprinkler Heads)

Rule 24-2 provides relief, without penalty, from interference by an immovable *obstruction*, but it also provides that, except on the *putting green*, intervention on the *line of play* is not, of itself, interference under this Rule.

However, on some courses, the aprons of the *putting green* are so closely-mown that players may wish to putt from just off the green. In such conditions, immovable *obstructions* on the apron may interfere with the proper playing of the game and the introduction of the following Local Rule providing additional relief, without penalty, from intervention by an immovable *obstruction* would be warranted:

"Relief from interference by an immovable *obstruction* may be taken under Rule 24-2.

In addition, if a ball lies *through the green* and an immovable *obstruction* on or within two club-lengths of the *putting green* and within two club-lengths of the ball intervenes on the *line of play* between the ball and the *hole*, the player may take relief as follows:

The ball must be lifted and dropped at the nearest point to where the ball lay that (a) is not nearer the *hole*, (b) avoids intervention and (c) is not in a *hazard* or on a *putting green*.

If the player's ball lies on the *putting green* and an immovable *obstruction* within two club-lengths of the *putting green* intervenes on his *line of putt*, the player may take relief as follows:

The ball must be lifted and placed at the nearest point to where the ball lay that (a) is not nearer the *hole*, (b) avoids intervention and (c) is not in a *hazard*.

The ball may be cleaned when lifted.

Exception

A player may not take relief under this Local Rule if interference by anything other than the immovable *obstruction* makes the *stroke* clearly impracticable.

PENALTY FOR BREACH OF LOCAL RULE:
Match play – Loss of hole;
Stroke Play – Two strokes."

NOTE

The Committee may restrict this Local Rule to specific holes, to balls lying only in closely-mown areas, to specific obstructions, or, in the case of obstructions that are not on the putting green, to obstructions in closely-mown areas if so desired. "Closely-mown area" means any area of the course, including paths through the rough, cut to fairway height or less.

b   Temporary Immovable Obstructions

When temporary obstructions are installed on or adjoining the *course*, the *Committee* should define the status of such obstructions as movable, immovable or temporary immovable obstructions.

If the *Committee* defines such obstructions as temporary immovable obstructions, the following Local Rule is recommended:

"1   Definition

A temporary immovable obstruction (TIO) is a non-permanent artificial object that is often erected in conjunction with a competition and is fixed or not readily movable. Examples of TIOs include, but are not limited to, tents, scoreboards, grandstands, television towers and lavatories.

Supporting guy wires are part of the TIO, unless the *Committee* declares that they are to be treated as elevated power lines or cables.

2   Interference

Interference by a TIO occurs when (a) the ball lies in front of and so close to the TIO that the TIO interferes with the player's *stance* or the area of his intended swing, or (b) the ball lies in, on, under or behind the TIO so that any part of the TIO intervenes directly between the player's ball and the *hole* and is on his *line of play*;

interference also exists if the ball lies within one club-length of a spot equidistant from the *hole* where such intervention would exist.

> **NOTE**
>
> A ball is under a TIO when it is below the outermost edges of the TIO, even if these edges do not extend downwards to the ground.

3   Relief

A player may obtain relief from interference by a TIO, including a TIO that is *out of bounds*, as follows:

(a)   **Through the Green:** If the ball lies *through the green*, the point on the *course* nearest to where the ball lies must be determined that (a) is not nearer the *hole*, (b) avoids interference as defined in Clause 2 and (c) is not in a *hazard* or on a *putting green*. The player must lift the ball and drop it, without penalty, within one club-length of the point so determined on a part of the *course* that fulfills (a), (b) and (c) above.

(b)   **In a Hazard:** If the ball is in a *hazard*, the player must lift and drop the ball either:

(i)   Without penalty, in accordance with Clause 3(a) above, except that the nearest part of the *course* affording complete relief must be in the *hazard* and the ball must be dropped in the *hazard*, or, if complete relief is impossible, on a part of the course within the *hazard* that affords maximum available relief; or

(ii)   Under penalty of one *stroke*, outside the *hazard* as follows: the point on the *course* nearest to where the ball lies must be determined that (a) is not nearer the *hole*, (b) avoids interference as defined in Clause 2 and (c) is not in a *hazard*. The player must drop the ball within one club-length of the point so determined on a part of the *course* that fulfils (a), (b) and (c) above.

The ball may be cleaned when lifted under Clause 3.

> **NOTE 1**
>
> If the ball lies in a *hazard*, nothing in this Local Rule precludes the player from proceeding under Rule 26 or Rule 28, if applicable.
>
> **NOTE 2**
>
> If a ball to be dropped under this Local Rule is not immediately recoverable, another ball may be *substituted*.
>
> **NOTE 3**
>
> A *Committee* may make a Local Rule (a) permitting or requiring a player to use a dropping zone when taking relief from a TIO or (b) permitting a player, as an additional relief option, to drop the ball on the opposite side of the TIO from the point established under Clause 3, but otherwise in accordance with Clause 3.

PREFERRED LIES

A player must mark the position of the ball first before preferring the lie. The player is not allowed to move the ball with a club.

Exceptions

If a player's ball lies in front of or behind the TIO (not in, on or under the TIO), he may not obtain relief under Clause 3 if:

Interference by anything other than the TIO makes it clearly impracticable for him to make a *stroke* or, in the case of intervention, to make a *stroke* such that the ball could finish on a direct line to the *hole*;

Interference by the TIO would occur only through use of a clearly unreasonable *stroke* or an unnecessarily abnormal *stance*, swing or direction of play; or

In the case of intervention, it would be clearly impracticable to expect the player to be able to strike the ball far enough towards the *hole* to reach the TIO.

A player who is not entitled to relief due to these exceptions may, if the ball lies *through the green* or in a *bunker*, obtain relief as provided in Rule 24-2b, if applicable. If the ball lies in a *water hazard*, the player may lift and drop the ball in accordance with Rule 24-2b(i), except that the *nearest point of relief* must be in the *water hazard* and the ball must be dropped in the *water hazard*, or the player may proceed under Rule 26-1.

Ball in TIO Not Found

If it is known or virtually certain that a ball that has not been found is in, on or under a TIO, a ball may be dropped under the provisions of Clause 3 or Clause 5, if applicable. For the purpose of applying Clauses 3 and 5, the ball is deemed to lie at the spot where it last crossed the outermost limits of the TIO (Rule 24-3).

Dropping Zones

If the player has interference from a TIO, the *Committee* may permit or require the use of a dropping zone. If the player uses a dropping zone in taking relief, he must drop the ball in the dropping zone nearest to where his ball originally lay or is deemed to lie under Clause 4 (even though the nearest dropping zone may be nearer the *hole*).

NOTE

A Committee may make a Local Rule prohibiting the use of a dropping zone that is nearer the hole.

PENALTY FOR BREACH OF LOCAL RULE:

Match play – Loss of hole;
Stroke Play – Two strokes."

c   Temporary Power Lines and Cables

When temporary power lines, cables or telephone lines are installed on the *course*, the following Local Rule is recommended: "Temporary power lines, cables, telephone lines and mats covering or stanchions supporting them are *obstructions*:

1   If they are readily movable, Rule 24-1 applies.

2   If they are fixed or not readily movable, the player may, if the ball lies *through the green* or in a *bunker*, obtain relief as provided in Rule 24-2b. If the ball lies in a *water hazard*, the player may lift and drop the ball in accordance with Rule 24-2b(i), except that the *nearest point of relief* must be in the *water hazard* and the ball must be dropped in the *water hazard* or the player may proceed under Rule 26.

3   If a ball strikes an elevated power line or cable, the *stroke* is cancelled and the player must play a ball as nearly as possible at the spot from which the original ball was played in accordance

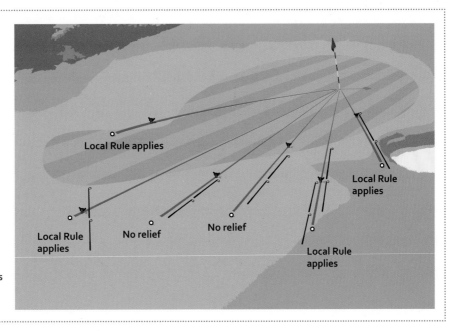

A player is entitled to relief from an immovable obstruction under Rule 24-2. If the specimen Local Rule is introduced, a player is also entitled to relief for intervention to his line of play provided:
(a) (i) the immovable obstruction is on or within two club-lengths of the putting green, and
(ii) the ball lies within two club-lengths of the immovable obstruction; or
(b) the ball lies on the putting green and the immovable obstruction within two club-lengths of the putting green intervenes on his line of play.

Local Rule applies

Local Rule applies

Local Rule applies

No relief

No relief

Local Rule applies

with Rule 20-5 (Making Next Stroke from Where Previous Stroke Made).

NOTE

Guy wires supporting a temporary immovable obstruction are part of the temporary immovable obstruction, unless the *Committee*, by Local Rule, declares that they are to be treated as elevated power lines or cables.

Exception

A *stroke* that results in a ball striking an elevated junction section of cable rising from the ground must not be replayed.

4   Grass-covered cable trenches are *ground under repair*, even if not marked, and Rule 25-1b applies.

PENALTY FOR BREACH OF LOCAL RULE:

Match play – Loss of hole;
Stroke Play – Two strokes."

5   Water Hazards - Playing Ball Provisionally Under Rule 26-1

If a *water hazard* (including a *lateral water hazard*) is of such size and shape and/or located in such a position that:

(i)   it would be impracticable to determine whether the ball is in the *hazard* or to do so would unduly delay play, and

(ii)   if the original ball is not found, it is known or virtually certain that it is in the *water hazard*,

the *Committee* may introduce a Local Rule permitting the play of a ball provisionally under Rule 26-1. The ball is played provisionally under any of the applicable options under Rule 26-1 or any applicable Local Rule. In such a case, if a ball is played provisionally and the original ball is in a *water hazard*, the player may play the original ball as it lies or continue with the ball played provisionally, but he may not proceed under Rule 26-1 with regard to the original ball.

In these circumstances, the following Local Rule is recommended:

"If there is doubt whether a ball is in or is *lost* in the *water hazard* (specify location), the player may play another ball provisionally under any of the applicable options in Rule 26-1.

If the original ball is found outside the *water hazard*, the player must continue play with it.

If the original ball is found in the *water hazard*, the player may either play the original ball as it lies or continue with the ball played provisionally under Rule 26-1.

If the original ball is not found or identified within the five-minute search period, the player must continue with the ball played provisionally.

PENALTY FOR BREACH OF LOCAL RULE:

Match play – Loss of hole;
Stroke Play – Two strokes."

6   Dropping Zones

The *Committee* may establish dropping zones on which balls may or must be dropped when the *Committee* considers that it is not feasible or practicable to proceed exactly in conformity with Rule 24-2b or Rule 24-3 (Immovable Obstruction), Rule 25-1b or 25-1c (Abnormal Ground Conditions), 25-3 (Wrong Putting Green), Rule 26-1 (Water Hazards and Lateral Water Hazards) or Rule 28 (Ball Unplayable).

Generally, such dropping zones should be provided as an additional relief option to those available under the Rule itself, rather than being mandatory.

Using the example of a dropping zone for a *water hazard*, when such a dropping zone is established, the following Local Rule is recommended:

"If a ball is in or it is known or virtually certain that a ball that has not been found is in the *water hazard* (specify location), the player may:

(i)   proceed under Rule 26-1; or

If there are temporary immovable obstructions, such as TV towers, on the course, the Committee should introduce a Local Rule providing for relief from such temporary immovable obstructions.

ii)   as an additional option, drop a ball, under penalty of one stroke, in the dropping zone.

PENALTY FOR BREACH OF LOCAL RULE:

Match play – Loss of hole;

Stroke Play – Two strokes."

NOTE

When using a dropping zone the following provisions apply regarding the dropping and re-dropping of the ball:

a)   The player does not have to stand within the dropping zone when dropping the ball.

b)   The dropped ball must first strike a part of the course within the dropping zone.

c)   If the dropping zone is defined by a line, the line is within the dropping zone.

d)   The dropped ball does not have to come to rest within the dropping zone.

e)   The dropped ball must be re-dropped if it rolls and comes to rest in a position covered by Rule 20-2c(i-vi).

f)   The dropped ball may roll nearer the *hole* than the spot where it first struck a part of the *course*, provided it comes to rest within two club-lengths of that spot and not into any of the positions covered by (e).

g)   Subject to the provisions of (e) and (f), the dropped ball may roll and come to rest nearer the *hole* than:

○   its original position or estimated position (see Rule 20-2b);

○   the *nearest point of relief* or maximum available relief (Rule 24-2, 25-1 or 25-3); or

○   the point where the original ball last crossed the margin of the *water hazard* or *lateral water hazard* (Rule 26-1).

Distance-Measuring Devices

If the *Committee* wishes to act in accordance with the Note under Rule 14-3, the following Local Rule is recommended:

"(Specify as appropriate, e.g. In this competition, or For all play at this *course*, etc.), a player may obtain distance information by use of a distance-measuring device. If, during a *stipulated round*, a player uses a distance-measuring device to gauge or measure other conditions that might affect his play (e.g. elevation changes, wind speed, etc.), the player is in breach of Rule 14-3."

PART B
Conditions of the Competition

Definitions

All defined terms are in *italics* and are listed alphabetically in the Definitions section – see pages 13-23.

General

Rule 33-1 provides, "The *Committee* must establish the conditions under which a competition is to be played." The conditions should include many matters such as method of entry, eligibility, number of rounds to be played, etc. which it is not appropriate to deal with in the Rules of Golf or this Appendix. Detailed information regarding these conditions is provided in "Decisions on the Rules of Golf" under Rule 33-1 and in "Guidance on Running a Competition".

However, there are a number of matters that might be covered in the Conditions of the Competition to which the Committee's attention is specifically drawn. These are:

1   Specification of Clubs and the Ball

The following conditions are recommended only for competitions involving expert players:

a   List of Conforming Driver Heads

On its website (www.randa.org) the *R&A* periodically issues a List of Conforming Driver Heads that lists driving clubheads that have been evaluated and found to conform with the Rules of Golf. If the *Committee* wishes to limit players to drivers that have a clubhead, identified by model and loft, that is on the List, the List should be made available and the following condition of competition used:

"Any driver the player carries must have a clubhead, identified by model and loft, that is named on the current List of Conforming Driver Heads issued by the *R&A*.

Exception

A driver with a clubhead that was manufactured prior to 1999 is exempt from this condition.

---

*PENALTY FOR CARRYING, BUT NOT MAKING STROKE WITH, CLUB OR CLUBS IN BREACH OF CONDITION:

Match play – At the conclusion of the hole at which the breach is discovered, the state of the match is adjusted by deducting one hole for each hole at which a breach occurred; maximum deduction per round – Two holes.

Stroke play – Two strokes for each hole at which any breach occurred; maximum penalty per round – Four strokes (two strokes at each of the first two holes at which any breach occurred).

Match play or stroke play – If a breach is discovered between the play of two holes, it is deemed to have been discovered during play of the next hole, and the penalty must be applied accordingly.

Bogey and par competitions – See Note 1 to Rule 32-1a.

Stableford competitions – See Note 1 to Rule 32-1b.

*Any club or clubs carried in breach of this condition must be declared out of play by the player to his *opponent* in match play or his marker or a fellow-competitor in stroke play immediately upon discovery that a breach has occurred. If the player fails to do so, he is disqualified.

PENALTY FOR MAKING STROKE WITH CLUB IN BREACH OF CONDITION:

Disqualification."

b List of Conforming Golf Balls

On its website (www.randa.org) the *R&A* periodically issues a List of Conforming Golf Balls that lists balls that have been tested and found to conform with the Rules of Golf. If the *Committee* wishes to require players to play a model of golf ball on the List, the List should be made available and the following condition of competition used:

"The ball the player plays must be named on the current List of Conforming Golf Balls issued by the *R&A*.

PENALTY FOR BREACH OF CONDITION:

Disqualification."

c One Ball Condition

If it is desired to prohibit changing brands and models of golf balls during a *stipulated round*, the following condition is recommended: "Limitation on Balls Used During Round: (Note to Rule 5-1)

(i) "One Ball" Condition

During a stipulated round, the balls a player plays must be of the same brand and model as detailed by a single entry on the current List of Conforming Golf Balls.

Note

If a ball of a different brand and/or model is dropped or placed it may be lifted, without penalty, and the player must then proceed by dropping or placing a proper ball (Rule 20-6).

PENALTY FOR BREACH OF CONDITION:

Match play – At the conclusion of the hole at which the breach is discovered, the state of the match is adjusted by deducting one hole for each hole at which a breach occurred; maximum deduction per round – Two holes.

DISTANCE-MEASURING DEVICES

Where the Committee have introduced the Local Rule permitting the use of distance-measuring devices, the player is prohibited from gauging or measuring other conditions that might affect his play (e.g. elevation changes, wind speed etc).

Stroke play – Two strokes for each hole at which any breach occurred; maximum penalty per round – Four strokes (two strokes at each of the first two holes at which any breach occurred).

Bogey and Par competitions – See Note 1 to Rule 32-1a.
Stableford competitions – See Note 1 to Rule 32-1b.

ii) Procedure When Breach Discovered

When a player discovers that he has played a ball in breach of this condition, he must abandon that ball before playing from the next *teeing ground* and complete the round with a proper ball; otherwise, the player is disqualified. If discovery is made during play of a hole and the player elects to substitute a proper ball before completing that hole, the player must place a proper ball on the spot where the ball played in breach of the condition lay."

2. Caddie (Note to Rule 6-4)

Rule 6-4 permits a player to use a *caddie*, provided he has only one *caddie* at any one time. However, there may be circumstances where a Committee may wish to prohibit *caddies* or restrict a player in his choice of *caddie*, e.g. professional golfer, sibling, parent, another player in the competition, etc. In such cases, the following wording is recommended:

"Use of Caddie Prohibited

A player is prohibited from using a *caddie* during the *stipulated round*."

"Restriction on Who May Serve as Caddie

A player is prohibited from having _____ serve as his *caddie* during the *stipulated round*.

---

*PENALTY FOR BREACH OF CONDITION:

Match play – At the conclusion of the hole at which the breach is discovered, the state of the match is adjusted by deducting one hole for each hole at which a breach occurred; maximum deduction per round – Two holes.
Stroke play – Two strokes for each hole at which any breach occurred; maximum penalty per round – Four strokes (two strokes at each of the first two holes at which any breach occurred).
Match play or stroke play – If a breach is discovered between the play of two holes, it is deemed to have been discovered during play of the next hole, and the penalty must be applied accordingly.
Bogey and par competitions – See Note 1 to Rule 32-1a.
Stableford competitions – See Note 1 to Rule 32-1b.
*A player having a *caddie* in breach of this condition must immediately upon discovery that a breach has occurred ensure that he conforms with this condition for the remainder of the *stipulated round*. Otherwise, the player is disqualified."

3   Pace of Play (Note 2 to Rule 6-7)

The *Committee* may establish pace of play guidelines to help prevent slow play, in accordance with Note 2 to Rule 6-7

4   Suspension of Play Due to a Dangerous Situation (Note to Rule 6-8b)

As there have been many deaths and injuries from lightning on golf courses, all clubs and sponsors of golf competitions are urged to take precautions for the protection of persons against lightning. Attention is called to Rules 6-8 and 33-2d. If the *Committee* desires to adopt the condition in the Note under Rule 6-8b, the following wording is recommended:

"When play is suspended by the *Committee* for a dangerous situation, if the players in a match or group are between the play of two holes, they must not resume play until the *Committee* has ordered a resumption of play. If they are in the process of playing a hole, they must discontinue play immediately and not resume play until the *Committee* has ordered a resumption of play. If a player fails to discontinue play immediately, he is disqualified, unless circumstances warrant waiving the penalty as provided in Rule 33-7.

The signal for suspending play due to a dangerous situation will be a prolonged note of the siren."

The following signals are generally used and it is recommended that all *Committees* do similarly:

Discontinue Play Immediately: One prolonged note of siren.
Discontinue Play: Three consecutive notes of siren, repeated.
Resume Play: Two short notes of siren, repeated.

5   Practice
a   General

The *Committee* may make regulations governing practice in accordance with the Note to Rule 7-1, Exception (c) to Rule 7-2, Note 2 to Rule 7-2 and Rule 33-2c.

b   Practice Between Holes (Note 2 to Rule 7)

If the *Committee* wishes to act in accordance with Note 2 to Rule 7-2, the following wording is recommended:

"Between the play of two holes, a player must not make any practice stroke on or near the *putting green* of the hole last played and must not test the surface of the *putting green* of the hole last played by rolling a ball.

PENALTY FOR BREACH OF CONDITION:
Match play – Loss of next hole.
Stroke play – Two strokes at the next hole.
Match play or stroke play – In the case of a breach at the last hole of the stipulated round, the player incurs the penalty at that hole."

6 Advice in Team Competitions (Note to Rule 8)

If the *Committee* wishes to act in accordance with the Note under Rule 8, the following wording is recommended:

"In accordance with the Note to Rule 8 of the Rules of Golf, each team may appoint one person (in addition to the persons from whom *advice* may be asked under that Rule) who may give *advice* to members of that team. Such person (if it is desired to insert any restriction on who may be nominated insert such restriction here) must be identified to the *Committee* before giving *advice*."

7 New Holes (Note to Rule 33-2b)

The *Committee* may provide, in accordance with the Note to Rule 33-2b, that the *holes* and *teeing grounds* for a single round of a competition being held on more than one day may be differently situated on each day.

8 Transportation

If it is desired to require players to walk in a competition, the following condition is recommended:

"Players must not ride on any form of transportation during a *stipulated round* unless authorised by the *Committee*.

---

*PENALTY FOR BREACH OF CONDITION:

Match play – At the conclusion of the hole at which the breach is discovered, the state of the match is adjusted by deducting one hole for each hole at which a breach occurred; maximum deduction per round – Two holes.

Stroke play – Two strokes for each hole at which any breach occurred; maximum penalty per round – Four strokes (two strokes at each of the first two holes at which any breach occurred).

Match play or stroke play – If a breach is discovered between the play of two holes, it is deemed to have been discovered during play of the next hole, and the penalty must be applied accordingly.

Bogey and par competitions – See Note 1 to Rule 32-1a.
Stableford competitions – See Note 1 to Rule 32-1b.
*Use of any unauthorised form of transportation must be discontinued immediately upon discovery that a breach has occurred. Otherwise, the player is disqualified."

9 Anti-Doping

The *Committee* may require, in the conditions of competition, that players comply with an anti-doping policy.

10 How to Decide Ties

In both match play and stroke play, a tie can be an acceptable result. However, when it is desired to have a sole winner, the *Committee* has the authority, under Rule 33-6, to determine how and when a tie is decided. The decision should be published in advance.

The *R&A* recommends:

"Match Play

A match that ends all square should be played off hole by hole until one side wins a hole. The play-off should start on the hole where the match began. In a handicap match, handicap strokes should be allowed as in the *stipulated round*.

Stroke Play

(a) In the event of a tie in a scratch stroke play competition, a play-off is recommended. The play-off may be over 18 holes or a smaller number of holes as specified by the *Committee*. If that is not feasible or there is still a tie, a hole-by-hole play-off is recommended.

(b) In the event of a tie in a handicap stroke play competition, a play-off with handicaps is recommended. The play-off may be over 18 holes or a smaller number of holes as specified by the *Committee*. It is recommended that any such play-off consist of at least three holes.

In competitions where the handicap stroke allocation table is not relevant, if the play-off is less than 18 holes, the percentage of 18 holes played should be applied to the players' handicaps to determine their play-off handicaps. Handicap stroke fractions of one half stroke or more should count as a full stroke and any lesser fraction should be disregarded.

In competitions where the handicap stroke table is relevant, such as four-ball stroke play and bogey, par and Stableford competitions, handicap strokes should be taken as they were assigned for the competition using the players' respective stroke allocation table(s).

(c) If a play-off of any type is not feasible, matching score cards is recommended. The method of matching cards should be announced in advance and should also provide what will happen if this procedure does not produce a winner. An acceptable method of matching cards is to determine the winner on the basis of the best score for the last nine holes. If the tying players have the same score for the last nine, determine the winner on the basis of the last six holes, last three holes and finally the 18th hole. If this method is used in a competition with a multiple tee start, it is recommended that the "last nine holes, last six holes, etc." is considered to be holes 10–18, 13–18, etc.

For competitions where the handicap stroke table is not relevant, such as individual stroke play, if the last nine, last six, last three holes scenario is used, one-half, one-third, one-sixth, etc. of the handicaps should be deducted from the score for those holes. In terms of the use of fractions in such deductions, the *Committee* should act in accordance with the recommendations of the relevant handicapping authority.

In competitions where the handicap stroke table is relevant,

SUSPENSION OF PLAY DUE TO A DANGEROUS SITUATION

Where the Committee signal a suspension of play for a dangerous situation, the players must discontinue play immediately. If a player plays a stroke after the signal, he is disqualified.

uch as *four-ball* stroke play and bogey, par and Stableford ompetitions, handicap strokes should be taken as they were ssigned for the competition, using the players' respective stroke llocation table(s)."

1   Draw for Match Play

lthough the draw for match play may be completely blind or ertain players may be distributed through different quarters r eighths, the General Numerical Draw is recommended if natches are determined by a qualifying round.

General Numerical Draw

For purposes of determining places in the draw, ties in qualifying rounds other than those for the last qualifying place are decided by the order in which scores are returned, with the first score to be returned receiving the lowest available number, etc. If it is impossible to determine the order in which scores are returned, ties are determined by a blind draw.

GENERAL NUMERICAL DRAW

UPPER HALF			LOWER HALF			UPPER HALF			LOWER HALF			UPPER HALF			LOWER HALF		
	64 qualifiers						32 qualifiers						16 qualifiers				
1	vs.	64	2	vs.	63	1	vs.	32	2	vs.	31	1	vs.	16	2	vs.	15
32	vs.	33	31	vs.	34	16	vs.	17	15	vs.	18	8	vs.	9	7	vs.	10
16	vs.	49	15	vs.	50	8	vs.	25	7	vs.	26	4	vs.	13	3	vs.	14
17	vs.	48	18	vs.	47	9	vs.	24	10	vs.	23	5	vs.	12	6	vs.	11
8	vs.	57	7	vs.	58	4	vs.	29	3	vs.	30						
25	vs.	40	26	vs.	39	13	vs.	20	14	vs.	19	UPPER HALF			LOWER HALF		
9	vs.	56	10	vs.	55	5	vs.	28	6	vs.	27		8 qualifiers				
24	vs.	41	23	vs.	42	12	vs.	21	11	vs.	22	1	vs.	8	2	vs.	7
4	vs.	61	3	vs.	62							4	vs.	5	3	vs.	6
29	vs.	36	30	vs.	35												
13	vs.	52	14	vs.	51												
20	vs.	45	19	vs.	46												
5	vs.	60	6	vs.	59												
28	vs.	37	27	vs.	38												
12	vs.	53	11	vs.	54												
21	vs.	44	22	vs.	43												

INCIDENTS

A Local Rule for preferred lies or "winter rules" is commonly used by Committees to counter poor conditions on the course. The specified area in which to place the ball under this Local Rule can vary as there is no hard-and-fast Rule. Some Committees will stipulate within six inches, others a score card-length or perhaps even one club-length. It is for the Committee to determine and clarify in the Local Rule. Therefore, a player should check in advance of the competition the distance the placement has to occur, to avoid any unnecessary penalties.

This is something PGA Tour golfer Ryuji Imada would have been advised to do in order to avoid a monstrous 26-stroke penalty at the 2010 Mission Hills Star Trophy in China. Imada assumed he could prefer the lie of the ball within a club-length of its original position, as is standard on the PGA Tour. But the Local Rules for this particular tournament stated that the placement had to occur within the length of one score card.

Imada's fellow-competitor alerted him to the mistake during the round and, prior to signing for his score, Imada informed tournament officials that he thought he had breached the Local Rule. He was assessed a two-stroke penalty for each of the 13 times he had preferred the lie outwith the prescribed distance.

Imada acknowledged that only he was to blame as he had failed to read the Local Rules sheet, and he finally signed for a first-round total of 24 over par, 97!

Tiger Woods incurred a costly penalty at the Abu Dhabi Championship in 2013. After hitting his tee shot into ice plants at the 5th hole, he asked his fellow competitor Martin Kaymer to take a look at the lie.
"I called Martin over to verify that the ball was embedded," said Woods. "We both agreed, but evidently it was in sand."

Woods proceeded to take relief under the Local Rule for embedded ball, dropped the ball and played on. Rule 25-2 provides relief, without penalty, for a ball embedded in its own pitch-mark in any closely mown area through the green. However, by Local Rule, the Committee may extend this provision to anywhere through the green.

The European Tour had this Local Rule in effect but Woods and Kaymer had failed to notice the Exception contained within the Local Rule – a player may not take relief under this Local Rule if the ball is embedded in sand in an area that is not closely-mown.

As Woods' ball was embedded in sand in an area that was not closely-mown through the green, he was not entitled to take relief. By taking the drop he had breached the Local Rule. The two-stroke penalty was confirmed prior to Woods signing his score card and his bogey five was changed to a triple-bogey seven.

Tiger Woods and Martin Kaymer examine Woods' lie at the 2013 Abu Dhabi Championship.

APPENDICES II, III AND IV
Definitions

All defined terms are in *italics* and are listed alphabetically in the Definitions section - see pages 13–23.

The *R&A* reserves the right, at any time, to change the *Rules* relating to clubs, balls, devices and other equipment and make or change the interpretations relating to these *Rules*. For up to date information, please contact the *R&A* or refer to www.randa.org/equipmentrules.

Any design in a club, ball, device or other equipment that is not covered by the *Rules*, which is contrary to the purpose and intent of the *Rules* or that might significantly change the nature of the game, will be ruled on by the *R&A*.

The dimensions and limits contained in Appendices II, III and IV are given in the units by which conformance is determined. An equivalent imperial/metric conversion is also referenced for information, calculated using a conversion rate of 1 inch = 25.4 mm.

APPENDIX II

Design of Clubs

A player in doubt as to the conformity of a club should consult the *R&A*.

A manufacturer should submit to the *R&A* a sample of a club to be manufactured for a ruling as to whether the club conforms with the *Rules*. The sample becomes the property of the *R&A* for reference purposes. If a manufacturer fails to submit a sample or, having submitted a sample, fails to await a ruling before manufacturing and/or marketing the club, the manufacturer assumes the risk of a ruling that the club does not conform with the *Rules*.

The following paragraphs prescribe general regulations for the design of clubs, together with specifications and interpretations. Further information relating to these regulations and their proper interpretation is provided in "A Guide to the Rules on Clubs and Balls".

Where a club, or part of a club, is required to meet a specification within the *Rules*, it must be designed and manufactured with the intention of meeting that specification.

1 Clubs
a General

A club is an implement designed to be used for striking the ball and generally comes in three forms: woods, irons and putters distinguished by shape and intended use. A putter is a club with a loft not exceeding ten degrees designed primarily for use on the *putting green*.

The club must not be substantially different from the traditional and customary form and make. The club must be composed of a shaft and a head and it may also have material added to the shaft to enable the player to obtain a firm hold (see 3 below). All parts of the club must be fixed so that the club is one unit, and it must have no external attachments. Exceptions may be made for attachments that do not affect the performance of the club.

b Adjustability

All clubs may incorporate features for weight adjustment. Other forms of adjustability may also be permitted upon evaluation by the *R&A*. The following requirements apply to all permissible methods of adjustment:

(i) the adjustment cannot be readily made;

(ii) all adjustable parts are firmly fixed and there is no reasonable likelihood of them working loose during a round; and

(iii) all configurations of adjustment conform with the *Rules*.

During a *stipulated round*, the playing characteristics of a club must not be purposely changed by adjustment or by any other means (see Rule 4-2a).

c Length

The overall length of the club must be at least 18 inches (0.457 m) and, except for putters, must not exceed 48 inches (1.219 m).

For woods and irons, the measurement of length is taken when the club is lying on a horizontal plane and the sole is set against a 60 degree plane as shown in Fig. I. The length is defined as the distance from the point of the intersection between the two planes to the top of the grip. For putters, the measurement of length is taken from the top of the grip along the axis of the shaft or a straight line extension of it to the sole of the club.

d Alignment

When the club is in its normal address position the shaft must be so aligned that:

(i) the projection of the straight part of the shaft on to the vertical plane through the toe and heel must diverge from the vertical by at least 10 degrees (see Fig. II). If the overall design of the club is such that the player can effectively use the club in a vertical or close-to-vertical position, the shaft may be required to diverge from the vertical in this plane by as much as 25 degrees;

(ii) the projection of the straight part of the shaft on to the vertical plane along the intended *line of play* must not diverge from the vertical by more than 20 degrees forwards or 10 degrees backwards (see Fig. III).

Except for putters, all of the heel portion of the club

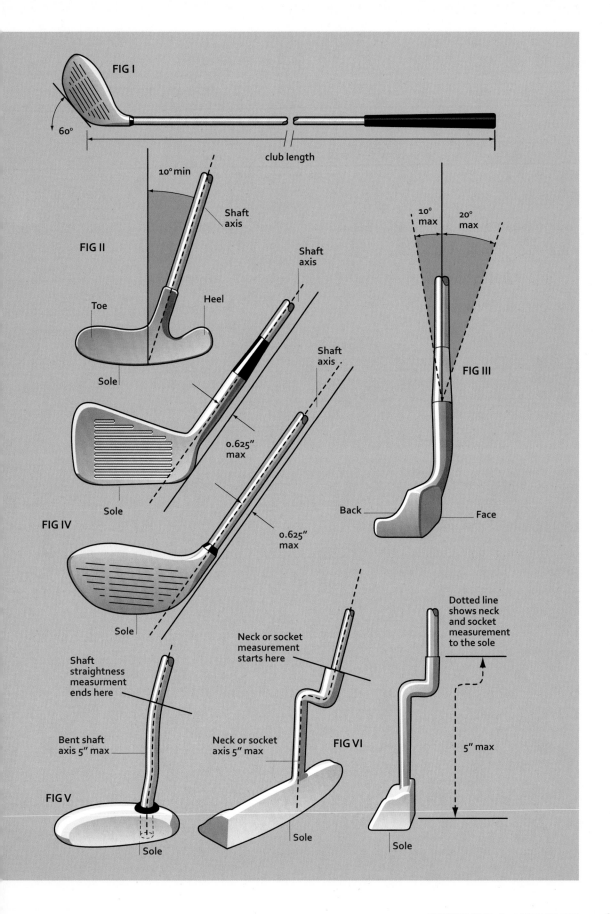

FIG I

60°

club length

FIG II

10° min

Shaft axis

Toe

Heel

Sole

Shaft axis

0.625" max

Sole

FIG III

10° max

20° max

FIG IV

Shaft axis

0.625" max

Back

Face

Sole

Sole

Shaft straightness measurment ends here

Bent shaft axis 5" max

FIG V

Sole

Neck or socket measurement starts here

Neck or socket axis 5" max

FIG VI

Sole

Dotted line shows neck and socket measurement to the sole

5" max

Sole

must lie within 0.625 inches (15.88 mm) of the plane containing the axis of the straight part of the shaft and the intended (horizontal) *line of play* (see Fig. IV).

2 Shaft

a Straightness

The shaft must be straight from the top of the grip to a point not more than 5 inches (127 mm) above the sole, measured from the point where the shaft ceases to be straight along the axis of the bent part of the shaft and the neck and/or socket (see Fig. V).

b Bending and Twisting Properties

At any point along its length, the shaft must:

(i)   bend in such a way that the deflection is the same regardless of how the shaft is rotated about its longitudinal axis; and

(ii) twist the same amount in both directions.

c Attachment to Clubhead

The shaft must be attached to the clubhead at the heel either directly or through a single plain neck and/or socket. The length from the top of the neck and/or socket to the sole of the club must not exceed 5 inches (127 mm), measured along the axis of, and following any bend in, the neck and/or socket (see Fig. VI). **Exception for Putters:** The shaft or neck or socket of a putter may be fixed at any point in the head.

3 Grip (see Fig. VII)

The grip consists of material added to the shaft to enable the player to obtain a firm hold. The grip must be fixed to the shaft, must be straight and plain in form, must extend to the end of the shaft and must not be moulded for any part of the hands. If no material is added, that portion of the shaft designed to be held by the player must be considered the grip.

(i)   For clubs other than putters the grip must be circular in cross-section, except that a continuous, straight, slightly raised rib may be incorporated along the full length of the grip, and a slightly indented spiral is permitted on a wrapped grip or a replica of one.

(ii) A putter grip may have a non-circular cross-section, provided the cross-section has no concavity, is symmetrical and remains generally similar throughout the length of the grip. (See Clause (v) below).

(iii) The grip may be tapered but must not have any bulge or waist. Its cross-sectional dimensions measured in any direction must not exceed 1.75 inches (44.45 mm).

(iv) For clubs other than putters the axis of the grip must coincide with the axis of the shaft.

(v)   A putter may have two grips provided each is circular in cross-section, the axis of each coincides with the axis of the

shaft, and they are separated by at least 1.5 inches (38.1 mm).

4 Clubhead

a Plain in Shape

The clubhead must be generally plain in shape. All parts must be rigid structural in nature and functional. The clubhead or its parts must not be designed to resemble any other object. It is not practicable to define plain in shape precisely and comprehensively. However, features that are deemed to be in breach of this requirement and are therefore not permitted include, but are not limited to:

(i) All Clubs

o   holes through the face;

o   holes through the head (some exceptions may be made for putters and cavity back irons);

o   features that are for the purpose of meeting dimensional specifications;

o   features that extend into or ahead of the face;

o   features that extend significantly above the top line of the head;

o   furrows in or runners on the head that extend into the face (some exceptions may be made for putters); and

o   optical or electronic devices.

(ii) Woods and Irons

o   all features listed in (i) above;

o   cavities in the outline of the heel and/or the toe of the head that can be viewed from above;

o   severe or multiple cavities in the outline of the back of the head that can be viewed from above;

o   transparent material added to the head with the intention of rendering conforming a feature that is not otherwise permitted; and

o   features that extend beyond the outline of the head when viewed from above.

b Dimensions, Volume and Moment of Inertia

(i) Woods

When the club is in a 60 degree lie angle, the dimensions of the clubhead must be such that:

o   the distance from the heel to the toe of the clubhead is greater than the distance from the face to the back;

o   the distance from the heel to the toe of the clubhead is not greater than 5 inches (127 mm); and

o   the distance from the sole to the crown of the clubhead, including any permitted features, is not greater than 2.8 inches (71.12 mm).

These dimensions are measured on horizontal lines between vertical projections of the outermost points of:

o   the heel and the toe; and

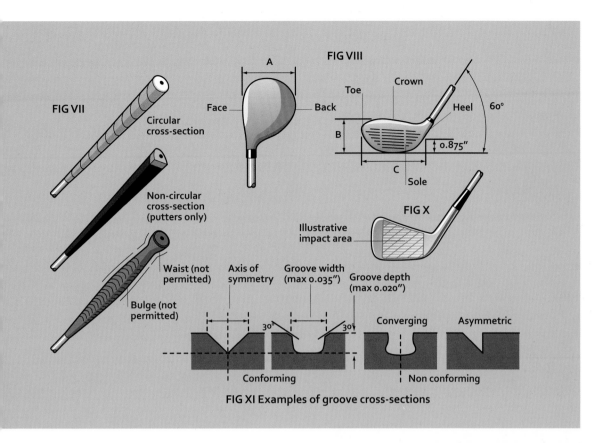

FIG VII

Circular cross-section

Non-circular cross-section (putters only)

Waist (not permitted)

Bulge (not permitted)

Face

A

Back

FIG VIII

Toe

Crown

Heel

60°

B

0.875"

C

Sole

FIG X

Illustrative impact area

Axis of symmetry

Groove width (max 0.035")

Groove depth (max 0.020")

30°

30°

Converging

Asymmetric

Conforming

Non conforming

FIG XI Examples of groove cross-sections

the face and the back (see Fig. VIII, dimension A); and on vertical lines between the horizontal projections of the outermost points of the sole and the crown (see Fig. VIII, dimension B). If the outermost point of the heel is not clearly defined, it is deemed to be 0.875 inches (22.23 mm) above the horizontal plane on which the club is lying (see Fig. VIII, dimension C).

The volume of the clubhead must not exceed 460 cubic centimetres (28.06 cubic inches), plus a tolerance of 10 cubic centimetres (0.61 cubic inches).

When the club is in a 60 degree lie angle, the moment of inertia component around the vertical axis through the clubhead's centre of gravity must not exceed 5900 g cm^2 (32.259 oz in^2), plus a test tolerance of 100 g cm^2 (0.547 oz in^2).

(ii) Irons

When the clubhead is in its normal address position, the dimensions of the head must be such that the distance from the heel to the toe is greater than the distance from the face to the back.

(iii) Putters (see Fig. IX)

When the clubhead is in its normal address position, the dimensions of the head must be such that:

the distance from the heel to the toe is greater than the distance from the face to the back;

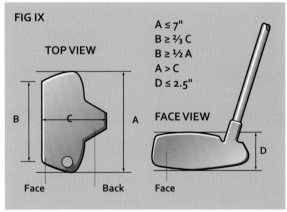

FIG IX

$A \leq 7"$
$B \geq \frac{2}{3} C$
$B \geq \frac{1}{2} A$
$A > C$
$D \leq 2.5"$

TOP VIEW

B

C

A

Face

Back

FACE VIEW

D

Face

FIG XII

$\frac{A}{W + S} \leq 0.0030 \ in^2/in$

W

S

30°

30°

A

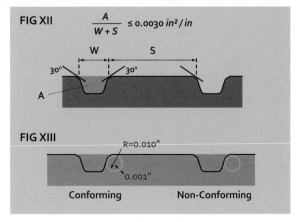

FIG XIII

R=0.010"

0.001"

Conforming

Non-Conforming

- the distance from the heel to the toe of the head is less than or equal to 7 inches (177.8 mm);
- the distance from the heel to the toe of the face is greater than or equal to two thirds of the distance from the face to the back of the head;
- the distance from the heel to the toe of the face is greater than or equal to half of the distance from the heel to the toe of the head; and
- the distance from the sole to the top of the head, including any permitted features, is less than or equal to 2.5 inches (63.5 mm).

For traditionally shaped heads, these dimensions will be measured on horizontal lines between vertical projections of the outermost points of:
- the heel and the toe of the head;
- the heel and the toe of the face; and
- the face and the back;

and on vertical lines between the horizontal projections of the outermost points of the sole and the top of the head. For unusually shaped heads, the toe to heel dimension may be made at the face.

c. Spring Effect and Dynamic Properties

The design, material and/or construction of, or any treatment to, the clubhead (which includes the club face) must not:

(i) have the effect of a spring which exceeds the limit set forth in the Pendulum Test Protocol on file with the *R&A*; or

(ii) incorporate features or technology including, but not limited to, separate springs or spring features, that have the intent of, or the effect of, unduly influencing the clubhead's spring effect; or

(iii) unduly influence the movement of the ball.

NOTE
(i) above does not apply to putters.

d. Striking Faces

The clubhead must have only one striking face, except that a putter may have two such faces if their characteristics are the same, and they are opposite each other.

5. Club Face
a. General
The face of the club must be hard and rigid and must not impart significantly more or less spin to the ball than a standard steel face (some exceptions may be made for putters). Except for such markings listed below, the club face must be smooth and must not have any degree of concavity.

b. Impact Area Roughness and Material
Except for markings specified in the following paragraphs, the surface roughness within the area where impact is intended (the "impact area") must not exceed that of decorative sandblasting, or of fine milling (see Fig. X).

The whole of the impact area must be of the same material (exceptions may be made for clubheads made of wood).

c. Impact Area Markings
If a club has grooves and/or punch marks in the impact area they must meet the following specifications:

(i) Grooves
- Grooves must be straight and parallel.
- Grooves must have a symmetrical cross-section and have sides which do not converge (see Fig. XI).
- *For clubs that have a loft angle greater than or equal to 25 degrees, grooves must have a plain cross-section.
- The width, spacing and cross-section of the grooves must be consistent throughout the impact area (some exceptions may be made for woods).
- The width (W) of each groove must not exceed 0.035 inches (0.9 mm), using the 30 degree method of measurement on file with the *R&A*.
- The distance between edges of adjacent grooves (S) must not be less than three times the width of the grooves, and not less than 0.075 inches (1.905 mm).
- The depth of each groove must not exceed 0.020 inches (0.508 mm).
- *For clubs other than driving clubs, the cross-sectional area (A) of a groove divided by the groove pitch (W+S) must not exceed 0.0030 square inches per inch (0.0762 mm²/mm) (see Fig. XII).
- Grooves must not have sharp edges or raised lips.
- *For clubs that have a loft angle greater than or equal to 25 degrees, groove edges must be substantially in the form of a round having an effective radius which is not less than 0.010 inches (0.254 mm) when measured as shown in Fig. XIII, and not greater than 0.020 inches (0.508 mm). Deviations in effective radius within 0.001 inches (0.0254 mm) are permissible.

(ii) Punch Marks
- The maximum dimension of any punch mark must not exceed 0.075 inches (1.905 mm).
- The distance between adjacent punch marks (or between punch marks and grooves) must not be less than 0.168 inches (4.27 mm), measured from centre to centre.
- The depth of any punch mark must not exceed 0.040 inches (1.02 mm).

Q & A

Are there any limits on club length?

Yes. The overall length of the club shall be at least 0.457 m (18 inches) and, except for putters, must not exceed 1.219 m (48 inches).

Can a golf club be designed to be adjustable?

Yes, any club may be designed to be adjustable. However, the adjustment mechanism must conform to the following conditions set forth in Appendix II, 4b:

(i) The adjustment cannot be readily made. This means that the adjustment must require the use of a special tool rather than purely the hands or something that would commonly be kept in a golfer's pocket or golf bag (for example, a coin or a pitch-mark repair tool).

(ii) All adjustable parts must be firmly fixed and there must be no reasonable likelihood of them working loose during a round. Mechanisms that are fixed by friction fit alone would not normally be permitted.

(iii) All configurations of adjustment must conform to the Rules. Therefore, if a putter is designed to be adjustable for lie, it must not be possible to position the shaft at an angle less than 10 degrees from the vertical (see Appendix II, 1d).

How do I find out if an item of golfing equipment I have designed conforms to the Rules or not?

The R&A can only render a formal ruling on an item of golfing equipment if a sample is submitted for examination. However, informal opinions, based on a description, diagrams and/or photographs can sometimes be given. The R&A strongly recommends that new design ideas should be communicated or submitted as early as possible in the development process and certainly prior to beginning production of any golf club, device or component. Even though a final ruling cannot be made without the benefit of a sample, costly errors can be prevented if communication with The R&A is made as soon as possible. If a manufacturer fails to submit a sample or begins manufacturing and/or marketing an item of equipment prior to receiving an R&A ruling, the manufacturer assumes the risk of a possible ruling that the item of equipment does not conform with the Rules. Equipment submissions or enquiries should be directed to: Equipment Standards, The R&A, St Andrews, Fife, KY16 9JD, Scotland.

What are the Rules relating to grooves and punch marks?

Additional specifications relating to club face grooves and punch marks were introduced into the Rules of Golf in 2010. However, they only apply to new models of clubs, manufactured after 1 January 2010.

A Committee that wishes to limit players to only using clubs that meet the new specifications, including clubs manufactured prior to 2010, may adopt a condition of competition. Further information on this condition can be found in Decision 4-1/1 and an Informational Database of clubs can be found on The R&A's website (www.randa.org), along with a copy of the evaluation protocol. The Rules, specifications and interpretations relating to all clubs and golf balls can be found on The R&A's website and in The R&A's publication *A Guide to the Rules on Clubs and Balls*.

- o   Punch marks must not have sharp edges or raised lips.
- o   *For clubs that have a loft angle greater than or equal to 25 degrees, punch mark edges must be substantially in the form of a round having an effective radius which is not less than 0.010 inches (0.254 mm) when measured as shown in Figure XIII, and not greater than 0.020 inches (0.508 mm). Deviations in effective radius within 0.001 inches (0.0254 mm) are permissible.

NOTE 1

The groove and punch mark specifications above indicated by an asterisk (*) apply only to new models of clubs manufactured on or after 1 January 2010 and any club where the face markings have been purposely altered, for example, by re-grooving. For further information on the status of clubs available before 1 January 2010, refer to the "Equipment Search" section of www.randa.org.

NOTE 2

The Committee may require, in the conditions of competition, that the clubs the player carries must conform to the groove and punch mark specifications above indicated by an asterisk (*). This condition is recommended only for competitions involving expert players. For further information, refer to Decision 4-1/1 in "Decisions on the Rules of Golf".

d   Decorative Markings

The centre of the impact area may be indicated by a design within the boundary of a square whose sides are 0.375 inches (9.53 mm) in length. Such a design must not unduly influence the movement of the ball. Decorative markings are permitted outside the impact area.

e   Non-Metallic Club Face Markings

The above specifications do not apply to clubheads made of wood on which the impact area of the face is of a material of hardness less than the hardness of metal and whose loft angle is 24 degrees or less, but markings which could unduly influence the movement of the ball are prohibited.

f   Putter Face Markings

Any markings on the face of a putter must not have sharp edges or raised lips. The specifications with regard to roughness, material and markings in the impact area do not apply.

APPENDIX III

The Ball

A player in doubt as to the conformity of a ball should consult the *R&A*.

A manufacturer should submit to the *R&A* samples of a ball to be manufactured for a ruling as to whether the ball conforms with the *Rules*. The samples become the property of the *R&A* for reference purposes. If a manufacturer fails to submit samples or, having submitted samples, fails to await a ruling before manufacturing and/or marketing the ball, the manufacturer assumes the risk of a ruling that the ball does not conform with the *Rules*.

The following paragraphs prescribe general regulations for the design of the ball, together with specifications and interpretations. Further information relating to these regulations and their proper interpretation is provided in "A Guide to the Rules on Clubs and Balls".

Where a ball is required to meet a specification within the Rules, it must be designed and manufactured with the intention of meeting that specificiation.

1   General

The ball must not be substantially different from the traditional and customary form and make. The material and construction of the ball must not be contrary to the purpose and intent of the *Rules*

2   Weight

The weight of the ball must not be greater than 1.620 ounces avoirdupois (45.93 g).

3   Size

The diameter of the ball must not be less than 1.680 inches (42.67mm).

4   Spherical Symmetry

The ball must not be designed, manufactured or intentionally modified to have properties which differ from those of a spherically symmetrical ball.

5   Initial Velocity

The initial velocity of the ball must not exceed the limit specified under the conditions set forth in the Initial Velocity Standard for golf balls on file with the *R&A*.

6   Overall Distance Standard

The combined carry and roll of the ball, when tested on apparatus approved by the *R&A*, must not exceed the distance specified under the conditions set forth in the Overall Distance Standard for golf balls on file with the *R&A*.

APPENDIX IV

Devices and Other Equipment

A player in doubt as to whether use of a device or other equipment would constitute a breach of the *Rules* should consult the *R&A*.

A manufacturer should submit to the *R&A* a sample of a device or other equipment to be manufactured for a ruling as to whether its use during a *stipulated round* would cause a player to be in breach of Rule 14-3. The sample becomes the property of the *R&A* for reference purposes. If a manufacturer fails to submit a sample or, having submitted a sample, fails to await a ruling before manufacturing and/or marketing the device or other equipment, the manufacturer assumes the risk of a ruling that use of the device or other equipment would be contrary to the *Rules*.

The following paragraphs prescribe general regulations for the design of devices and other equipment, together with specifications and interpretations. They should be read in conjunction with Rule 11-1 (Teeing) and Rule 14-3 (Artificial Devices, Unusual Equipment and Abnormal Use of Equipment).

Tees (Rule 11)

A tee is a device designed to raise the ball off the ground. A tee must not:
- be longer than 4 inches (101.6 mm);
- be designed or manufactured in such a way that it could indicate *line of play*;
- unduly influence the movement of the ball; or
- otherwise assist the player in making a *stroke* or in his play.

2. Gloves (Rule 14-3)

Gloves may be worn to assist the player in gripping the club, provided they are plain.

A "plain" glove must:
- consist of a fitted covering of the hand with a separate sheath or opening for each digit (fingers and thumb); and
- be made of smooth materials on the full palm and gripping surface of the digits.

A "plain" glove must not incorporate:
- material on the gripping surface or inside of the glove, the primary purpose of which is to provide padding or which has the effect of providing padding. Padding is defined as an area of glove material which is more than 0.025 inches (0.635 mm) thicker than the adjacent areas of the glove without the added material;

NOTE
Material may be added for wear resistance, moisture absorption or other functional purposes, provided it does not exceed the definition of padding (see above).

- straps to assist in preventing the club from slipping or to attach the hand to the club;
- any means of binding digits together;
- material on the glove that adheres to material on the grip;
- features, other than visual aids, designed to assist the player in placing his hands in a consistent and/or specific position on the grip;
- weight to assist the player in making a *stroke*;
- any feature that might restrict the movement of a joint; or
- any other feature that might assist the player in making a *stroke* or in his play.

3. Shoes (Rule 14-3)

Shoes that assist the player in obtaining a firm *stance* may be worn. Subject to the conditions of competition, features such as spikes on the sole are permitted, but shoes must not incorporate features:
- designed to assist the player in taking his *stance* and/or building a *stance*;
- designed to assist the player with his alignment; or
- that might otherwise assist the player in making a *stroke* or in his play.

4. Clothing (Rule 14-3)

Articles of clothing must not incorporate features:
- designed to assist the player with his alignment; or
- that might otherwise assist the player in making a *stroke* or in his play.

5. Distance-Measuring Devices (Rule 14-3)

During a *stipulated round*, the use of any distance-measuring device is not permitted unless the *Committee* has introduced a Local Rule to that effect (see Note to Rule 14-3 and Appendix I; Part A; Section 7).

Even when the Local Rule is in effect, the device must not be used for any purposes that are prohibited by Rule 14-3, including but not limited to:
- the gauging or measuring of slope;
- the gauging or measuring of other conditions that might affect play (e.g. wind speed or direction);
- recommendations that might assist the player in making a *stroke* or in his play (e.g. club selection, type of shot to be played, green reading or any other advice related matter); or
- calculating the effective distance between two points based on elevation changes or other conditions affecting shot distance.

A multi-functional device, such as a smartphone or PDA, may be used as a distance-measuring device, but it must not be used to gauge or measure other conditions where doing so would be a breach of Rule 14-3.

ACKNOWLEDGEMENTS

The R&A and the Publishers would like to thank Sunningdale Golf Club for allowing us to use the courses for the photography in this book and for all their help and assistance during the photography session. We would also like to thank St Andrews Links Trust for the use of The Castle Course.

Photographic Acknowledgements
All photographs are by Kevin Murray (16, 19, 26, 41, 46, 56, 71 bottom, 75, 84, 90, 118 above, 119, 120, 141, 143, 144, 146, 147, 153) and Tom Miles (11, 13, 15, 24, 28, 31, 34, 39, 53, 55, 59, 62, 63, 65, 66, 69, 70, 71 above, 72, 77, 83, 85, 103, 106, 109, 112, 118 below, 132, 133, 136 right, 142, 151, 178) for Octopus Publishing Group with the exception of the following:

AFP Adrian Dennis 100; **Alamy** Wayne Hutchinson 128; **Robyn Beck** 114; **Congressional Country Club** Michale G Leemhuis 161; **Peter Dazely** 127 right; **Getty Imgages** 27, 127 left; David Cannon 42, 61, 81, 164; Stanley Chou 45 right; Adrian Dennis/AFP 14 below; Stephen Dunn 117; Mike Ehrmann 51; Stuart Franklin 14 above, 30, 165; Chris Graythen 168; Richard Heathcote 97, 115; Harry How 148; Ross Kinnaird 36, 45 left, 95, 154; Matthew Lewis 67; Warren Little 73, 136 left, 139; Donald Miralle 10, 176; Dean Mouhtaropoulos 15, 88; Doug Pensinger 140; Andrew Redington 22, 86, 110, 183; Jamie Squire 20, 76; Matt Sullivan 37; Ian Walton 126; **Steve Grayson** 104; **MCT** Charlotte Observer 23; **R&A** Ross Kinnaird 87, 167.

An Hachette UK Company
www.hachette.co.uk

First published in Great Britain in 2003

This revised and updated edition published in 2015 by Hamlyn, a division of Octopus Publishing Group Ltd, Carmelite House, 50 Victoria Embankment, London, EC4Y 0DZ
www.octopusbooks.co.uk

Distributed in Canada by Manda Group, 664 Annette Street, Toronto, Ontario, Canada M6S 2C8

Text copyright © R&A Rules Limited 2003, 2005, 2008, 2009, 2011, 2015
Design copyright © Octopus Publishing Group Ltd 2003, 2005, 2008, 2009, 2011, 2015

Specially commissioned photography by Tom Miles and Kevin Murray for Octopus Publishing Group
Illustrations by Sudden Impact Media

ISBN: 978-0-600-63065-4

A CIP catalogue record of this book is available from the British Library.

Printed and bound in China.

10 9 8 7 6 5 4 3 2 1